THE
Novel-writer's
TOOLKIT

THE
Novel-writer's
TOOLKIT

Your ultimate guide to writing and publishing a successful novel

Edited by Caroline Taggart

D&C
David and Charles

A DAVID & CHARLES BOOK
Copyright © David & Charles Limited 2011

David & Charles is an F+W Media Inc. company
4700 East Galbraith Road
Cincinnati, OH 45236

First published in the UK in 2011

Text copyright © F+W Media Inc. 2011

The material in this book has been previously published in *The Everything Guide to Writing a Novel*, published by Adams Media, 2004, *Writer's Market UK 2008*, *Writer's Market UK 2009*, *Writer's Market UK & Ireland 2010*, all published by David & Charles Ltd.

A catalogue record for this book is available from the British Library.

ISBN-13: 978-1-4463-0050-3 paperback
ISBN-10: 1-4463-0050-1 paperback

Printed in China by RR Donnelley
for David & Charles
Brunel House, Newton Abbot, Devon

Senior Acquisitions Editor: Freya Dangerfield
Desk Editor: Felicity Barr
Project Editor: Caroline Taggart
Proofreader: Ame Verso
Senior Designer: Victoria Marks
Production Controller: Bev Richardson

David & Charles publish high quality books on a wide range of subjects.
For more great book ideas visit: **www.rubooks.co.uk**

CONTENTS

INTRODUCTION

It may or may not be true that everyone has a novel in them: if you have bothered to pick up this book, it's likely that you hope there is a novel in *you*. It's also likely that you find something about the process of writing a novel and getting it published a little bit daunting.

If so, you have come to the right place. *The Novel-Writer's Toolkit* aims to answer all those questions that are buzzing around in the back of your mind, from 'How do I start?' to 'How do I find an agent or a publisher?'

The book is divided into three parts. The first is designed to make your novel as good as it can possibly be. It deals with the practicalities of being a writer ('plonk yourself in front of the computer and stay there' is not a bad place to start). There are suggestions on creating plot, characters, setting and dialogue and, eventually, on editing your work so that it is ready to send into the outside world.

Part Two contains invaluable advice from industry insiders, from what an editor is looking for to how to prepare an outline and compose a covering letter that will make a busy agent want to read more. It describes what happens to your manuscript once it has been accepted, considers some aspects of copyright and other legal matters, and gives a salesperson's view of what makes a book sell.

Finally, the Directory lists agents and publishers who deal with novels – professionals who are potentially interested in your work. The information in each entry is intended to help you decide who might be right for you, so that you don't send a graphic novel to someone who is interested only in literary fiction, or vice versa. There are also details of literary consultancies and writing courses, useful organizations and online resources, competitions, prizes, grants, festivals, conferences and more.

As an aspiring writer, you can imagine that there is nothing more exciting than having a published book with your name on the cover. It's up to you to finish the job, but here are – we hope – all the tools you need.

ACKNOWLEDGEMENTS

The articles in Part Two and those quoted in Part One originally appeared in *Writer's Market UK*, 2008, 2009 or 2010 editions, published by David & Charles. Their authors are:

Dominic Brendon, currently Key Account Director at the large international publisher Simon & Schuster. Previous to that he was sales director at Kyle Cathie Limited, a smaller independent publisher with a string of bestsellers behind it. His early background was with a London-based bookselling chain where he did 13 years at the coal face.

Simon Brett, who started his professional career as a comedy producer, first for BBC radio and then for London Weekend Television, before becoming a full-time writer. He has published over 80 books, many of them crime novels or psychological thrillers, including the Charles Paris, Mrs Pargeter and Fethering series. His humorous writings include the bestselling *How To Be A Little Sod*. For radio and television he has written many plays and series, like *After Henry* and *No Commitments*.

Sara Crowley, shortlisted for the Faber/Book Tokens 'Not Yet Published Award' in 2007, and winner of the Waterstone's 2009 Bookseller's Bursary. Her short stories have won prizes and been widely published. She blogs at http://asalted.blogspot.com/.

Caro Fraser, author of the bestselling Caper Court series of legal novels and of six stand-alone novels, including *A Little Learning* and *A World Apart*. She is currently working on the eighth in the Caper Court series. Her website is www.caro-fraser.co.uk.

Jane Friedman, for 12 years editorial director of Writer's Digest Books, America's leading publisher of 'how to' and inspirational books for writers of all sorts. She now teaches in the e-media department at the University of Cincinnati and speaks at writing and publishing events. Visit www.janefriedman.com.

Sophie Hannah, a bestselling crime writer. Her latest novel is *Lasting Damage* (Hodder, 2011) and her website is www.sophiehannah.com.

Penelope Hoare, former Deputy Publisher of Chatto & Windus, an old-established traditional publishing house, now part of Random House, which in its turn is part of the giant international company Bertelsmann. Chatto & Windus owns the Hogarth Press, the publishing company founded by Leonard and Virginia Woolf, and as an imprint still retains its own personality and high standards.

Dr Hilary Johnson, who has edited a writers' magazine, taught creative writing and judged writing competitions. She has been organizer of The Romantic Novelists' Association's New Writers' Scheme and worked as a publisher's reader. For many years she has run her own highly regarded Authors' Advisory Service and is a scout for a leading literary agent. Visit www.hilaryjohnson.demon.co.uk.

Jonathan Pegg, who founded his own agency in 2009 after 12 years at Curtis Brown where he was a senior agent. Prior to becoming an agent he was an agent's assistant, foreign rights executive, and publicist for books. He has worked with a range of prestigious authors, and his interests include both fiction (literary fiction, thrillers, historical and quality commercial) and a broad range of non-fiction. Visit www.jonathanpegg.com.

Jem Poster, the author of a collection of poetry, *Brought to Light* (Bloodaxe, 2001) and two novels, *Courting Shadows* (Sceptre, 2002) and *Rifling Paradise* (Sceptre, 2006). He is Professor and Director of Creative Writing at Aberystwyth University.

Caroline Taggart, editor of *Writer's Market UK 2009* and *2010* and a bestselling author in her own right. Her latest book, *The Book of English Place Names*, is published by Ebury Press.

Much of the information in Part One first appeared in The Everything Guide to Writing a Novel *by Joyce and Jim Lavene (Adams Media, 2004).*

Part 1 Writing Your Novel

For many would-be writers, finding ideas isn't the problem – the hard part is turning them into full-length novels of publishable quality. An idea that seems brilliant for the first few pages may run out of steam; characters and dialogue come out wooden; or there may simply not be enough hours in the day to sit down and write. This section addresses the question of making your work as good as it can possibly be.

THE REALITIES OF BEING A NOVELIST

Organizing Your Life – and Your Ideas

Jim Rohn, a motivational speaker, once said, 'It takes what it takes.' He was referring to finding the right place to live your life. For most writers, that 'place' is writing a book. It's a dream that can become reality, but not without some hard work.

It Takes Time

Some people find writing more arduous than others. You may be like Monet, able to finish any project quickly and easily, or more like Michelangelo, taking years to complete what others do in months. Either way, writing a novel is a demanding process. Not only do you have to produce the words in the first place, but you also have to make them the best words they can possibly be: there is always something to be revised or edited. Telling a long, complex tale requires time and patience. If you can't imagine yourself spending hours in front of your computer when other members of your household are asleep or out enjoying themselves, it may be better to focus on some other dream.

It Takes Commitment

Most beginning novelists have lives: families, jobs, responsibilities of one sort or another. You may have a partner who doesn't understand your compulsion to write, or well-meaning friends who remind you that you will probably never be published. But if you want to make a success of your writing, you have to make a commitment to it.

Commitment means parking yourself on the chair in front of the computer and staying there. It means finding time for character analysis and revamping your plot when you'd rather be playing football or going out shopping. It means staying up late, getting up early on Sundays and bank holidays, giving up afternoon naps. In fact, if you have a busy life already, it may sometimes seem as if you are giving up sleep altogether.

There is also a financial commitment. If you sign up for a creative writing course, or buy books on writing, or send your manuscript to a professional literary consultant, the cost mounts up. Not to mention the paper and postage involved in sending work out to agents and publishers. Starting a novel can be daunting if you realize what you are letting yourself in for, but the better prepared you are for the task, the better your chances of completing it. Thousands of writers start writing a novel every day. Only a few finish, and even fewer get their work published.

Writing Discipline

Most successful writers have a routine; a daily way of weaving their writing into their lives so that it is a job like any other. Here are five starting points from which to proceed:

- Have a plan and set lots of goals. What are you going to write, and by when?

- Set aside specific times for writing. Many of us are at our best early in the morning, but some work best at night. Either end of the day is usually good, as those are the times when you are most likely to get peace and quiet. Get into a pattern of working and stick to it.

- Set yourself a specific minimum number of words to aim for; even if it's only 50 you'll still see your manuscript growing over time.

- Make good use of any unexpected 'spare' time. Have your notebook or laptop with you at all times. If that train or plane is going to be delayed, don't just sit there – write.

- Consider joining a writers' group, either face to face or online: many set deadlines by which all members are expected to produce a piece of work for discussion, which may be just the impetus you need.

Stay Organized

Organization is a skill that anyone can learn. Because writers are essentially small business people, it's important for them to learn it as early on in their careers as possible. If you do manage to sell a book, you'll be glad you kept those receipts, letters and notes. They prove to the tax authorities that you're serious about your career – and enable you to set legitimate expenses against the tax you pay.

Your computer can keep track of appointments, phone numbers and all sorts of information related to your notes, your research and your writing. But for letters, receipts and other miscellaneous bits of paper, there's nothing like a filing cabinet. Keep a folder for receipts, another for correspondence (or several if you have several projects on the go and want to keep their correspondence separate) and a third one for all your random notes. Keeping your ideas and other writing-related information close at hand and in an orderly fashion can save you hours of hunting through the glove compartment and your other handbag – and that gives you more time to write.

It Takes Good Material

There is no hard-and-fast rule to help you decide whether you have a novel in you. But it's an important question to ask yourself: do you have enough material to create 300–400 pages of printed text? Many would-be novelists find as they start writing that they run out of steam after only a few pages – their novel is really only a short story. Nothing wrong with that, of course, but by taking the time to examine what you want to write before you start, you can save yourself the heartbreak of beginning a manuscript that is never going to be completed.

You know all this? And you aren't put off? OK, let's look at what else you are letting yourself in for.

What Is a Novel?

The writing field is full of rules and regulations – a number of them crop up later in this book. Some of them you can break, some you can't, and the length of a novel is one of the ones you can't. That's because today's novel is defined largely by word count. For most styles of novel, the bare minimum is 50,000 words, the maximum for a beginner

100,000 words. I say for a beginner because many modern novels – Vikram Seth's *A Suitable Boy*, Stieg Larsson's *The Girl with the Dragon Tattoo*, the later Harry Potters – are much longer than that. But they are the exceptions: as a rule of thumb publishers are looking for novels of about 85,000–100,000 words, and you don't want to make the uphill task of getting published more difficult by asking them to make an exception in your case. If you are typing in double spacing in A4 format, 250–300 words will fill a page, so if you end up with a manuscript of about 300 pages you won't be far wrong.

What Is a Genre?

The word is originally French and means a type or sort. It's used in the book world to mean a type or style of novel – mystery, science-fiction, fantasy, romance – each with its own characteristics. A traditional romantic novel always has a happy ending: boy gets girl. A good science-fiction story must contain elements of understandable science: it must obey *some* rules, even if they are strained to the limits of the author's imagination.

Within these broad genres, there are many, many sub-genres: under 'mystery' or 'crime' you find the hard-boiled private-eye stories of Mickey Spillane, the amateur sleuths of Agatha Christie or Simon Brett, and the insider's-look-at-the-forensics of Patricia Cornwell or Kathy Reichs. If you are writing genre fiction it is important to understand these niches and therefore to understand your market. Is your mystery novel a police procedural like Ed McBain's or a techno-thriller *à la* Tom Clancy? Is your science-fiction story psychological or does it depend on your characters meeting weird and wonderful beings from another world? Or both? A good look at the market and plenty of objective homework categorizing your novel will be time well spent.

Some writers are rebels, defying classification for their work. Are Anne Rice's vampire novels horror or romance? Readers have their own opinions. It's not against the rules to write a book that contains elements of more than one genre, as long as you understand the combination and have given some thought to the market.

What Is a Mainstream Novel?

A mainstream novel tends to be more eclectic and less simple to identify than a genre novel. It doesn't obey the genres' rules.

Perhaps the easiest way to define it is to consider what it lacks. Ian McEwan's *On Chesil Beach*, for example, is partly a romance, but it doesn't have a happy ending. So it doesn't follow the formula set out for romantic novels. Sebastian Faulks' *Engleby* has elements of the thriller – a girl has disappeared and we don't know how or why – but the novel's scope is much broader and deeper than that of the average genre whodunit. Mainstream authors are free to follow their instincts and truly write what their hearts dictate. That's why it is harder for mainstream novels to be successful, but why the best of them are so deeply satisfying.

Finding Ideas

Most writers don't have a problem coming up with ideas for novels. They're more likely to have a problem picking and choosing between all the ideas that occur to them. It's a bit like having five children who all need shoes. You don't have the money to buy shoes for all of them – or the time and energy to write five novels at once – so you have to decide which child needs shoes most urgently or which story simply won't wait to be written.

> Faced with a choice between ideas, choose the one that makes you feel as if you could drag yourself out of bed at five in the morning to write it. The one that's burning a hole in your brain. The others will wait. Mentally put them to one side for now and start working on the story that's most important to you.

Use Your Imagination

A good imagination can get you started. A great imagination can take you to the moon. Tap into the wellspring of your imagination – if you've been neglecting it with too much reality, you'll probably have to work on it. Give yourself time to dream every day. Find a quiet corner and allow yourself to imagine all the possibilities around you.

A story idea may spring from your imagination fully formed. Or it may just be the germ of a story. Elizabeth Kay had the idea for her fantasy trilogy *The Divide* when she visited Costa Rica and saw the 'magical' effect of the Continental Divide, separating the Atlantic from the Pacific. What better place to create another world, in which fabulous creatures are real and her human hero is the mythical being? Then she used her imagination to add a wealth of detail and to invent strong, believable characters who had adventures and triumphed over their difficulties.

Reality as Inspiration

Many authors create their novels from something that really happened to them. Others watch the news and scan the papers for events. They write down scraps of ideas that strike them as story possibilities. Creating fiction from real life is nothing new. Even writers with fantastic imaginations sometimes need a jump start.

Of course, some fiction genres depend on reality. Police mysteries have to have some grain of truth in the way the police force operates. One of the (many) reasons why

PD James' novels are so successful is that she used to work in the Police Department and later the Criminal Policy Department of the Home Office, so she could draw on this experience for the background to her crime novels, even though her imagination creates the plot and characters. This applies to non-genre writing too: Ken Kesey, author of *One Flew Over the Cuckoo's Nest*, once worked on a psychiatric ward, and David Lodge wrote his novel *Deaf Sentence*, about a man losing his hearing, when the same thing happened to him. This real-life experience brings an authentic background to the fictional stories these authors create.

Building a Novel

The very definition of a novel creates expectations. There are certain things that every reader, in every country in the world, expects to find when he or she buys a work of fiction. They include:

- **Characters:** the people or other beings who inhabit the novel.
- **Plot:** the road map that takes the characters from one place to another.
- **Setting:** the world, real or imagined, where the plot takes place.
- **Dialogue and narrative:** the way all the aspects of the story are expressed.

Then there are the themes – the ideas or concepts that you want to get across. Is your hero looking for himself by exploring his past? Are you telling a love story in a light-hearted manner, but trying to make a serious point – about loneliness, self-respect or loyalty, for example? Not until you know the answers to these questions can you begin to understand your characters and their goals. And if you don't understand your characters, you have no chance of writing a good novel.

WHAT'S IT ALL ABOUT?

Outlining and Plotting

How do you find out if your idea for a novel has 'legs'? You start by taking that idea and seeing if you can turn it into a plot.

Thinking Your Story Through

Telling yourself the story of your novel is an effective way of understanding what you want to say and how you want to say it. Many writers treat this exercise as if they were a parent telling a child a bedtime story. They go to bed at night repeating their ideas in an almost once-upon-a-time format. This has the advantage of giving their subconscious a chance to work on the story as well.

Think about the details of your plot. It is all very well knowing that you want to drive from Exeter to Carlisle, but if you have never done it before and you don't have a map or a satnav you are likely to get lost. So, you may know who your heroine and your hero are and that they are going to end up together, but what is going to happen to them along the way?

What If...?

A writer should always be asking, 'What if...?' or 'What happens?' These questions are the catalyst for the thought processes that develop plot, character and setting.

What happens when a bored housewife goes on holiday to Greece and meets a sweet-talking con man? Or when a gangster falls in love with a girl from the other side of town? Questions like this can give you the beginning of a plot, but so can such day-to-day activities as going for a bike ride (what happens if you get a flat tyre in the middle of nowhere and a stranger offers you a lift?), going to work (what happens when a new colleague starts muscling in on your job?) or going to the local coffee shop (what happens if two strangers strike up a conversation?).

All these starting points can be used to spark stories of love, hate or redemption. It's up to you to stretch that idea to make a story, to build a framework on which your novel can depend. That first question may have got you going, but thousands of other questions must follow: what happens when the people in the coffee shop exchange phone numbers? What happens when it is not the girl in the coffee shop but her flat mate who answers the phone? And so on.

Don't be afraid to question your plot. Make sure every aspect of it makes sense. If the answers to your questions aren't in there, think about them and add them. Give your plot depth and clarity. After all, if you don't understand what is going on, you can't expect your readers to.

Why: Motivations and Explanations

As the creator of the world that becomes your novel, it's important for you to ask why. Just because you think of a basic plot, that doesn't mean you'll instantly understand every aspect of what takes place over the next 80,000 words. Whether you are dealing with a murder or a trip to the moon, it's important to know why what is happening is happening in the story.

'Why?' is of course a fundamental part of character motivation and we'll go into that further in the next chapter. But for the moment, imagine that your neighbour has painted his house pink. He's a quiet man who never causes trouble: what's he doing with a pink house in a sea of white and grey? Is it a cry for attention? Did he do it for a bet? You may never know, but asking this sort of question begins the process of looking for motivation.

A writer of murder mysteries may be thinking, 'It's to cover up the bloodstain by the back door.' A science-fiction writer may wonder if the paint is an alien phosphorescent that will tell a passing UFO to pick him up. A mainstream writer will be imagining that this quiet, shy man just wants to be noticed by his uncaring neighbours.

You can see how asking the same question from different points of view can produce totally different answers and thus totally different plots. The reason your plot flows in any direction may be the result of asking, 'What if…?'

Looking for the Weak Spots

A sure way to find the holes in your story is to hear it read or told aloud. Maybe that's why so many writers would rather avoid this step and go straight to the computer. Once you've seen the hole – in your plot or your characterization or whatever – you feel obliged to patch it; if you never see the hole, you can let yourself believe that it isn't there.

As we'll see in more detail in the next chapter, every realistic, convincing character has flaws: otherwise they become literarily 'too good to be true'. That isn't what we are talking about here. The weak spots you are looking for at this stage are the unintentional mistakes that can destroy a book: the sleuth knowing something that he couldn't possibly know or the plot completely running out of steam before you are halfway through.

It's important that the writer knows the explanations behind everything that happens in the novel, even if she hasn't shared it with the reader – yet. Obviously, most mystery writers know who the killer is from the word go, but they don't normally tell the reader in the first chapter. But revealing – in that Hercule Poirot-style final scene – that the killer is a character the reader has never heard of before just won't work. As a writer you aren't only a creative artist; you are also the master architect of your novel and it is your job to make sure that everything in the story makes sense – otherwise the book will come crashing down round everyone's ears.

Here's one sure way to test if a character or plot point is essential: take it (or him or her) out. If the story collapses, the character or idea is important. If not, you may need to weed it out or build it up to strengthen the work.

Putting Things Right

While it may seem impossible to alter an idea that's already in place, asking 'What if...?' helps in that situation as well. Don't be afraid to make sweeping changes if you find yourself wrestling with something that just isn't working. What if you altered the setting? What if Paris became New York and the 1890s became the 1920s? Look at it from a different angle and you may come up with something fresh and sparkling.

This may, of course, mean rethinking a lot of ideas that you felt were concrete. It may mean ditching the research you did into 1890s fashion and music. But although you lose those ideas, you gain new ones. Playing with ideas is much the same as children playing with building blocks. You may cry for a moment when your masterpiece is destroyed, but you move right on to building a new one. The trick is not to fall so deeply in love with any idea that you can't contemplate tearing it apart and putting it back together again. Yes, it will be painful. But what you come up with may be better.

The writer's job is not just to write; it's also to rewrite and rethink and revamp. There are millions of ideas and thousands of words to choose from, and no single one of them is the only perfect option.

To Plan or Not to Plan?

The late Sidney Sheldon once said that no author should ever know how the book was going to end. Some writers work that way. They allow the plot to meander like a river until they feel it has reached its goal. They believe that knowing too much about what is going to happen can ruin their creativity and make the book flat.

You can't argue with Mr Sheldon's success, but not all authors would agree. Many prefer to begin with a clear picture of the book's plot from beginning to end. Sometimes a character or a secondary plot line may not work out the way they envisaged, but overall they know where they're going and how they want to get there.

For some people, particularly beginners, having a plan, knowing the goal, is the only way they can hope to finish the project. If you decide to plan your ending, remember you can always change it if you don't like it. If you decide not to plan and you don't like what emerges, you can always change that too. All that matters is that you provide your readers with a satisfactory conclusion.

Be True to Yourself

Even at this early stage, second opinions can be valuable, but you need to get the opinion of someone you trust. Friends and family members may not be able to give you an honest reaction, for fear of hurting your feelings or because they are so impressed that you are writing a novel at all. Joining a reading or writing group can be a wonderful way to get feedback on your work, but can also be a disaster. Be sure that you are in sync with the people who will be helping you shape your work. It's not true that a bad critique is better than no critique at all.

Should you make changes just because someone else tells you that it would be better if you did? Should you make the hero dark instead of fair, or leave out the wedding scene to make the plot move along more briskly? You're the only one who can make these decisions. But try to look at your work with the objectivity of a surgeon rather than the loving devotion of a parent. Would it benefit from these changes? Would the characters become more believable or the plot more exhilarating? If so, do it. Throw in a little something extra. Make it better.

Writing Groups

Aspiring novelist Sara Crowley, spending a lot of her time at home with small children, describes how her online writing group helps her:

What is missing when you are trying to do it yourself is anyone to bounce ideas off and compare notes with. Your work isn't being discussed in a group setting, and no teacher is on hand with advice and instructions. Sometimes a storyline is so clear in your head that you can't imagine anyone not seeing exactly what you mean, and yet I have now learned that this is an incredibly common problem. It is hard to get the necessary distance to see one's own work with clarity.

That is where online writers' groups come in. There are groups, large and small, that operate by posting work online for critique and discussion. The other writers in the group then offer their feedback, which can be an effective way of highlighting issues that you had overlooked. Rewriting your work before sending off submissions means that editors get to see it at its best. Be wary, though, of editing too much and losing sight of your original story just to please those online critics, and remember that all writing is subjective — a person who dislikes your story may simply not be a fan of that particular style.

Three Recommended Sites for Writers

Blogger: www.blogger.com
WriteWords: www.writewords.org.uk/groups
The Workhouse: www.fictionworkhouse.com

Developing Secondary Plots

Very few novels contain only one plot. A secondary plot can strengthen and add to the main plot, introducing a dilemma or character that adds tension, comedy or complications to the lives of the main characters. It can be used as a red herring to draw readers' eyes away from what's really going on. It can be a device that helps to take the main plot where it needs to go. In a romance, a subplot could be a budding relationship between two side characters. The relationship complicates the main romance between the hero and heroine because these secondary characters are their parents.

It's not unusual for a novel to contain many different subplots. As long as all the loose ends are tied up by the end of the book, that's fine. But as you add additional plots, consider how they relate to the main one and how they advance the storyline. You don't want a side plot that doesn't have anything to do with telling the main story.

It's possible to have too much of a good thing. The plot should never overpower the characters. They should always create their world together.

HEROES, VILLAINS AND OTHERS

Creating Your Characters

Characters make the book. A great character can inspire a series; a less than great one can sink your novel. If you want your novel to work, create characters who will make the reader care what happens to them. The people in your novel must be as real as the people you see and deal with every day.

It's impossible to say what makes a character unforgettable. What is it about James Bond that has kept him alive and spying for so long? What makes us remember Philip Marlowe in Raymond Chandler's detective novels or Jack Ryan in the thrillers of Tom Clancy? Wouldn't you love to create characters so real, so intriguing that they will be used in countless books and films? Not everyone achieves it, but it is what every writer is striving for when he creates characters.

Heroes and Villains

Most novels have at least two main characters – the protagonist, who is the hero (of whichever sex) of the story, and the antagonist, the bad guy who puts obstacles in the way of the hero achieving his goal. Of course in a romance you'll normally have a hero and a heroine but the novel will probably be written from the heroine's point of view and for a lot of the time the 'hero' may actually be the antagonist – the one who doesn't realize that he has been in love with the heroine all the time.

The Protagonist: the Story's Hero

If your protagonist is a well-written character, readers will love him. They won't mind if he's a little rough round the edges – think Philip Marlowe again – or even if she is her own worst enemy – Jane Austen's Emma. He or she can be downtrodden but indomitable (Jane Eyre), quirky (John Mortimer's Horace Rumpole) or downright evil (Hannibal Lecter in *The Silence of the Lambs*). It doesn't matter. What the reader wants is a personality so strong, so fascinating, that she can't look away.

If your protagonist is to be memorable, readers have to believe that he is capable of dealing with the antagonist and coming out on top. Think of Sherlock Holmes and Professor Moriarty battling it out at the Reichenbach Falls. They have to be able to empathize with him and imagine themselves doing all those remarkable things. Think of Clark Kent, an ordinary, lovable guy when he isn't being Superman. A good hero can save the world many times over. A bad hero may save the world but no one will remember his name.

The Antagonist: the Hero's Nemesis

This is usually the character that readers love to hate, whether it is Goldfinger versus James Bond or Fagin versus Oliver Twist. But the antagonist doesn't have to be evil – he's simply a main character who happens to work against the story's hero. The best kind of antagonist is one that the hero can stand up to but not easily overpower. In *The Silence of the Lambs*, Hannibal Lecter is an unforgettable protagonist, but Agent Clarice Starling is his match. He is never really able to overpower her. Thomas Harris' novel is an unusual – and immensely successful – example of the protagonist, the person around whom the story revolves, being not only a villain but a supervillain, while the antagonist, the one who stands in his way, is on the side of right. But it is because Hannibal is in awe of Clarice, because we see her from that point of view, that we become fascinated with her as well. The result is a strong antagonist character.

This can work just as well in the more conventional set-up when the antagonist is the villain. Jim Hawkins is the hero of Robert Louis Stevenson's *Treasure Island*: he is the book's narrator and the thrust of the plot is whether or not he will escape from the pirate gang. But the truly charismatic character, the one that everyone remembers, is the antagonist Long John Silver.

Point of View

Knowing whose 'angle' of the story to give is one of the most difficult things for beginning novelists to get right. Jane Friedman, former editorial director of Writer's Digest Books in the US, gives this advice:

> Don't go from first-person point of view ('I') to third-person point of view ('he' or 'she') in the same story or novel. Choose one and stick with it. A more difficult problem is switching viewpoints between characters. Beginners should choose one viewpoint character and not switch to another. That means: you may get inside one person's head (such as your protagonist's) and relate that person's feelings throughout the course of the story – but you should never reveal what's going on inside other characters' heads. One of the most common problems for new writers is abruptly switching between characters' viewpoints in the same scene.
>
> I have heard people ask a thousand times why it is that all guides on writing declare against shifting viewpoint when successful writers allow their viewpoint to shift about. The reason is that successful writers who break such rules succeed not because of their breaking the rules, but because their style, characterization or mastery of the craft overcomes the inherent problems involved with the shifting of the viewpoint.

What Makes Them Tick?

In real life you probably often wonder what makes people do the things they do. What makes a runner get up at four o'clock in the morning and run 10 kilometres? Why does a teenager strew the floor of his room with so much dirty laundry that he can hardly reach his bed? Why does your boss insist on passing you over for promotion when you work so much harder than anyone else?

As with the man with the pink house we met earlier, asking questions like this is the first step towards understanding the people around you. The same applies to the characters you are creating. If they are to be realistic, they must be driven by the same sorts of motivation that drive real people.

Well-developed characters have goals, dreams, ambitions. They may consciously set goals for themselves, or be unclear what their goals are but still impatient or frustrated about not achieving them. Your main character may be a passionately committed detective who is obsessing day and night about solving a case. But he may also be worried that he smokes too much and that this is damaging his health. While he tries to give up smoking he becomes short-tempered and this has an effect on his marriage. Another goal is added: to save his relationship. Understanding your characters' goals can help you understand them as people.

Motivation doesn't have to be complicated: not everyone is set on world domination or beset by a longing to explore strange new worlds. A character may be motivated by greed, anger, frustration, love, fear or the need to win a promotion in order to keep up with the mortgage payments. Readers will identify more easily with characters who share their day-to-day motivations.

What Stands in Their Way?

Conflict is what keeps you and your characters on your toes. It keeps the plot moving forwards, because it creates obstacles for your characters to overcome – and that is what plot is all about. It shows the reader what the character is made of – does he have the tenacity, the ingenuity, the honesty to deal with this obstacle?

Look around you for examples of obstacles that stop people from getting what they want and observe what people do in order to achieve their goals. Are they ruthless? Cunning? Manipulative? What you see in real life might inspire you in your writing.

Internal and External Conflict

Conflict can be internal – emotions inside the mind of the character that stop her achieving what she wants – or external – a disaster or a bad guy who gets in the way. We all face internal barriers – fear, anger, love, hate – every day, so readers will recognize them when your character suffers from them. Hamlet couldn't make up his mind what to do about avenging his father's murder: that's one of the greatest internal conflicts ever written. In your case, it may take other forms. Is your character unable to chase the villain on the roof because she's afraid of heights? Fear can be a powerful internal conflict – and not just the fear of falling and breaking your neck. The fear of rejection can keep a woman from asking a man in her office out for coffee. She thinks about it for so long, it achieves epic proportions in her mind. Finally, that fear causes her to stalk him. Another plot hatches!

External conflict, on the other hand, shows how your character handles the outside world. It doesn't have to be huge – not every novel has an earthquake or a plane crash in it. But just because external conflicts are small, it doesn't mean they don't affect the character. As long as it keeps your character from getting what she wants, a shower of rain at the wrong moment, ruining an expensive new hairdo, can be conflict.

A Mix of Conflicts

Most genre books require both external and internal conflict. In romances, the internal conflict is likely to be the heroine's changing feelings, while the external conflict may be that her house is being completely refitted (contemporary, as in Nora Roberts' *Tribute*) or that gossips in the village spread word that she is a witch (historical, as in Catherine Cookson's *Tilly Trotter*). In a mystery, conflict may be balanced by the sleuth's inner workings or personal feelings and the terrible events going on around him.

With some books, such as pure 'adventure' stories, external conflict is more important than internal. These books thrive on action and don't insist on the hero doing a great deal of soul-searching.

On the other hand, some mainstream novels rely almost entirely on internal conflict: the hero's problems are to do with facing up to his own shortcomings rather than diving to the bottom of the sea to rescue treasure from a shipwreck.

Strengths and Weaknesses

Every character, whether hero, villain or something in between, has to have strengths and weaknesses. Is your protagonist a superhero who can pick up cars in one hand and rescue a busload of children with the other? Probably not. She might be a poor girl trying to get on in life by working hard, like Griet in Tracy Chevalier's *Girl with a Pearl Earring*. Character strengths vary from character to character. Even though Frodo in JRR Tolkien's *Lord of the Rings* trilogy has no great physical or mental prowess, his inner goodness is enough to carry him to victory against the forces of darkness. A character's strengths can make an ordinary person into a hero and a minor villain into a supervillain.

Weaknesses too can be large or small, but you have to have them. With no flaws at all, your character will turn out to be perfect – and boring. Readers will find themselves unable to sympathize with him or her. It's difficult to get emotionally involved with characters who have no flaws: they're just too unrealistic.

A good example of a character flaw that can be used to set off the story's conflict is a quick temper. McMurphy in *One Flew Over the Cuckoo's Nest* has a short fuse that helps to move the plot forwards on a number of occasions. Obstinacy is another. In Stephen R Donaldson's *Lord Foul's Bane*, the main character, Thomas Covenant, is transported to another dimension. But his stubbornness prevents him from believing that what he sees is real, creating all manner of conflict that carries him through the novel.

Then There are the Subsidiary Characters

You can't write a novel with only a hero and a heroine or a hero and a villain. They have to have friends, family, colleagues, people they meet in the street or in the supermarket. These subsidiary characters can move the plot along, help with character development, provide a change of pace, lighten the tension and give depth to the setting. Some of them will be highly developed, like the heroine's best friend or the murder victim's alluring widow. Others may appear in only one scene, contribute their mite to the plot and then be heard of no more. But they all have to be authentic.

Think of some of the great minor characters in literature: Mr Collins and Lady Catherine in *Pride and Prejudice*, Uriah Heep and Mr Micawber in *David Copperfield*, Eeyore and Tigger in *Winnie-the-Pooh*. They all have exaggerated characteristics, from Mr Collins' pomposity and Mr Micawber's optimism to Eeyore's gloominess, but they are all true to themselves. Everything that has been said in this chapter about creating your main characters applies – on a smaller scale – to everyone else who appears on your canvas.

A word of warning: be careful to keep your secondary characters from stealing the show. The main plot should belong to the primary characters. Sometimes minor characters are so much fun to write that you lose track of where they belong – which is in the background.

What Makes Them Unique?

You've thought about your characters. You understand what motivates them and who they are. You've give them strengths and weaknesses. But can they play the piano?

What makes everyone unique – in the real world or in the fictitious one that you are creating – is a combination of different characteristics. The past haunts or enriches your characters. They move forwards with confidence or despite terrible fears. But, just like you, your characters are more than the sum of their fears and desires. They have lives. They work or go to school. They spend Saturday mornings doing up their classic motorbike. Now is the time to have some fun with them, to build them into people who may not be real but are nevertheless realistic.

Your mystery sleuth may be a closet romance reader. Your tough-as-nails secret agent may like to play the saxophone when he isn't saving the world. Think of Rex Stout's detective Nero Wolfe, who grew orchids in a plant-room in his New York brownstone and took 45 minutes to cook perfect scrambled eggs. These habits weren't always necessary to the plot, but they were quirks that helped to bring the character to life.

Something that starts out as a quirk may also become part of your character's development. Say you show your hero getting dressed, putting on a blue shirt. You look in his wardrobe and see that he has 25 blue shirts: he never wears any other colour. That's quirky. But what if you find that he is superstitious about it – he wore a blue shirt the day he sat his final exams and passed with flying colours, so he doesn't believe he can succeed dressed any other way? Then what if he is offered the job of his dreams, but the company has a strict dress code that insists on white shirts? That ceases to be quirky and becomes another obstacle for your character to overcome – suddenly it's part of the plot. As we saw earlier, this is the sort of thing that happens when you ask, 'What if…?'

Having said that, be careful that your characters' quirks don't get out of hand. Make them believable and natural for the character, but don't let them overpower the story. And make sure that they enhance the character and make him more interesting rather than annoying.

Does Breakfast Matter?

You probably know a lot about your characters by now. You know how tall they are, what colour their hair is, whether they dress smartly or casually. Many 'experts' on creative writing say that you must know absolutely everything about your characters. However, Sophie Hannah, bestselling author of psychological thrillers, takes a different view:

When I read 'How To...' articles and books about writing, the sections on characterization are the parts I agree with least. Invariably, the advice will go something like this: 'You need to know your characters inside out and be able to answer the following questions about them: what do they like to eat for breakfast? What is their favourite colour? Are they night owls or early risers?' Usually, the list of questions is endless, and enough, in my opinion, to crush anyone's creative enthusiasm.

When you begin a work of fiction, you need to feel energized and excited about every aspect of it, including the characters with whom you'll be spending so much time. You must be eager to get to know them — ideally, you should feel magnetically drawn to them — and so to force yourself to answer a list of (often irrelevant) questions about them seems to me to be a silly task to set yourself, as silly as saying to someone who has just fallen in love, 'If you've met a gorgeous stranger who you hope might be "the one", the first thing to do is sit down and fill in a complicated tax return with him.'

Why should we strive to know the characters in our novels inside out? In real life, we don't know anyone inside out, not even those closest to us. People are unpredictable and full of secrets; many lack self-awareness and have an image of their own character that is entirely out of kilter with the reality. Sometimes the people who seem most stable are presenting a façade to the world, which might eventually crack to reveal an entirely different personality underneath. Often (as with the falling in love example above) we are keenest to spend time with — to try to get a grip on — those who are in some way elusive to us.

This is true in fiction as in life. Therefore, writing fiction is going to be far more compelling for any writer struggling with the fascinating ambiguities presented by a character he/she has invented. In writing the novel, or story, you are striving to know your characters. To a certain extent you'll succeed and to a certain extent you'll fail — ideally, by the end of the writing process, your characters will still feel slightly intangible and out of your reach. That, in my view, is how you know you've created a genuinely plausible and rounded character. You can answer questions about how early someone likes to get up or what their favourite colour is till the cows come home — and yes, some of these details might be useful to include — but what do they really tell you about the core of a person? The taste in music, the messy versus tidy — these are peripheral details, not real character. They're the sorts of thing you can easily tick off on a checklist, and, in doing so, give yourself the illusion that you know someone.

I know the preferred getting-up times of all my close relatives, for example, but I'm not sure how a single one of them would react if I killed someone in a hit-and-run accident and begged them not to tell the police.

I've often heard writers asked, 'Which is more important to you: character or plot?' Most writers choose character. I've only ever heard one answer, 'Plot, plot, plot' — that was the American thriller writer Jeffery Deaver. It's a crazy question, because plot and character are inextricably linked. The best way to start a novel is with a character in a compelling or intriguing situation. There's no character in the world unique and amazing enough to sustain readers' interest if they're not doing anything particularly fascinating, or if not much is at stake for them. Equally, the most gripping plot will fall flat if the characters acting it out are one-dimensional....

Naming Your Characters

In the real world, there are many people who aren't done justice by their names. Could David Bowie have achieved all he did if he had stuck to his original name of David Jones? Since you are the creator of your world, you have the power to give characters and places names that fit them.

Many writers say that their characters come with names, while others take weeks to come up with just the right one. However your characters and places come to you, be sure their names fit. (If you're stuck for inspiration, consult www.babynames.com or any of a number of other websites that specialize in names and their meanings.)

A name can become part of a character. Your romance heroine might be called Laetitia after a long-dead great-aunt and spend most of her waking hours trying to live it down. On the other hand, an action hero named Jefferson after the US president or Achilles after the Greek general may have trouble living *up* to his name. Always consider the impact your character's name will have on your reader: Mary is more likely to conjure up a plain, stay-at-home girl like Mary Bennet in *Pride and Prejudice* than an exotic beauty in an alien world. At the same time, avoid stereotypical names: not every prostitute is called Désirée and not everyone in 19th-century America had an Aunt Polly.

Common Mistakes

When you create characters, there are very few things that you absolutely have to avoid. With the exception of misplaced flaws and exaggerated strengths, most readers will forgive an interesting character most things.

However, there are some things you would do best to avoid when it comes to revealing your characters to the reader. Don't be overzealous in ramming home how beautiful the heroine is or how terribly shy Aunt Sally has become in her old age. Any character trait can be overdone and this can be just as bad as a character who lacks basic personality.

Allow your characters to unfold before the reader. Show the way boys react to your heroine, shy of asking her out because someone so gorgeous is bound to have a boyfriend already. Have Aunt Sally confide to a friend that she hates going even to the supermarket now that she doesn't have Uncle Jack to go with her. In other words, don't *tell* the reader what each person is like. Let them *get to know* them through other characters and their own actions.

Skip the Stereotypes

If you are writing comedy, using a representation of a person or group can be amusing. You can even exaggerate the stereotype for comic effect. Think of Phoebe in the TV series *Friends* – not just a dumb blonde but a totally off-the-wall wacky dumb blonde. But if you're writing a serious novel, avoid clichés such as the prostitute with a heart of gold, the fast-talking, in-your-face reporter, the City trader who'll do anything to clinch the deal and a host of other 'stock' characters.

It's not that you don't find these types of people in real life. And it's not that some highly successful writers don't have them in their novels. But as a beginner, it's best to try for a fresh approach to your characters. Does your beautiful blonde have to be dumb? (Or your dumb and beautiful character have to be blonde?) What would happen if your reporter had a lisp or your City trader was dashing home after work every day to care for an elderly parent? By staying away from stereotypes, you give your characters room to grow. They are free to be extraordinary, charismatic individuals who will surprise and enchant your readers.

SETTING

The Details of Where and When

If you think that when and where a story is set doesn't matter, think again. Whether the background is a creepy Yorkshire moor or a distant desert planet, setting creates the picture you are trying to portray. If you don't believe it, try taking the story about the desert planet and setting it in Wuthering Heights. How many things that you thought were basic to your plot and characters would you have to change?

Time and Place

Think of the setting for your novel as if it were the setting of a diamond ring. The diamond may be the most important part of the scene, but where you put it adds to or subtracts from its overall effect. The diamond, in this case, is your brilliant combination of plot and character. It's a masterpiece of sparkling wit and intricate facets that will mesmerize readers. Now, are you going to put that diamond in a lovely antique setting, large and heavily carved, or in something lightweight and comfortable, more in keeping with modern times? Or do you fancy a hi-tech platinum setting, one that challenges the mind and questions the future?

Whatever your choice, remember that the setting is the showcase for your work. Give your story the perfect background and your characters will shine.

Often the location of your story – both time and place – will come to you as part of the idea. *Gone with the Wind* could not have been set anywhere else but in the Deep South during the American Civil War. Philip Kerr's *Berlin Noir* is about a policeman in Berlin during the rise of Nazism – that geographical and political background is intrinsic to the plot. In both these examples, time and place are fixed so firmly that they rule out any other options. On a good day this can happen to you.

On a bad day, the character you thought could live only in Berlin in the 1930s suddenly takes a turn. He has to go to Cuba to escape persecution by the Nazis. You don't know anything about Cuba except what you hear on the news. You find yourself doing research. That's OK. Be flexible. If your character has to go to Cuba, let him go. He can always come home again.

Historical Settings

Every place, every time period is different. Historical settings allow some things to happen that couldn't happen in the present day. You can explore the world with Francis Drake or take part in the French Revolution. If you're a mystery writer, your sleuth can use his sense of curiosity and knowledge of the world to solve crimes, like Ellis Peters' Brother Cadfael. He doesn't need to worry about DNA. But he does need to know about the herbs that might have been used as poisons in 12th-century Shrewsbury.

If you decide that your perfect setting is Italy in the 1400s, expect to do a lot of research (unless, of course, you are a historian whose specialism is Renaissance Italy). But don't let that put you off if this is the right place for your novel. Certainly, if your main character is an Italian priest who knows Christopher Columbus, you have no choice but to set your story in 15th-century Italy.

Remember that accuracy is important to your plot's believability. This is true whatever you are writing about, but particularly so if you choose a historical setting. It may seem unlikely that readers will know much about 12th-century herbalism or 15th-century Italy and that getting the details right doesn't matter. But if your background lacks conviction, both you and your reader will lose the illusion that your story is real. Not only that, but some of your readers *will* know about the period you have chosen – and if you get it wrong, you can be sure they will write and complain.

Contemporary Settings

Maybe your sleuth is a monk like Cadfael, but he lives in a modern-day monastery and uses a computer to solve crimes. With a contemporary setting you don't need to research a historical period, but you still need to research certain aspects of your plot and character. What is the daily routine of a monastery like? How much freedom does your hero have to come and go? Do you know as much as he will need to know about using a computer? With other contemporary settings, you may need to swot up on stockbroking or sky-diving, bus timetables in Oxford or how yummy mummies organize the school run. You need to get this sort of detail right just as much as you would have needed to know about working conditions or travel arrangements if you had stuck with 15th-century Italy.

And What About the Future?

The future is wide open. Because no one knows for sure what's going to happen, in a futuristic novel your characters can go anywhere and do anything. They can live on an Earth that has become a barren wasteland or on a distant planet that is a garden paradise free of hunger and disease. The choice is yours. Just remember that, as you create the world of tomorrow, it has to be as detailed and as convincing as if you were writing about life today or 500 years ago.

Geographic Location

Wherever you set your novel, past, present or future, it has to *seem* real. Your characters could be in the glamorous world of New York fashion, as in Lauren Weisberger's *The Devil Wears Prada*, or part of an immigrant community in London's East End, as in

Monica Ali's *Brick Lane*. You could put your characters in the First World War trenches, as in Sebastian Faulks' *Birdsong*, or make one of them a detective in ancient Rome, like Lindsey Davis' *Falco*. Whatever suits your plot and creates the perfect setting for the characters in your novel to reach their goals is fair game.

Many authors set their stories in exotic places because they have lived in or travelled to these places. James A Michener's own travels were the inspiration for *South Pacific*. Paul Scott served in India during the Second World War; the India of that period became the setting for his *Raj Quartet* (later the television series *The Jewel in the Crown*).

If you haven't travelled to these places, you have to draw on the experience of someone who has. You need details. You want your readers to feel the heat of the jungle or the cold of the lifeless tundra. You have to know what animals exist there. You have to be able to evoke the smells and sounds, or the lack of them. What does the water taste like? What colours are the flowers, and in what season do they appear? Many of your readers will never travel to these locations: you have to make them feel that they've been there.

So First of All, Do Your Research

Many writers hate this word. They don't want to think about what they're writing: they just want to write it. If this is your attitude, the best advice is: don't write anything that requires research (see *Your Own Back Yard*, opposite). If you stay exclusively in your field of knowledge, you don't have to look up anything. The same goes for worlds that you create. All the information you need about them is stored in your own mind.

But if you want to write about a gunslinger in the Wild West, even if all you do if watch lots of old Westerns on TV, you still have to get a feel for the period and know what you're talking about.

If you want to write about Cairo, there's nothing like going there. You can taste the food, visit the pyramids, feel the sand. But this isn't always possible – or practical, if you are setting only one brief scene in Cairo.

That's why the internet is such an important resource. You can contact people around the world with just a few clicks of a mouse. You can visit museums and see virtual exhibits, view photographs of places you haven't visited and even look at live cameras. As far as research is concerned, writers have never had it so good or so easy. For far less than the cost of a trip to Peru, anyone with access to the web can read all about the history of Machu Picchu, look at pictures of the site and find details of walks along the Inca Trail. It may not be as romantic or exciting as getting on a plane and going there, but for many people, it's as close as they can get to the real thing.

Of course, many generations of writers have used books for research and their local librarian has been their best friend. It's worth checking whether your local library has an inter-library loan service, so that you can get hold of specific titles that they don't have in stock. Most libraries will perform this service for a very modest fee.

Travel books that describe contemporary places around the world are a favourite: if, say, your character has an hour to kill in Rome waiting for a connection and you want her to visit a church near the station, a travel guide may give you all the details you need.

If you need more detail than that, you're challenged by the internet and the accounts you find in books are dry, consult your local paper, library, literary festival or specialist bookshop for anyone giving a talk that might be useful to you. Many authors do 'events' all over the country to publicize their latest works and travel writers generally accompany these with photos of their experiences. You can learn a lot from what they have to say and there is almost always an opportunity to ask questions. This isn't a substitute for reading books for background, but it may help bring life to a subject that you know only at second hand.

Get Out More

You don't have to own a computer to use the web for research. Most public libraries have computers for their members to use, free of charge. Or you can go to an internet café and pay a pound or two for an hour's browsing wherever your imagination wants you to go.

Your Own Backyard

Teachers of creative writing often advise their students to write about people and places that they know. Let others write about perfumed harems and gilded palaces. You're going to write about taking your kids to school and going shopping – and you're going to make it sing.

It's not as far-fetched as it sounds. Mark Haddon's *The Curious Incident of the Dog in the Night-Time* doesn't take place in an extravagant setting. In terms of travel, all that happens is that the narrator, Christopher, goes from Swindon to London. But this unexotic location serves as a backdrop to Christopher's struggles to come to terms with the world around him. Similarly, David Mitchell's *Black Swan Green* takes place in a small village in Worcestershire, but the protagonist Jason's need to cope with his stutter and with being bullied at school is beautifully played out in this cosy setting. Many horror stories are set in the most ordinary circumstances and places. The rationale behind this is that something everyday suddenly becoming alien is particularly scary: think of Stephen King's *The Shining*, in which the hotel itself becomes a frightening character.

Here's what successful novelist Caro Fraser has to say about 'writing about what you know':

'Write about what you know' is one of those tired old adages guaranteed to polarize professional writers. In some it arouses spittle-flecked invective about the stifling of creativity and encouragement of dreary, introverted navel-gazing. There are even those who say it's particularly bad advice to give writers because, as a breed, we tend not to get out a lot. There are, on the other hand, those who believe it to be a sound precept, on the basis that if you're not writing from within the scope of your own experience, you can't possibly write with authenticity or with a truthful voice.

So, for the aspiring writer, is the advice good or bad — or what?

The answer probably lies somewhere in between. Let's first of all try to establish what is meant by 'writing what you know'. If it means using only the material of your own life, working solely with events and characters from within your personal experience, then that, at first glance, seems extremely restricting. However, if you possess the talents of Jane Austen, if you can handle social and domestic microcosms with dexterity and humour, and have a brilliant ear for dialogue and eye for detail, then what you 'know', in a strict sense, may be all you need. Yet even writers who are using only the material of their own life, like Austen, have to expand beyond the confines of their knowledge — that is, they need to manipulate and explore their experiences in creative ways that make them interesting to readers. It isn't so much what you know, as how you use it.

When I wrote The Pupil, the first in my series of Caper Court novels, I used the legal world as its setting. This wasn't because I especially wanted to write about lawyers or the law — my main interest is in people, exploring human emotions and motivations — but because setting the novel in a world with which I was familiar gave the story authenticity. I'm a barrister by training, so the legal world is one I understand. I'm familiar with lawyers' concerns, with law courts and with legal jargon. Leo Davies, perhaps my best-known character, is a successful, bisexual commercial barrister. I don't need to be bisexual to write him, because sexual impulses, passion, love, are universal emotions. All that's needed there is a little imagination and emotional empathy. But knowing what makes a commercial barrister tick enables me to write about Leo's world with a fluidity and confidence that I couldn't possibly bring to bear if I'd made him a brain surgeon. As a writer I believe it's important to get to the essential truth of a character, and it seems self-evident that this can only be achieved by properly understanding the motivations and preoccupation of that character.

Inside knowledge is invaluable if you decide to set your stories within a very particular world — take Patricia Cornwell and her experience of forensic science, or Dick Francis and his knowledge of horses and the world of racing. In such instances, 'what you know' allows you to manipulate your knowledge and use it deftly — even to subvert it for the purposes of plot. If you're not sure of your territory, your lack of confidence will transmit itself to the reader, and hamper your ability to develop plot and character. The point is, use what you know to its best advantage: your own life or experience may not strike you as a promising basis for fiction, but if you handle it with imagination and inventiveness, and create believable and empathetic characters about whom the reader can care, you may be surprised how much potential it possesses.

Details That Evoke the Setting

Whether your setting is exotic or homely, how do you add dimension to it? The five senses are a powerful place to start. What does the beach smell like? How does the sand feel between your toes? What do the waves sound like as they hit the beach? All these things represent the psychology of setting. They are the non-specific points of recognition that contribute to the reality of your locale.

Look at this piece from DH Lawrence's *Lady Chatterley's Lover* (it isn't all about sex, you know). The newly married Lady Chatterley, 'accustomed to Kensington or the Scotch hills or the Sussex downs', has moved to the industrial Midlands:

> With the stoicism of the young she took in the utter, soulless ugliness of the coal-and-iron Midlands at a glance, and left it at what it was: unbelievable and not to be thought about. From the rather dismal rooms at Wragby she heard the rattle-rattle of the screens at the pit, the puff of the winding-engine, the clink-clink of shunting trucks, and the hoarse little whistle of the colliery locomotives…. Even on windless days the air always smelt of something under-earth: sulphur, iron, coal, or acid. And even on the Christmas roses the smuts settled persistently, incredible, like black manna from the skies of doom.

Can't you just feel Her Ladyship's revulsion? Don't you know from this moment – and this is at a very early stage in the novel, the beginning of Chapter 2 – that her marriage is doomed and she is going to fall into the arms of the first handsome gamekeeper who comes her way?

Another small but important detail that can be used to evoke a setting is food, whether it is the exotic offerings of a Singapore street market or an overcooked Sunday roast on a duty visit to parents.

If you are going for a domestic setting, close your eyes and imagine your own home. What do you see? The easy chair in front of the television? The worn spot on the carpet where the dog lies? The comfort of your own bed after a hard day? These are just the sorts of details that will create a home for your characters too.

Creating the Backdrop

A setting is your novel's backdrop and you create it much as you would create a tapestry – by weaving together all kinds of details that fit into place to produce a larger picture. As you pull all your threads – your characters, dialogue and setting – together, ask yourself if they blend well or if anything clashes. If anything seems out of place, change it.

Even when you have all your information together, writing the whole thing may not be straightforward. Sometimes, even if you've asked all the questions and have all the answers, it won't all fit together. If you ever do jigsaw puzzles, you'll understand. Some pieces look as if they are exactly the right fit, yet when you try to put them into the slot they simply won't go. Other pieces don't look right but they fit anyway. Or, going back to the tapestry metaphor, you can see the whole picture in your mind's eye, yet somehow, when you start pulling the strings, everything falls apart.

When this happens to you, don't be afraid to let go of whatever doesn't work. It may be something large like how the murder is committed or how your hero happens to have amnesia. It may be something small like a side plot that was supposed to add humour but falls flat. Whatever it is, it can be rewritten, reworked, revised.

It's hard to be sure that everything is going to work before you start writing. Once you get going there is always a chance that your story will take on a life of its own and head off in a direction you hadn't planned. This could make one of your characters superfluous, or require you to create another. But the more time you spend thinking about the pieces and trying to put them together before you start, the better the chances that they will come out the way you want them to.

GETTING CHARACTERS TO TALK

Tricks for Writing Dialogue

One of the novel writer's most important resources is dialogue. You will need to use speech patterns to create impressions – to tell readers something about the character who is doing the talking.

Creating Realistic Dialogue

Start by listening to your character's voice in your head. What does he or she sound like? If you find this difficult, think about how you recognize the voices of friends and family on the phone. What makes one person's voice different from another's? What makes you like one voice more than another? Whatever the traits you identify, use them to make your character's speech memorable for your readers.

Next time you're at a party, listen to the people around you. Notice how you can hear Gloria's voice above any noisy crowd. She's an investment banker and she's always talking about what's happening in the City and whether interest rates are going to go up or down. Kevin talks like a caricature Irishman, using 'youse' as the plural of 'you' and asking 'if you would like a drink at all'. Mary never speaks above a whisper. She's a trauma nurse who frets over any injury, however small, and remembers to ask if you've had your flu jab. And Arthur whines when he speaks. His whining voice centres on how to tell one illness from another and how many rare diseases he's had this year.

Real Versus Realistic

Apply some of the things you overhear to your characters. And remember that there is a vast difference between *real* dialogue and *realistic* dialogue. Most of us talk a lot about mundane subjects such as the weather and supermarket prices. But unless the weather or the cost of living directly relates to your characters and plot, stay away from them. Also, most of us punctuate our speech with *ums*, *ers* and *you knows* – all of which become very boring if you copy them out word for word. When writing dialogue, omit these verbal fillers unless you want to show your character's nervousness.

A Night at the Cinema

Films are a good place to study effective dialogue, because they rely so heavily on it. Listen to the words being bandied back and forth between the characters. Ask yourself what works and what doesn't. Sloppy dialogue doesn't sound real. It doesn't have contractions. It doesn't pause for breath. It doesn't reflect the personality of the character. Sharp, crisp dialogue jumps off the page or out of the screen. It sparkles and makes the character shine. It's so good it can be the hook that drags the reader into the story all by itself. It moves the story forwards and keeps up the pace.

Reading Aloud

This is the crucial test of whether dialogue 'works' – does it sound right when you read it aloud? Say you have written a scene in which one character asks another a question:

'Susan, what is that that you are looking at?'

Grammatically, it's fine. But say it out loud and you'll find it's stilted; the double *that* makes it sound as if a Martian has taken over your mouth. Ask yourself what a real person – you, for instance – would actually *say* in those circumstances. How about:

'What are you looking at, Susan?'

The moment you speak these words aloud, you realize that they are punchier, more streamlined, more realistic. They have the same meaning, but they are much more effective as dialogue.

Dialogue That Fits

A tough cowboy walks into a saloon, wanting a drink. He doesn't say:

'If I don't get some whisky soon, I'm just going to die of thirst.'

No, that sounds like an elderly lady who persuades people to wait on her hand and foot by making herself sound feeble. Or possibly an over-the-top Southern belle.

What about:

> 'Could you please give me a small glass of whisky?'

No, that's a meek bank clerk who has never been in a bar before and doesn't know how to order.

> Tough cowboys talk tough. They say, 'Whisky. Now. And leave the bottle.'

It's important that dialogue reflects the characters' roles and personalities. Your reader will be reading the dialogue you write and hearing the voices in his or her head. The voices have to ring true or you will have lost one of the most powerful tools you have for showing who your characters are.

Dialogue That Rings True

In real life, people don't tell each other things that they know already, nor do they address each other by name all the time. That's what happens in bad radio plays, where dialogue has to convey all the information the listener needs and the writer isn't skilled enough to get it across any other way. In a novel, you have other options. Don't have one sister tell another that it is their mother's birthday next week – she knows that. Put it in dialogue that helps develop the characters:

> 'You aren't forgetting that it's Mum's birthday next week, are you? You know how upset she gets if we don't go for lunch.'

Or mix dialogue with narrative:

> 'You are coming next Wednesday, aren't you?'

> Wednesday is Mum's birthday and Sarah always goes into big-sister mode, assuming that I am going to forget.

> 'Yes, I'm coming. I'll be there at 12 to give you a hand with lunch.'

From these two pieces of dialogue we learn, first, that the mother is sensitive (perhaps hypersensitive?) about the attention her daughters pay her; and second, that there is tension between the two sisters. But we also know the narrator – the younger sister – doesn't want to rock the boat: she could have given Sarah a less conciliatory response. How people say things and what they choose to leave out can be just as important as what they say.

In real life, a lot of conversation is repetitive and unnecessary. In a novel, there is no room for meaningless conversation. Dialogue should always help advance the plot or tell the reader something about the character.

Male or Female?

Is there a certain way of speaking that can be defined as 'masculine' or 'feminine'? Over the telephone the pitch of the voice would normally give away the speaker's gender. But what about on the page?

'I saw her run down the street after the dog. She was wearing tight shorts and a low-neck sweater.'

'I saw her run down the street after the dog. She was wearing bright red shorts and a pink cashmere sweater.'

Without any context for this line of dialogue, you would be pretty confident that the first speaker was a man and the second a woman. But you could use the same line in different ways to convey something about the speaker:

'I saw her run down the street after the dog,' he said, an appreciative grin on his face. 'She was wearing tight shorts and a low-neck sweater.'

Or:

'I saw her run down the street after the dog. She was wearing bright red shorts and a pink cashmere sweater. I don't know how she can afford cashmere on her husband's salary.'

You are in danger of falling into sexual stereotyping here, but in the first example you have given a none-too-subtle indication of the man's lechery and in the second you have suggested a nosy and envious neighbour who probably nags her own husband about how little he earns.

If you want your reader to know what a character's voice is like, you have to describe it. A woman's voice might be sweet or shrill; if you want to give her a deep voice it could be husky or even manly. A man's voice could be deep and reassuring, a booming bass or a cultured baritone. While society looks for ways to make men and women equal, writers look for ways to tell them apart.

Because dialogue is unique to each character and each story, it's difficult to say what's right and wrong. What is right for a 1980s Scottish heroin user in Irvine Welch's *Trainspotting* would be ridiculous for a Victorian thief in Sarah Waters' *Fingersmith*, but that doesn't mean that either is better or worse than the other. Whatever your characters' ethnic or social origins, and whatever century and country they live in, they have to have something to say. Their words have to touch the reader. They have to make her laugh or cry at the right moment. They have to move the story forwards and/or reveal something important about whoever is speaking or being spoken about. And they have to do it in a way that is authentic to the character and his setting.

Dialogue Tags

At its simplest, a dialogue tag is 'he said' or 'she said'. It separates dialogue from narrative, indicating who said what, how they said it and what else was going on at the time. Today's fiction tends to use dialogue tags sparsely, relying on them only when they are necessary to enable the reader to keep track of what is going on – usually in a conversation between two or more people.

Finding the right number of dialogue tags to use in your work requires a common-sense approach. If you use too many, you'll interrupt the flow of dialogue and the storyline; too few and the reader won't be able to figure out who's talking.

Look at this example from Dickens' *Great Expectations*. The narrator, Pip, is a young boy; he and his guardian/brother-in-law Joe have fallen into conversation with a stranger in the local inn:

The stranger looked at me again…and said, 'He's a likely young parcel of bones that. What is it you call him?'

'Pip,' said Joe.

'Christened Pip?'

'No, not christened Pip.'

'Surname Pip?'

'No,' said Joe; 'it's a kind of family name what he gave himself when an infant, and is called by.'

'Son of yours?'

'Well,' said Joe, meditatively – not, of course, that it could be in anywise necessary to consider about it, but because it was the way at the Jolly Bargemen to seem to consider deeply about everything that was discussed over pipes; 'well – no. No, he ain't.'

This deceptively simple piece of dialogue moves the plot along by sparking our interest in the stranger: why is he asking so many questions? It adds to the impression we already have of Joe as a decent if not very quick-witted man. Even its use of dialogue tags adds to the character development: the repetition of the simple 'said Joe' reflects Joe's slow, measured speech. The only way to learn this technique is trial and error. When you've written enough dialogue of your own, you'll get the idea.

'Go Away,' He Sneered

A common pitfall is to use too many alternatives for 'said'. Try not to get too colourful:

'I'll see you in hell first,' he snarled.
'Oh, why does it always have to be me?' she moaned.
'Everyone must leave,' he ordered.

are fine every now and then, but soon become tiresome.

Questions of Pace and Space

Dialogue can be used to create a feeling of movement in the story. It helps the reader by – among other things – making the page look more open and easier to read. If you find that some spots in your book are not as lively or well paced as they could be, try adding some dialogue.

TELLING THE STORY
Getting It All Down On Paper

As a writer you are also an artist. You create emotions and characters. You paint a background and introduce the reader to your world. Everything on the page begins in your imagination. But it needs to have a structure.

You're almost ready to start writing, but now is the time to go back over that original idea, the one you have fleshed out with such great characters and lively dialogue, and make sure that everything is clear in your mind.

Formal Versus Informal Outlines

We talked earlier (see page 16) about whether or not you need to write an outline. You may feel that by now you know everything you need to know about where your story is going. There is no obligation to write a formal outline at this stage – that will come when you are ready to submit your work to an agent or publisher (see page 86). Anything you do now is for the sake of clarifying your own thinking.

If you do feel you want something structured, one way is to begin with:

Title: My Book
1. Characters
    a. Main characters
        1. Hero
        2. Villain
    b. Subsidiary characters

You could write a brief description of each character: the part they play in the story, what they look like, something about their goals and motivations. Create something you can glance at as you're writing in order to keep track of characters and avoid having Chapter 1's scuba diver turn into a mountaineer in Chapter 5.

Alternatively, or perhaps in addition to this, you could write out a summary of the plot, either chapter by chapter or incident by incident. A short paragraph or two for each one is usually enough – the point is to jog your memory about things you have already thought of, important details that will add to the authenticity and richness of your story.

Another option is to create a timeline. Start with the event that begins your story and move forwards. If it matters you can put in dates and times:

Tuesday morning: Dan fails to show up for work. His dead body is discovered in his garage, face down in a pool of oil. His friends Steve and Tom are suspicious because they know he was a hopeless mechanic and never did any work on his car.

Tuesday lunchtime: waiting to be interviewed by the police, Steve and Tom overhear Dan's wife Sylvia lying about where she was the night before.

Wednesday afternoon: etc. etc.

You can do this as a graph or just as a list of events, fleshing out the characters of Steve, Tom and Sylvia and adding details of the setting wherever it seems appropriate. If you prefer, you can put all these details on separate pieces of paper and spread them out over a table (preferably one that isn't going to be needed for breakfast any time soon) so that you can shuffle them around if need be. Some people even create a spreadsheet, because they have orderly minds and this is their way of keeping track of everything. There are no rules here: you are doing this for your own benefit and no one else ever needs to see it.

However you choose to outline, or even if you choose not to do it at all, you need to remember that there are three parts of your novel that are vitally important: the beginning, the middle and the end.

And if you think that adds up to 'all of it', you're absolutely right. So let's look at the impact that those three elements need to have.

The Beginning

The first words of any manuscript are the most important. They set the mood and lure the reader into the story, making him want to know what happens next. If the beginning fails, the reader will put the book down and never pick it up again. The beginning can be powerful, violent or passionate. It can be subtle like a gathering storm. It can be dialogue or narrative. But whatever its subject matter or mood, it must be exceptional. Consider:

'Have you split up now?'

'Are you being funny?'

People quite often thought Marcus was being funny when he wasn't.

Or:

When my mother died she left the farm to my brother, Cassis, the fortune in the wine cellar to my sister, Reine-Claude, and to me, the youngest, her album and a two-litre jar containing a single black Périgord truffle, large as a tennis ball and suspended in sunflower oil, which, when uncorked, still releases the rich dank perfume of the forest floor.

These are the opening lines of two very different books – Nick Hornby's *About a Boy* and Joanne Harris' *Five Quarters of the Orange* – but they share this indispensable characteristic: the reader is hooked. Who is Marcus? Why is he so often misunderstood? Why does Joanne Harris' narrator have siblings who are named after fruits and why is she bothering to tell us about the aroma of an enormous black truffle? If you can write a beginning that makes readers asks questions like this, they will read on.

Even though it is the beginning, your plot should begin in the middle. This may seem like a contrary idea, but you're trying to put your readers in the thick of things. You don't want to start with long explanations that take them into the plot. You want them to feel the icy finger of death on their necks, or to be standing at the edge of the volcano with your hero just before he slaloms down the lava flow.

Don't give readers a safe place to be. If your book starts out with afternoon tea in a Cotswold village, have someone spill the tea or make your characters gossip maliciously. Show that all is not as it seems. Engage readers in your plot from the word go.

Hooks

A 'hook' is an interesting part of the story meant to grab the reader's attention. Using a hook means that you start your piece in a way that will engage the reader and make her want to read more. A hook can be either a piece of dialogue or a description, as in the two examples quoted above. It is often emotional in nature, expressing fear, anger, passion or hatred. The key is to make sure the reader starts in the middle of the action. When you're starting a story, don't spend a lot of time establishing setting or character. If you start with action, you pique the reader's curiosity; you can work in setting and character later, once you've whetted the reader's appetite for more.

The Middle

Yes, it's essential to grab your readers in the beginning, but what you say next is important too. You've connected with your readers; now bring them into the story more deeply. Follow the plot points you established in your outline or summary. Don't be afraid to add anything that seems important that you didn't think of in the planning stage. Let the tension build as you add blocks to the story's foundation. Carefully take your readers from place to place.

Your plot should follow a logical line that your readers can follow easily. Or fairly easily. Of course you need tension. You need readers to be wondering what will happen next. But that isn't the same as wondering what is going on. Don't leave essential information out, assuming that readers will 'get it'. Sometimes they will, sometimes they won't, and there is nothing more frustrating than reading a book and suddenly feeling that you don't know what has just happened. Even in a mystery, don't leave readers stranded for long or let them fall too far behind.

Make sure that your characters' actions add to the feeling of movement in the plot. This doesn't always need to be literal movement. Sometimes a character might need to sit down and take a rest. Even Sherlock Holmes sat quietly and pondered when he had to. But that very fact could add to the tension as Dr Watson, who was narrating the stories, waited in growing frustration to hear what the Great Detective came up with. Whatever is going on, whether it is a lot or a little, the plot must continue to build, drawing readers closer as the story races like a runaway freight train towards its inevitable conclusion.

A book is said to have a 'sagging middle' if the main bulk of the text fails to grip. Somewhere between the margins of 50,000 and 75,000 words there exists a no-man's land that no writer wants to visit, the place where it is too soon to end but where the story has lost the glory of the beginning. It's as if the writer has got bored or can't figure out what to do next, so he kills time by not doing anything important with the characters or plot.

A 'sagging middle' will kill your novel stone dead. A good middle is like a series of surprise birthday parties. Readers shouldn't know what's coming next – but they can't wait to get there.

The End

Not every book has to have a surprise ending. An ending can be subtle, like a good wine, lingering with the reader for a while. But either way, everything must come together. All the loose strings should be tied up neatly. Don't end too abruptly, so that readers are sent scampering back through the book trying to figure out what happened. Remember that you and your readers are on a journey of discovery together: don't leave them out in the cold when it comes to understanding what happened and why.

Every novelist wants to write a novel that ends with the reader sighing, wiping away a tear or turning on all the lights in the house. The words that end a book should always come from the reader and they should be, 'That is the best book I have ever read.' They should want to rush out and buy every other book the author has written. That is ultimately what everyone writes for. That is the true power behind every story.

Writing a Rough Draft

Some writers think of a rough draft as another version of an outline; others see it as the first phase of writing proper. It may be nothing like the final version, but knowing that what they're writing down is more like an outline than the final text makes it easier for some writers to just start writing. And the resulting draft becomes the master plan for their novel. If you can get down the basic idea and aren't put off by the prospect of a lengthy rewrite process, this approach may work for you.

All you have to do is take the thread of your story and start writing. Don't worry about spelling, punctuation, grammar or paragraphs. Just run through until you've told the whole story from beginning to end. Doing this gives you an opportunity to find weak spots and loopholes in your characters and plot before you begin to write the manuscript proper. If you're one of those writers who must create the perfect draft first time out, repress your urge for perfection. Think of this as an exercise in writing what's on your mind.

If you simply can't bear to write anything 'rough', skip this stage and go straight to the discovery draft, overleaf – but first read the section *Turn Off Your Inner Editor* and particularly the warning about perfection being a form of procrastination on page 48.

What If You Get Into Trouble?

Oh no! Your plot has unravelled. Your main characters have flaws that can't be mended. Your setting is all wrong. Your dialogue sounds phoney. The whole thing is a disaster. The only solution is to throw it out and start again with a new idea.

There should be a word for this event. Every writer goes through it at some point, particularly beginners who don't yet have much confidence in their work. But giving up at this stage is like trading in your car because its tyres are worn out. Nine times out of ten, all you need to do is invest in new tyres.

OK, there are times – that one in ten left over from the nine times out of ten – when you do have to give up. But not – not ever – when you are working on a rough draft. This is still fine-tuning. No matter how many errors or flaws there are in your plot, you should at least try to mend them. Hopping from one manuscript to another without ever getting one to the stage where you are prepared to send it out into the world won't make you a better writer. The only way to become a better writer is to stick with what you have and fix what's wrong with it.

Your characters are weak? Go back to everything you know about creating characters and work out what makes them weak. Look through your notes about them. What can you change to make them stronger and more vibrant?

Your plot has bad spots? Where are they? What makes them bad? Why don't they work? Take each plot point and follow it through. You should be able to see where your brilliant ideas got muddled along the way.

Your setting is wrong? Change it. Change it to one that works for the characters and plot and one that you can write about with confidence. And next time, be sure to take extra time (or do extra research) before you decide where and when your novel is going to be set.

Your dialogue sounds like a B movie? Read each piece out loud. What's wrong with what's being said? Correct it by making it sound more natural and right for the character who is speaking.

If when you have done all this, you still hate it, that may be the time to give up. But I doubt it. It's a much better idea to carry on, to give your novel – and yourself – a chance to be brilliant.

The Discovery Draft

Whether or not you choose to write a deliberately rough draft as outlined on the previous page, you are going to have to write a first draft at some point. This is sometimes called the discovery draft. Think of it as a dress rehearsal for the finished product. Some writers like to write each paragraph as if it were the final draft, revising and refining as they go along. Many others feel that this is too much pressure and prefer to get the entire story down and then go back to make it perfect.

One thing you should be aware of, though, if you fall into the first category, is that first draft is *not* going to be perfect – you are going to have to reread, rethink, revise, rewrite. Frankly, you have a better chance of finishing a novel if you get the whole thing down first, then worry about making it perfect. Too many first-time writers are so concerned about crafting each sentence and phrase that they never get around to completing their story.

Getting Started

It's the big moment. You're going to sit down and write all your heaped-up ideas, the pictures in your mind, as short scenes, whether or not they come in order. Play with words the way a child plays in a playground, trying out various things any way you feel like it. Let all the research you've done come together. It doesn't have to be coherent. Shift it around like a jigsaw puzzle until you know exactly where everything goes.

This is your chance to let your writing be really creative. Throw wild colours at your canvas. Don't be shy. No one else has to see this version of your story. Writers talk about 'writer's trance', the moment when the story seems to take over and the words flow without their thinking about them. For most, this is the best writing they will ever do and it usually occurs during the rough or discovery draft.

Writing a first draft frees your mind from the world you inhabit at this moment. It allows you to move into the world you're creating. This is absolutely necessary if you hope to describe this world for your readers. If you don't believe that, try describing people and places you've never experienced. Try it using 100,000 words. If you've never been to India, for example, or done serious research on it, you'll find that words fail you after the first few hundred.

This place and these people you are excavating from your soul are real to you. The challenge is to make them real for the person reading your book. You can know all the pretty words and all the right ways to express them, but if you aren't writing as if you were really there, the reader won't be there either.

Your approach to writing this first draft will depend on your approach to writing an outline. If you haven't written anything very detailed yet, you'll just have to start writing. If you have a chapter-by-chapter breakdown, you will probably want to write your first draft in chapters too. Or if your book is character-driven – as most non-genre fiction is these days – you can write detailed studies of your entire cast of characters, saying something about who they are and what they contribute to the plot. Start with the main characters and progress to the ones that have only bit parts. Sketches for the secondary characters will not be as long or as detailed as they are for the main characters, but remember that these people add charm, wit and information to your book. The story may not revolve around them, but they make it more interesting.

By the time you finish, you should have a discovery draft of your story. It will have to be pieced together, but that is what revisions are for.

Whichever approach you choose, remember two things:

1. Spelling, punctuation, grammar and paragraph breaks are not important at this stage. Don't get bogged down worrying about semi-colons when you should be telling a story. Tidying this sort of thing up comes later.

2. If you don't like something you have written in your outline or character studies, or if you find that you want to put something in Chapter 3 that your outline had in Chapter 5 – just go with it. Change it. Rewrite it. Your outline and notes are there to help you, not to restrict the flow of your creativity. They're like a road map. If you find that the road you planned to drive along is closed, you take a different route, don't you? The same applies here. The important thing is to get to the end in the best possible way. Minor detours can strengthen your novel and give your characters a better way of getting from point A to point B.

Because there are no rules for this part of your work, you can relax. Have some fun. Enjoy your writing. Don't be afraid of making mistakes – explore the possibilities. Maybe you thought your hero empathized with the heroine because she was the product of a broken home, as he was. But in the discovery draft you realize it would create more interesting situations if she had a big family she was very close to. These are things you can't see until you start writing. Characters don't relate to one another in an outline, however detailed and organized that outline may be. They don't interact until you have them face to face in a situation.

Writer's Block

All writers dread it, but most suffer from it at some point. Your mind refuses to move a character another step forward. When this happens, most writers find it helpful to get away from their work for a while and focus on something else. An idea to resolve the situation may pop into your mind while you are loading the washing machine or taking the dog for a walk. Another option is to abandon (for the moment) the scene that is causing you problems and move on to the next. After a while, interest and enthusiasm usually return and you can go back and fill in the gaps.

Turn Off Your Inner Editor

Many writers are natural editors. All their lives they've irritated their families by correcting their spelling errors, and been annoyed by people using words wrongly. They notice if there is a question mark where there isn't a question. They point out mistakes they see on advertising hoardings or in the newspaper. It's all part of the love of language that makes writers want to write.

All this attention to detail (did somebody say nitpicking?) makes writers their own toughest critics. They may not be able to see holes in their plots or character flaws because they're too intimate with them. But the errors in spelling, grammar and punctuation that they see in their own work haunt them like a song they can't get out of their heads.

Get On With It!

Perfectionism is a form of procrastination. Don't get hung up on honing each and every word to make it perfect, if that's keeping you from completing your novel. You want your writing to be the best it can be, but you don't want editing to become your excuse for not finishing. Remember, successful writers are the ones who get published and publishers can't publish your novel if you don't finish it.

This will be difficult advice to follow if you are that sort of person, but you have to let those things go for the time being. Don't let your inner editor keep you from telling your story by making you worry too much about mistakes you can deal with in later revisions. Resist the urge to correct every minor detail. If you can't find the perfect word to describe the colour of a flower, just call it red or yellow and highlight it to remind yourself to come back to it later. It's not important right now.

On the other hand, if you have to change the fact that your murder victim died going over a cliff in his car, that will affect the rest of the plot. The clues that the detective is going to discover will be completely different if you decide the man was strangled in his bath. You need to work on this straight away. Changing what kind of car he's driving when he goes over the cliff isn't a major plot point. It can wait until you do revisions.

If you find a gap in your research – if you want to describe the dress Marie Antoinette was wearing but have forgotten to read up on 18th-century French fabrics – you could decide to stop writing and look it up, but that probably means the end of writing for the day, or at least a break in your flow. Instead, leave a gap or highlight the place in your document and carry on. Unless the details are at the core of your plot, that information can wait. Don't ruin your creative moment worrying about jacquard and brocade.

When You Finish

Finishing a rough draft, no matter how rough, is a huge accomplishment. What you should do next is simple: sit back and relax. Yes, you still have a lot of work ahead of you – it's possible that you'll need to make major revisions, do more research and then revise again. But for now, consider what you've accomplished. You've told your story from beginning to end. All the problems you created for your hero to solve have been solved. True love has conquered all. Your sleuth has found the killer. The world has been saved.

The best thing you can do now is take a break. Move away from your computer screen and refocus your eyes. Reacquaint yourself with your family. Stay in bed for an extra hour or two. If you are not working to a deadline, leave the manuscript alone for a while – a few days or even more. This will give you a fresh perspective when you come back to it.

Do More Research

Now is the time to look up the information you were missing. You may find your flower is scarlet or vermilion, golden or amber. You may discover that jacquard wasn't invented until ten years after Marie Antoinette's death. It's fine to go back and fill in this sort of gap, as long as you resist the temptation to start editing just yet.

This is also a good moment to reread all your reference materials and check for any errors you may have made in your background. Be thorough. Remember what we said earlier about setting: there *will* be someone among your readers who knows all about the subject, whatever it is, and even those who aren't familiar with it will probably spot a lack of authenticity.

It's Time to Edit

Taking even a few days off can give you an amazing amount of distance and objectivity when it comes to rereading your work. You notice all sorts of things you had never noticed before. At this point it is almost inevitable that most of them will be bad. The plot isn't as exciting as you thought it would be. The characters don't interact, or they react with the force of a sledgehammer. You didn't realize there could be so much bad dialogue in a single book. Your setting feels about as real as the backdrop of a silent film. You want to throw the whole thing away and start again.

Hold on. We've been through this before (see page 45). There are cures for almost anything that ails a rough draft. Remember, this was never meant to be the finished product. You were supposed to make mistakes. Now is the time to correct them.

Your hero seems weak? He stumbles when he should be walking confidently? He mumbles when he should be taking charge? Put it right. Figure out what is wrong and correct it. He's still your character. You have the final say in everything he does. If he stumbles, help him up. If he mumbles, change his dialogue. Consider how you saw him the first time he popped into your head. Reshape him to fit that image.

You don't like the dialogue? Your heroine sounds mild-mannered when she should be outspoken? Or abrasive when she's meant to be sweet? Go through her dialogue and pinpoint what you don't like about it. Change her words to suit what you first envisioned and what the plot needs. And make sure that the rest of her character changes with her.

Not enough plot? Your novel is supposed to be 100,000 words. Your rough draft is a mere 50,000 and even so the plot runs out before the end. Go back and find the place where your plot starts winding down. What can you do to give it more oomph? Do you need to add an incident (another murder) or complication (an old girlfriend comes back into the hero's life)? Or do you need a larger, more important subplot? Either approach could help.

Too much plot? This can be even worse than not enough. Half-solved theories, partially developed characters and storylines that go nowhere are the hallmarks of this problem. You want to keep your readers engaged. You want to give them plenty of action and excitement. But too much excitement that doesn't fit in and makes the book too busy isn't good either. It leaves readers feeling as if they have been run over by a car at an intersection. They wonder what happened and how they failed to see the oncoming vehicle. Correcting this mistake can be as easy as removing an unnecessary subplot or character. Focus on what's important to the story. Make that exciting and you won't need anything else.

A weak ending? Go back to your original premise and revise with the idea that the reader has to be as excited at the end of the story as you were when you began to write it. If she doesn't know what happened, she may be frantically looking back through the book trying to figure out where she lost the thread. Letting the reader down gently is a fine art. When she finishes a book, she wants to feel satisfied with the conclusion. She wants the story to have played itself out. If the characters seem rushed or the plot seems cut off, she'll feel cheated. Not let down gently – just let down.

Some writers dread writing the last scene, because it means they have to let go of a character they have come to love. But you can't drag the book out just so that you can stay in the world you have created. You may be able to write another book with the same characters. First you have to finish this one. If you find yourself staring at a blank final page, ask yourself what your reader would like to see here. What would give a sense of ending and completion? What would make her come back to read about this character again? The answers to these questions should help you finish the story, even if you don't want to.

AS GOOD AS IT CAN BE...
Some Basics of Structure and Style

In the previous chapter we considered what might need correcting in your story and the way you tell it. Once you've dealt with that, it is finally time to polish your structure and presentation. Here are a few basics that you should keep in mind.

Chapter Breakdown

A novel doesn't have the same structural rules as, say, a sonnet or a haiku, but there is a more-or-less accepted framework. The most macro element of this framework is generally the chapter.

A chapter may be as long or as short as necessary. Some writers prefer to keep all their chapters about the same length, say 5,000 words, which would mean an average-length book had 15–20 chapters. Other writers vary chapter size: one may be 1,200 words (only about three or four printed pages) while another is 6,000. This may be dictated by the pace of the book or the way the plot develops: you don't want to break off in the middle of the most exciting part to say 'Chapter 10' just because you have reached the required number of words in Chapter 9. Most publishers don't mind about chapter length, as long as the book has the right number of words in total.

How much happens in a chapter is up to you, too. Sometimes a lot, sometimes a little. The hero may meet the heroine, fall in love, have a misunderstanding and break up, all in the space of a chapter. At other times a whole chapter may be consumed by the hero driving from his office to the nursing home where his elderly mother lives, worrying about what sort of mood she will be in today.

How to Begin and How to End

How many times have you been reading in bed, or over a cup of coffee during a break in your working day and said to yourself, 'I'll just get to the end of this chapter'? And then found yourself three pages into the next chapter without realizing it? That's because the writer has been clever with chapter endings.

Except for the end of the book, when you have to tie up all the loose ends, never end a chapter by solving anything. If your hero is having a problem catching up with the bad guy, don't let him catch him on the last page of a chapter, unless the bad guy has a gun in his hand. Chapter endings should be dynamic and energetic, taking the reader's breath away and forcing her to continue reading.

The first sentence in every chapter should draw the reader into the story, just as the first sentence in the book did. Starting with dialogue or a strong piece of action may persuade the reader not to go to sleep just yet.

Paragraphs

Each chapter is further broken down into paragraphs. Paragraphs are versatile and flexible; they may be a page long or just a few sentences. But unless you are writing dialogue (see below), they should be more than one sentence. As a rule, a single sentence cannot stand as a separate paragraph of narrative text.

If you haven't done it automatically as you wrote your first draft, breaking your manuscript into paragraphs should be done with an eye for both sense and readability. Huge blocks of text can be off-putting. Many readers will give up – or at least skip a few lines – rather than wade through that much information. You may be reluctant to break a single thread of thought that runs through a page-long paragraph. Henry James famously wrote in very long paragraphs, but even with a great stylist such as him, many people find him difficult to read for this very reason. It's for the good of your story that you offer it to your readers in a way that they can take it in.

This doesn't mean that you should never use a long paragraph. Paragraphs don't all have to be the same length. Long paragraphs can be right for creating mood, but shorter paragraphs convey more movement. Excitement and agitation can be expressed with short, choppy paragraphs.

Use paragraph breaks every time you change the mood or place. Give your reader plenty of room to absorb all your words.

Dialogue Format

Each line of dialogue constitutes its own paragraph. For instance:

> She walked into the house and closed the door.
> Her mother looked up. 'Back already?'
> 'Yes.'
> 'Well, there's nothing to eat. I wasn't expecting you.'

This is where you break the rule about single-sentence paragraphs. The convention is that each new speaker has a new paragraph. That's because it is so easy for a reader to get lost when more than one character is speaking. Always keep in mind that you want to make it as easy for the reader as possible. She may be reading in a room full of crying toddlers, or on a crowded bus on the way to work. A fascinating story will go a long way towards keeping her attention. But a well-ordered page helps too.

Don't worry that there is too much of what publishers call 'white space' on a page of dialogue. Readers can cope with that. They may even welcome it after an extended piece of 'moody' narrative where you indulged in a few longer paragraphs. It would be far worse to have the dialogue jumbled together without paragraphing. A dialogue paragraph means the reader instantly recognizes when a different character is speaking, even without dialogue tags.

Sentence Structure

Each paragraph is made up of sentences. There are plenty of books about grammar and sentence structure: what concerns us here is how you use sentences to the best advantage. Sentences can be long or short, but each one should make sense and get to the point.

So how do you write good sentences? Use strong verbs and interesting nouns. Be sure that you have something to say. Do what feels natural. Watch out for awkward ways of saying something and strive to make them clearer and easier to understand. Compare these two paragraphs:

He'd always been afraid of lifts. As a child, he avoided them. Later, they became a necessary evil. Now he faced the ultimate challenge. His new job required him to get into a lift that went up ninety-nine floors.

He gulped as he faced his new enemy. A lift that went up ninety-nine floors. Yes, he was afraid of lifts. He had always managed to avoid them as a child. But now he had no choice. He had to get into that lift or not go to work.

There is nothing grammatically wrong with the first version. It conveys the same information as the second. But the second is more active and punchy Don't be afraid of using sentence fragments such as 'A lift that went up ninety-nine floors' if it enhances your text.

As for sentence length, look at these two examples:

When I came back from the East last autumn I felt that I wanted the world to be in uniform and at a sort of moral attention forever; I wanted no more riotous excursions with privileged glimpses into the human heart. Only Gatsby, the man who gives his name to this book, was exempt from my reaction – Gatsby, who represented everything for which I have an unaffected scorn. If personality is an unbroken series of successful gestures, then there was something gorgeous about him, some heightened sensitivity to the promises of life, as if he were related to one of those intricate machines that register earthquakes ten thousand miles away.

Dolly stole a glance down the staircase. There were soldiers milling around below, dozens of them, wearing the colours of the palace guard. One of them spotted her and began to shout – the Queen? Is the Queen up there?

Dolly stepped quickly back, out of his line of sight. Who were these soldiers? What did they want? She could hear their feet on the stairs now. Somewhere close by, the Princess began to cry, in short, breathless gasps. Augusta thrust the baby into her arms – here, Dolly, here, take her, she won't stop. The baby was screaming, flailing her fists. Dolly had to turn her face away to keep from being struck.

The first of these, from F Scott Fitzgerald's *The Great Gatsby*, has 110 words and three sentences. The second, from Amitav Ghosh's *The Glass Palace*, has 112 words and 12 sentences. The first is lyrical, evocative, haunting. You read the long sentences slowly and ponder what great sorrow they foreshadow. The second is action-packed and anxious. You read them quickly, you want to get on with the story: where is the Queen? Is she all right? Will Dolly and the baby escape?

Try these effects with your own work. Choose your sentence length to suit your story. Vary it to change pace and mood.

Making Every Word Count

Deciding what to put in and what to leave out is tough. Deciding what to leave in and what to take out when you are editing is even tougher. Writers tend to fall in love with their words and ideas. That is one reason why it helps to put your work aside for a while before coming back to revise it: you need to distance yourself from it just a little, so that you can judge it more dispassionately.

As a writer, you should be prepared to sacrifice anything in the name of clarity. If the reader has no idea what you are talking about, then the greatest story ever told has no meaning. Telling a tale clearly and brilliantly should be the goal of every writer.

With this in mind, stay away from fancy words that the average person doesn't know and doesn't want to know. Don't say 'masticate' when all you mean is 'chew' or 'peruse' when you mean 'read'. Your reader wants to read your story: she isn't interested in the breadth of your vocabulary. Also, in addition to being irritating, the more you use big words, the more likely you are to use them incorrectly. Never, ever use a word unless you are absolutely certain of its meaning. Don't say disinterested when you mean uninterested, or fortuitous when you mean fortunate. Say what you mean, mean what you say is one of your most important mantras.

Brevity: the Writer's Virtue

Being succinct is an art. Even in a book of 100,000 words, it is important to keep the story fresh and vital. Say what needs to be said in each scene or piece of dialogue, then move on. Don't belabour the point. If you feel the story or a scene is being dragged out for too long, the chances are that the reader will think so too.

Some writers feel it's their responsibility to educate their readers, whether it is about spirituality, world events or whatever. They feel the need to drive their point home over and over again in a way that would make a children's book on good manners look interesting. Being preachy when you write will alienate more people than it attracts. If you are able to get some small point that you believe in across, then good for you. But be entertaining first. Let readers pick up on your moral if they like, without having it hammered down their throats.

Overwriting Descriptions

Overlaying your work with too many metaphors and lavish descriptions will make it feel like a Victorian drawing room. Think of all those lace doilies over velvet cushions. Rugs on top of carpets, bric-a-brac on every surface, pictures all over the walls. The Victorians didn't know the expression 'less is more'. The result was nice and comfy most of the time, but sometimes it became stifling.

Watch out for flowery phrases describing simple things and for page-long descriptions of the room in which the heroine finds herself. Description is fine in small doses. But if your long sentences of description are turning into long pages, cut it back. Find ways of injecting some of it into conversation. Remember that you have a whole book to fill. You can add little details all the way through it. Unless it is crucial to your plot development, there's no need tell us on page 2 that the flowers in your alien world smell like chocolate. They'll be just as sweet if you mention them on page 139.

Overstating Your Point

As I said a moment ago, it is OK for your book to have a message as long as it doesn't become an obsession. Readers don't care about your obsessions unless you are Captain Ahab chasing a great white whale. You can make them feel guilty about eating meat or voting Conservative if it is something to do with the story – but not otherwise.

The same applies to something as simple as how sexy and beautiful your heroine is. Readers can only stand to be given information like that so many times. After a while, instead of empathizing with her, they begin to want her to fall over a cliff. This is not the reaction you want.

Over-Explaining the Story

Mystery novels aren't the only places where you can explain too much. Even if yours isn't the sort of book where over-explaining 'gives the game away', any novel that tells too much about the plot, the characters or the setting is flawed. You're trying to give your readers a *feel* for the place, the time or the people. You don't need to spend 25 pages telling them everything you know about it – and they certainly don't want to know. Caro Fraser puts it this way:

> One of the dangers of working largely from research is that you can get carried away by your own discoveries. There is a temptation, when researching some incidental aspect of a novel, to use a wealth of interesting information and fact in the novel itself. Most of it isn't needed. It may have helped you to write with confidence, but the reader can usually do without it. More than a few writers fall into the trap of imagining that their sudden, profound depth of knowledge about

some esoteric subject will be just as fascinating to the reader as it is to them. In one of my novels I had to create a character who develops dementia, and I spent a lot of time researching dementia and its effects on the individual. At the end of the day, however, I took what I had learned and used my imagination to create what I hoped was a believable characterization. The research stayed in my notes.

How do you know if you've explained too much? Look for repetition: that's the hallmark. But also ask yourself if a particular fact or description is in there for a reason. If you find that you have detailed the kind of thread that was used in a Roman toga without advancing the plot or developing a character, you've overdone it – take it out.

Show, Don't Tell

This is a mantra of creative-writing classes that you have probably heard many times. Only occasionally will the reader accept text that simply tells what has occurred without describing it. In your rough draft, there are probably passages where you simply said what happened or what the characters did or how they felt without really involving the reader. Now is the time to go back and rewrite.

For example, you might have said that the heroine was worried about climbing the mountain because of the risk of an avalanche. That doesn't engage your reader: it's too passive. Try livening it up with a bit of dialogue:

'Are you sure it's safe to climb today?' She looked up at the mountain that seemed to touch the sky. 'Those snow packs look pretty heavy. It wouldn't take much to bring them down.'

Both ways accomplish the same thing: the reader knows that the mountain is high and covered with snow. But the second way doesn't read like a travelogue. It draws the reader in, helping her to see through your character's eyes.

Of course there are times when you simply have to 'tell'. One of these is during tense or fast-moving scenes:

They struggled for the gun. Max kicked it across the room. But Sam shoved him against the door and pulled out a knife.

Scenes like this don't have time to be pleasant or descriptive. In fact it's important that they aren't. Your concern here is not to break the tension or mood with unnecessary description. In this case, terse, staccato words and sentences work best. Stick to the bare minimum and tell your readers what's happening. Think of it as a live commentary on a football game: you're excited, possibly scared; so are your characters and with any luck your readers will be too.

The Cutting-Room Floor

In real life there is a surfeit of words. People don't consider that what they're saying might be repetitive or unimportant, as you realize every time you eavesdrop on someone else's mobile-phone conversation on the bus. They don't have to think about how everything they say and do fits together to make a coherent whole.

Writing isn't like that. Writers observe real life in order to learn more about people and situations. They *mimic* real life. But even a 100,000-word novel is too small to encompass everything that happens in a single day in the real world. Nor would you want to encompass it – as we said in the chapter about dialogue, too much of what happens to most of us on a daily basis is too mundane, and frankly too boring, to be included in a novel.

That's why writers have to choose their words carefully. They have a limited amount of space in which to tell their story. Think of it as being on a budget, only instead of money it is words that are restricted. You need to consider how much narrative you are going to spend on any given scene. That doesn't necessarily mean allocating a fixed number of words (though if you are the type who has already chosen to write a detailed outline, you may find this works for you). What most writers do is write the scene, then go back and tighten it. Cut anything that is rambling, or that comes under the headings of overwriting, over-explaining or overstating your point. Don't use six words where one will do. Not every scene needs to have action or tension that propels it forwards, but every scene needs to know why it's in the book and what its function is for the storyline.

Shortening Dialogue

This goes back to the two hard-and-fast rules mentioned earlier:

1. Read it out loud and see if it sounds natural.
2. Don't have your characters tell each other something that they both already know. They wouldn't do that in real life.

Look at this example of total information overload:

> *'Mary, where are those fuzzy red slippers that you gave me last year for Christmas when I was sick with the flu and my aunt was visiting from Scotland?'*

If you find your dialogue rambles on in this way, get out your scissors immediately!

How could you present this passage differently? First of all, decide if it is important for the reader to have all this information. Does it matter what colour the slippers are, or that they were a Christmas present from Mary? Do we need to know that the speaker had the flu last Christmas, or that her aunt was visiting, or that the aunt came from Scotland? If not, take out the surplus stuff.

Even if all this information is essential, it could be conveyed in a more lively, less stilted way. How about:

'Mary, have you seen my red fuzzy slippers? I was just thinking about last Christmas when you gave them to me. Do you remember? Aunt Phyllis was visiting from Scotland and I had the flu. I was so feeble I couldn't bend down to put the slippers on and you had to do it for me.'

It's longer, but much less tedious.

Personal Style

Many writers define style as a personal voice that distinguishes their writing from anyone else's. For many successful writers, their 'style' is what attracted a publisher to them in the first place and what makes their fans stay loyal.

But style is also used as an excuse for deviations from writing norms. If you choose to have paragraphs three pages long or use no dialogue tags at all, you can call that your 'style'. Certainly this can make your writing original, but if it moves it too far outside the mainstream – or makes it too difficult for most people to read – it can also make it more liable to be rejected. If no one understands your style, you have two options: give up hope of publication, or change it.

To work, your style should be a natural extension of who you are. That's why different people write differently. Style reflects how you see the world around you and how you express that vision back to others. It doesn't mean that you always have to write in the same way about the same things. Writers can change their style – from one book to another, or as they grow older and see the world in a different way. Many successful writers, including Agatha Christie and Ruth Rendell, have published novels under more than one name to alert their readers to their different approaches or different subject matter. Graham Greene's attitude to religion changed over the course of his life and that is reflected in his writing. None of that means that any way you choose to write is unnatural. The words that come to you and the characters you create are part of you – and part of your style.

But don't use this as a crutch. You can always improve your style. If you work to make your writing better, that better style will become natural to you. There is always something new to learn.

Keeping Track

As you edit, try to work through your book consecutively. If a scene from later on in the novel comes to you, write it down in note or rough-draft form and then forget about it until it is its turn. Keeping track of where you are in a story is hard enough; trying to write scenes from all over the plot could end with you being completely confused and your story losing its life. That is what we have been working very hard to avoid. By the time you have worked through everything in this chapter you shouldn't be tearing your hair out or losing interest in your book altogether; you should have a polished draft, ready for a final edit.

NEARLY THERE...

The Final Edit

Editing your work is a serious job. Some writers really enjoy this part of the process; others hate it, because it means looking out for flaws and they hope they've got rid of them all by now. If you refuse to accept the possibility that your manuscript has mistakes in it, hire an editorial consultant (see pages 195–197) to put you straight.

Reading Aloud

If you choose to do the job yourself, one approach is to read your manuscript aloud. This may sound simple, but it isn't. It takes stamina and focus to read through a 100,000-word book as if it were a children's story. You have to stay alert, because if you don't pick up errors as you go, the exercise becomes pointless. It might take you a week or more, depending on how much time you have and how strong your vocal cords are.

As you read, words that don't sound right will show up quickly. Bad dialogue will become easy to spot. Too much narrative will put you to sleep as surely as it will any other reader.

You can correct mistakes as you go, while they are fresh in your mind. Or, if you prefer, you can take notes and make the changes later, when you have finished reading. The advantage of this is that you may find errors that compound each other. If you try to correct them as you go, you'll end up coming back again as you spot something else that needs changing.

Ring the Changes

One way to make your work seem fresh as you read it for the umpteenth time is to put it into another format. If you have always worked on screen, print out a hard copy and read that. Or change the typeface so that it *looks* different. This may help you to pick up errors you've missed so far.

Finding Flaws

This can be a painful process, but the more you practise the easier it becomes. To start with, you are looking for things that just don't feel right, as if you had walked into your living room and found that someone had moved a piece of furniture – it's subtle, but still noticeable. Typical examples include:

- Too many characters introduced too quickly in the opening pages.
- Telling your reader what's going to happen before it happens.

- Backstory introduced too early, before the reader is drawn into the narrative.
- Mentioning a character's name more than once or twice on the first page.
- Confusion about whose voice is telling the story.
- The plot unravels too quickly.

This may seem like a daunting list, but you'll get better and faster at spotting mistakes as you go along. Learn right away to have confidence in your judgement. But also learn all you can about editing. Read books about it. Read other novels in your field and criticize them. What's right about them? What's wrong? Go to lectures given by writers and editors. They can help you hone ways to find mistakes in your work.

Your Own Bad Habits

Looking for your personal demons in your text can be a strange experience. How many times did you use the word *finally* in the course of your novel? Some writers use the search mode on their computer to help pinpoint their overuse of specific words.

Inconsistencies

It has been known – in a published novel, no less – for the heroine's name to change from Eleanor in Chapter 1 to Emily in Chapter 2. That's an extreme example of neither the author nor the editor doing her job, but less glaring inconsistencies will put editors and readers off. For example:

- A detective in Victorian times cannot rely on DNA evidence.
- A heroine who started out blonde shouldn't turn into a redhead unless we have seen her going to the hairdresser's.
- A hill that started off being 500 metres high can't grow into a 5000-metre mountain.
- A character can't get from London to Edinburgh in two hours unless he is a superhero or has his own private jet.
- A rose garden can't be looking its best if your setting is Christmas time.

Keep your notes handy as you edit, particularly if you need to check historical or technical facts. Don't let this sort of mistake slip through because you didn't bother to get it right.

Sentence Structure

As you read, think how your sentence structure looks. Is it sloppy or neat? Can you tell the difference between times of great excitement and times when things are going smoothly? Are your sentences grammatical and correctly punctuated? Are they set up in the best way to ensure that readers get the idea you want them to have? This may seem trivial in comparison to solving a murder case, but readers will appreciate your storyline better if they can make sense of your sentences.

This is another instance where reading your words aloud should give you a better understanding. If you have to catch your breath when you've finished reading a sentence, it's too long. If you feel you have to speak faster to get through it, it's too long. Break it up into smaller sentences. You don't have to lose the idea or the train of thought. Just make it more accessible to the reader.

Checking Spelling

Spelling correctly is an important way to make a good first impression on an agent or editor. It shows that you cared enough to make sure everything was in good shape. Remember, you have spent quality time creating this work. Don't let it go out the door without being the best it can be.

Spell checkers are wonderful things, but they can't tell when you have inadvertently used the wrong word. They don't know the difference between *to*, *too* and *two*, or between *there* and *their*. It's up to you – not your computer – to read through carefully and make sure you don't make this sort of mistake.

Checking Style

The computer also can't tell if you are using the right words to make your point. It can be hard to know if words are too difficult for your readers to understand. People who read tend to have above-average IQs, but that doesn't mean that a professor or a lawyer wants to read unfamiliar words for pleasure. Read other authors who write in your field and compare their vocabulary with yours.

If in doubt, keep it simple. You don't have to talk down to your readers. You're just trying to give them a good read without straining their brains to understand what you are saying. If you want to write textbooks, go and write textbooks – but don't put that sort of language in your novel.

And Finally...

Are you satisfied? Is your book really and truly as good as you can make it? Then now is the time to venture out into the publishing world – and that is what the next section is all about.

Part 2
Insiders' Information

The articles in this section are written by publishing professionals, giving their perspectives on what agents and publishers are looking for and what might happen to you and your book when you are offered a contract. See pages 6–7 for biographical details of these contributors.

STUDYING CREATIVE WRITING

The Course Options Available

Jem Poster

Most of those who think of discovering themselves as writers also imagine being discovered as writers by others: dreams of literary achievement are usually partly – and sometimes primarily – dreams of commercial success and/or critical acclaim. The ambition to be published is natural and entirely understandable, but it's worth remembering that there are many forms of creative fulfilment. No reputable creative writing course will offer you a guarantee of success in the crowded field of literary publishing but all good courses will help you to advance in your understanding of the craft of writing. For some, this will give readily measurable results – an agent, a publisher, good sales figures – while for others the benefits may be more modest, but no less important: for a student who begins with limited confidence and ability, the eventual production of a handful of well-written poems can represent a very real achievement.

I'm emphasizing this point because even the most basic statistical analysis will make it clear that many of those who complete programmes of creative writing study don't in fact go on to achieve literary success in the public sphere. But if you bear in mind that publication isn't the only measure of a course's value, you'll be open to the full range of possible benefits.

Short Courses

Many aspiring writers will already have attended at least one short creative writing course but if you haven't yet done so, this might be a good starting point. Short courses offer an opportunity to get the flavour of working with a small group under tutorial guidance. The best known are those run by the Arvon Foundation at their four UK centres; and you might also look at the courses at Ty Newydd, the National Writers' Centre for Wales, which works in close collaboration with Arvon. Keep an eye open, too, for courses organized as part of literary festivals: the Cheltenham Festival of Literature sometimes offers two-day courses, while the Oxford Literary Festival offers a six-day residential programme.

It would perhaps be unwise to base any significant decision solely on your experience of a single short course, but it's fair to say that if you've enjoyed one or more of them (and particularly if enjoyment has been accompanied by a noticeable improvement in your writing ability), then there's a good chance that you're ready for a more sustained programme of study.

Longer Courses

If you feel that you want to commit to a more prolonged creative writing course, a good option would be one of the part-time certificates or diplomas organized for mature students by the continuing education departments of a number of universities. In London, for example, there's Birkbeck's two-year certificate course, while those living in or near Oxford might take advantage of the two-year diploma course offered by Oxford University's Department for Continuing Education. Other continuing education departments offer similar opportunities. Because these courses are designed to accommodate those with domestic or professional commitments, classes tend to take place in the evenings and at weekends.

Technically, certificate courses operate at first-year undergraduate level and diploma courses at second-year level: the former might therefore seem most suitable for beginners and the latter for more advanced writers. However, there is often some flexibility on entrance requirements, and the standard is in any case defined partly by the quality of your fellow students – so don't automatically assume that you're restricted to one or the other.

Useful Websites for Short Courses

The Arvon Foundation: www.arvonfoundation.org
The Cheltenham Festival of Literature: www.cheltenhamfestivals.com
The Oxford Literary Festival: www.sundaytimes-oxfordliteraryfestival.co.uk
Ty Newydd: www.tynewydd.org

University Degree Courses

Undergraduate (BA) programmes mix creative writing with literary study. There are historical reasons for this – creative writing programmes have usually grown out of existing English departments – but there are also sound practical reasons. It's simple: good creative writers need to be good analytical readers and the intermingling of the two strands is both natural and necessary.

The programme of study is likely to last for three years, and to be dominated by participants of standard undergraduate age (18–21), though mature students are usually welcome. The courses differ significantly from one university to another, so it's difficult to generalize; all offer guidance on the elements of good writing, while helping students to understand the relationship of their own work to a wider literary tradition.

Masters (MA) programmes offer more specialized training in the craft of writing and they are more likely than undergraduate courses to emphasize the goal of publication. Since they assume a certain level of critical and creative expertise, it follows that the majority of successful applicants will be graduates in English or closely related disciplines – classics or modern languages, for example. But you shouldn't be deterred if your previous degree is in a subject only loosely related to English studies: if you have a good degree in any subject and can show a convincing portfolio of creative work, it's well worth discussing your situation with the institution concerned in the hope that it will consider an application.

Useful Websites for Longer Courses

Birkbeck College: www.bbk.ac.uk/study/ce/creativewriting
Bristol University: www.bristol.ac.uk/english/cw-diploma
Oxford University Department for Continuing Education:
www.conted.ox.ac.uk
Sussex University: www.sussex.ac.uk/cce

It's often possible to study for an MA on a part-time basis, but those with other commitments will usually need to juggle them carefully since – unlike the certificate and diploma courses discussed above – MA courses normally require daytime attendance. Courses last for a year (two years in part-time mode).

PhD programmes in creative writing are not as widely available as MA programmes, but are offered by a substantial number of universities, including Aberystwyth, Bath Spa, Lancaster, Manchester and St Andrews. Typically, a PhD student will spend three years on a major creative project (a novel, a collection of short stories or a substantial collection of poems) together with a critical account that both analyses and contextualizes that work. PhD study tends to be less communally focused than the programmes of study discussed opposite, but a good department will ensure that there are ample opportunities for meeting up with other students.

An MA in creative writing may not be a prerequisite for PhD study, but it arguably provides the best grounding. You'll certainly need to provide evidence of a high level of prior attainment both as a creative writer and as a critical thinker. If you're interested in the possibility but have doubts about your eligibility, don't hesitate to discuss the matter with a representative of the department concerned.

Useful Websites for Degree Courses

Aberystwyth University: www.aber.ac.uk/english
Bath Spa University: www.bathspa.ac.uk
University of East Anglia: www.uea.ac.uk
Glamorgan University: www.glam.ac.uk
Lancaster University: www.lancs.ac.uk/fass/english
Manchester University: www.arts.manchester.ac.uk/newwriting
St Andrews University: www.st-andrews.ac.uk
Warwick University: www.warwick.ac.uk

What Form will the Teaching Take?

Except in the case of PhD programmes, you can normally expect the workshop to figure centrally in your course of study: a workshop is essentially a small-group discussion focusing on writing produced by course members. A good creative writing tutor will ensure that group work of this kind is simultaneously stringent and supportive – that is, it offers suggestions for the improvement of the work under review while at the same time acknowledging its strengths. A successful, well-run group will operate collaboratively rather than competitively, working towards insights which will be useful to all of its members.

Try to find out the probable size of workshop groups when you check the course details: somewhere between 8 and 15 students is appropriate. You might also want to find out whether the course provides one-to-one tutorials: a programme that offers individual tuition as part of its provision has obvious advantages over one that doesn't.

Who Are the Teachers?

These will be writers, often well-known ones. The short courses tend to draw on a wide range of writers, ringing the changes each year. University departments are likely to have a stable core of full-time creative writing staff, often augmented by part-time tutors; again, all are likely to be practising writers.

It's worth looking closely at the published work of these tutors before making your decision: if you like the work of a particular writer, it's probable that you will enjoy the classes he or she teaches.

A word of warning, however: the presence of a particular writer's name on the list of a university department's teaching staff is no guarantee that he or she will be teaching extensively (or even at all) on the course you sign up for. If this matter is important to you, be sure to make the necessary enquiries in advance.

A tutor's publishing profile is a significant indicator but not the only one. In the case of university courses, it's important to be taught by appropriately qualified tutors: academic qualifications don't outweigh creative achievements, but if good writers are also academically well qualified they are likely to be in a stronger position to offer academic guidance.

How Will I Benefit?

As I suggested in my introduction, it's conceivable that the benefits of creative writing study will be tangible and obvious; but even if you don't end up with a contract for your novel or poetry collection, you're likely to have benefited in other ways. As a student on a creative writing course, you'll usually be expected to produce work by a particular time or date. This may sound intimidating, even restrictive, but it can actually be surprisingly empowering to know that other people are waiting to see your work. And then there's the feedback you get on that work – not to mention the feedback you'll be invited to give to other members of your group: again, this may seem intimidating at first, but as your critical awareness develops, you'll find yourself appreciating the subtleties of the writing process in new and increasingly sophisticated ways.

The ability to write and speak well is an immensely important social and professional skill. Many employers are, for obvious reasons, interested in job applicants with well-developed powers of expression, while social relationships almost invariably benefit from the participants' ability to say what they mean in suitably nuanced language. A well-taught course in creative writing will, at the very least, offer you fresh insights into language and the ways in which we use it; it will almost certainly heighten your awareness of the world around you and help you to express that awareness; and it's always possible that – as with any serious programme of study – it will radically change your life.

LEARNING TO WRITE

A Guide to What you Can and Can't be Taught

Simon Brett

Is it possible to teach anyone to write? The answer to that question would have to be no. You can't teach *anyone* to write. If the person has no interest in or aptitude for writing, then the task is impossible. And even when you're dealing with people who are motivated, there is still a question mark over whether they can actually be *taught*.

I speak as someone who has spent a lot of time conducting creative writing classes. I have been a tutor for the Arvon Foundation (see pages 64–65 and 71–72), I have led workshops in libraries and at literary festivals. I have taught courses in rural France and on the Greek island of Skyros. I have even run a week of workshops on short-story writing in Nigeria. And yet I'm still ambivalent about whether writing can be taught.

One thing I'm certain of, though, is that an experienced writer can facilitate the work of an aspiring writer. You can save people time; you can stop them from pursuing their craft in directions that will prove unrewarding. For example, you can point out that, however good a 72-minute radio play someone has written may be, there are no slots on BBC radio for 72-minute plays. Or you can gently suggest that writing a novel about a writer with writer's block is possibly not the most rewarding route to travel. Often all you're doing is giving aspiring writers a bit of confidence in their own abilities. Above all, you can encourage them in the belief that the ambition to write is not an unnatural one.

In the various courses I've conducted, I have observed that the participants get at least as much stimulus from each other as they do from the tutors. A few people grow up in literary families or even dynasties, but for the great majority wanting to write is a slightly unusual aspiration and feeling that urge can sometimes lead to a sense of isolation. Just being with other people who share the ambition has a very liberating effect.

> The prerequisite for any writer must be the desire to write. At school most students will at one stage or another have been set a creative writing task. For the majority the demand was sheer purgatory, for the few it was a moment of great excitement and liberation. The same majority would regard continuing to do such homework for the rest of one's life as a bizarre and masochistic concept. But for someone who wants to do it, writing offers an unrivalled sense of power when it's going well (and an unrivalled sense of despair when it's going badly).

Improving Your Skills

There is no lack of titles in the creative writing section of bookshops, but it's a striking fact that few of them seem to have been written by people you've ever heard of. The cruel question inevitably arises: if you know so much about the subject, why aren't you writing your own bestsellers rather than 'How To' manuals? So I'm afraid I don't have that much faith in books on creative writing.

The exception I would make to this general rule concerns works by William Goldman, screenwriter of *The Sting, Butch Cassidy and the Sundance Kid* and many other great films. His two books, *Adventures in the Screen Trade* and *Which Lie Did I Tell?*, are full not only of good jokes but also of great wisdom about the business of writing for the cinema – wisdom that applies to a lot of other literary forms too.

What I would recommend an aspiring writer to read, however, is as much fiction as they can lay their hands on. Read good writing, read bad writing – work out for yourself what the difference is. Read classics, read potboilers, read so-called literary fiction, read genre fiction – you will learn something from every word of it. Decide why you like some authors and dislike others, why some books are crystal clear and others deeply muddled. Identify the qualities you would like to see in your own writing and then try to reproduce them.

Seeking Help

That invaluable basis of broad reading may, however, still need to be built on by some form of teaching. So where should the aspiring writer turn for help in developing his or her skills? The answer, of course, depends on how much time the individual wants to invest. Twenty years ago, East Anglia was about the only university in the British Isles which offered a degree course in Creative Writing. Now there is an enormous number to choose from in other universities (see page 66 for more about these), and you should assess them from reading prospectuses and talking to people who have experienced them, just as you would choose any other course.

It should be pointed out, however, that gaining a degree in creative writing offers no guarantee of success in the commercial world of literature. Such training may help focus the energies of a talented writer but it won't help a no-hoper to get published.

Anyway, many aspiring writers don't have the time to devote to a full-time degree course. Most have to hold down a day job while they dream of the bestseller that will one day free them from the thrall of going out to work. For them the solution must be something part-time.

There are local Writers' Circles all over the country (information about those in your area can be found through your library or from www.writers-circles.com). They are of variable quality but they do offer the aspirant an opportunity to mix with like-minded people. Many also organize programmes of talks by professional writers, from whom useful tips may be gleaned. And the practice of completing set exercises and critiquing each other's work can be of benefit (though there is always the danger of the same people constantly repeating the same criticisms).

Short Courses

Another worthwhile experience for would-be writers who can spare the time is The Writers' Summer School at Swanwick in Derbyshire. This week-long event has been taking place every August since 1949. It exists, to quote from its website (www.wss. org.uk), 'to give writers at all levels of experience an opportunity to learn from expert tutors and excellent speakers in a comfortable and friendly atmosphere'. I have tutored and spoken there on many occasions and can vouch for the fact that it is a unique and nurturing environment.

Many local authorities also run creative writing courses, of which details can be found in libraries or on council websites. The quality of these tends to depend on the quality of the individual tutors involved, and it would be best to do a bit of homework before enrolling.

Then again, newspapers and magazines are full of advertisements for correspondence courses in creative writing, and there are also plenty to be found on the internet. I have never actually taken one of these myself, but the anecdotal evidence I have gleaned from those who have has not been encouraging. The general view is that the people running them are more concerned with taking your money than with turning you into a better writer.

The Crème de la Crème

The best courses I have encountered – and indeed been involved in – are those run by the Arvon Foundation (www.arvonfoundation.org). These take place in four large houses in the country, one in Devon, one in Yorkshire, one in Shropshire and one in Inverness-shire. They usually run from Monday evening till Saturday morning and different weeks concentrate on different aspects of writing – poetry, the novel, short stories, radio, television and so on. There is a maximum of 16 participants on each course, with two professional writers as tutors. The structure of individual courses differs, but generally speaking participants take part in group sessions and workshops, where they are set short writing exercises to be read out at the next session. Among the other valuable components in the programme are one-to-one tutorials with the professional writers. And in the middle of the week there is a visit for one evening from a guest reader, another writer whose work is relevant to the course but whose insights can open up a wider perspective on the subject.

Arvon's admission policy is very broad. Basically, places are awarded to the first 16 people who try to book. As a result, there is a wide range of skills and backgrounds among the participants who may vary, in my experience, from published novelists to the man who joined a course of mine 'because the Spanish course was full'.

The concentration during these Arvon weeks is intensified by the lack of outside distractions, and the experience of communal living never fails to create something greater than the sum of its parts. Unexpected talents are discovered and developed, and the participants frequently keep in touch with each other once the course has finished. (The participants in my most recent one have set up a Yahoo group and supportive emails are constantly flying back and forth between them.) As a tutor, I always return from a week at Arvon totally exhausted but with the feeling that something worthwhile has been achieved.

The courses are not cheap but there are various bursaries and grants available for qualifying applicants.

A final important thing that's worth saying about writing courses is that they can be just another form of procrastination. The members of no other profession are as skilled as writers in finding things to do other than what they should be doing. Going on a course is a very effective way of postponing the actual putting down of words on the page. As a tutor I have encountered many 'courseoholics'. More than once, when I have met truly talented people in such circumstances, I have given them one stern piece of advice: 'Never go on another course. You've already got as much as you're ever going to get from courses. From now on, just write!'

THE AGENT'S VIEW

A Guide to Finding and Working with an Agent

Jonathan Pegg

If I meet a first-time author with a view to representing them, they often seem hesitant about asking what they can expect from me. Yet there are many elements to this non-secret agency work beyond the licence to lunch imagined by my non-publishing friends, and equally as many considerations that I try to anticipate for the author at such meetings.

Since the whole purpose of a literary agent is to take care of publishing processes for their client, to the extent that many details can go without saying if an author's career is in good hands, the important question to begin with is how one agent differs from another. At the same time, the considerations involved in choosing an agent are meaningless without basic prior knowledge of publishing processes. So I have provided a ten-step guide to the least an agent does for their client, hoping to address not just the kinds of questions that first-time authors often have, but also the issue of which are reasonable or realistic questions to ask at an initial meeting.

Finding and Approaching a Literary Agent

It can be difficult to secure an agent's attention in the first place, so to begin with here is a very basic guide to going about that.

- First, look up the websites of the agents listed in this book's Directory (see pages 154–194).
- Check that the agency's commission rates are acceptable to you (see *The Agency Agreement*, overleaf).
- Study the agency's instructions for submitting material. Most will request you to enclose a stamped self-addressed envelope if you would like your material returned to you. A typical instruction for fiction might be to enclose a covering letter, biographical information, one-page synopsis and two or three chapters. Some agencies' sites go into more detail than I have done here and there is more information about how to prepare a submission on pages 82–87.
- It is reasonable to expect a swift acknowledgement. After that, be prepared to wait patiently for a further response – agencies receive a lot of manuscripts and it sometimes takes them up to two months to clear their backlog, although most will try to respond within four to six weeks. If they are potentially interested in taking you on, they should invite you for the introductory meeting I mentioned earlier.

Ten-Stage Guide to the Agent's Role

1. Preliminaries – Content Preparation

Agents vary in the amount of editorial guidance they will offer. Sometimes they will suggest further work as a prerequisite to formalizing the relationship with a written agreement (see box, below). If a formal agreement is produced before editorial suggestions have been made, it is reasonable to check whether an agent feels more work will be needed. It may be that they feel the material is ready for submission to publishers – after all, you should have got it into the best possible state before you sent it to them. But if they do think more work will be necessary, it is reasonable to ask roughly how much editorial guidance they will be prepared to give you. I say 'roughly' because it's difficult for an agent to say how much detail they'll go into without going into the detail itself!

The Agency Agreement

Reputable agencies offer a formal contract. This might be offered immediately or at a later date once the agent decides your work is ready for submission to publishers. The agreement is usually subject to a reasonable notice period invoked by either party, since a successful relationship is dependent on mutual enthusiasm. Most agencies charge between 10 and 15 per cent of earnings on deals done in the UK, and 20 per cent on international deals. Most also charge expenses such as photocopying, couriers or ordering finished copies of your book for the purpose of selling subsidiary rights but not phone calls, standard postage or entertaining. It is not advisable to sign with an agent who charges a reading fee or any other sort of fee (including fees if they are unsuccessful in placing your work with publishers).

2. Submission Strategy

The agent will decide in due course which publishers, and specifically which commissioning editors, are likely to be interested in – and most suitable for – any particular project. Sometimes an agent will submit a project to one editor at a time; sometimes they will make 'multiple submissions'. They are unlikely to have decided this until after the initial meeting, and it is probably unrealistic to request too much information about strategy at this stage for two reasons: first, the agent might understandably be reticent about giving away all their ideas before you have committed to them; second, the process does require flexibility.

Once a project has been submitted by an agent, it may be difficult to find another agent to take it on if it is rejected and the author loses steam, so it is worth trying to ascertain an agent's likely commitment and perseverance with regard to the project in question. Their response will be necessarily vague because the question of how many publishers they'll approach may depend on the kind of feedback they get, or indeed a number of circumstances, yet I personally believe it is only fair for an agent to be as clear as possible about their intentions so that you have a rough idea of where you stand with them – are they undertaking to stick with the project to the bitter end if necessary, or will it be a staged process in which they will review their commitment and the valid question of whether it is in your best interests to continue?

3. Pitching

The agent's next step is to represent your book to commissioning editors in a way that is appealing without being misleading. It is important that an agent enthusiastically 'gets' your work. Whether they do or not will probably be apparent from the way they talk about it to you. But if not, I think it is reasonable to ask an agent how, in broad terms, they see themselves characterizing your work. How would they summarize the book, and what strengths would they emphasize?

4. Exploitation of Subsidiary Rights

Should a publishing deal be secured, there are early decisions for an agent to make about which rights are included. From a publisher's point of view, the sale of subsidiary rights will often be an important means of recouping their investment in producing the book. So the question of which rights are being granted and which are being withheld will have some impact on the level of advance they are prepared to pay. The relative value of different rights will vary according to the project in question, and the agent will need to judge whether the advance is a fair return for the rights being requested.

If a publisher who has been granted the opportunity to sub-license these rights makes a successful sale, you will receive a portion as set out in the original publishing contract. However, as with the royalties from sales of the book, that share will initially go towards 'earning out' the up-front 'advance' sum the publisher has paid for the book, with the result that you may receive payments from sub-licensed subsidiary rights only some time later, if at all.

If, on the other hand, an agent handles the subsidiary rights, further up-front advances are guaranteed as soon as the sale is made. You are also one step closer to the publishing activities that will ensue, which results in you having much more control over what happens with your work.

So there are various considerations involved. Apart from the question of what a publisher is prepared to pay for subsidiary rights, another factor will be how energetically they will pursue the sales of these rights. This latter factor is equally true of your agent. So it is important to ascertain how an agent is set up for exploitation of the more important subsidiary rights such as US, translation and serialization.

A few will sell US and translation rights directly to publishers, some will work with a network of co-agents in the territories concerned, and some will have in-house foreign rights staff selling directly or via co-agents. Having dedicated staff selling your foreign rights is obviously attractive, but the impact on sales of the primary agent's enthusiastic familiarity with a book should never be underestimated. So there are pros and cons whichever way you look at it. In these days of easy telecommunications, what is important is for the agent to have sufficient knowledge of the market in question if they are working directly, and a good network of co-agents (together with sufficient knowledge to oversee them) if they are working indirectly.

I am sometimes asked whether money can be saved by coming to independent arrangements with agents in several territories. In my view the savings are small and such an arrangement may prevent you benefiting from the strategic overview your primary agent can provide.

5. TV/Film Representation

Some literary agencies will offer TV and film representation, and some will partner with independent specialist agents. There are advantages and disadvantages to each: in a larger agency with a TV department, there is the convenience of having all the activities under one roof, but the TV agent is unlikely to commit to all their book department's offerings. An independent literary agent may or may not be prepared to network with independent TV and film agents on your behalf, but if they are there is the advantage of a more bespoke service. If you've got aspirations in this direction, ask whether the agent feels that they are realistic and, if so, how they would help you.

6. Deal Negotiation

Rather than bombard the agent with too many questions about the deal initially, since they are somewhat hypothetical until the moment has arrived, it is worth remembering that at this point an agent's time is best spent focusing on making the deal happen in the first place. They probably have a rough idea of what they might expect by way of an advance, but be understandably reluctant to make precise predictions. However, it may be helpful for both parties to touch on the question of their attitude to advances.

Since agents work on commission, they share an author's financial interest, but a good agent will also take other things into consideration on their clients' behalf. Too high an advance might put you under unconstructive commercial pressure, and if a publisher ends up making a large loss on a book, this can affect your future opportunities. At the same time, it's worth bearing in mind that a publisher's marketing budget for a book is often guided by the advance they have paid, with a higher advance meaning more to recoup and therefore more reason to put resources into making a success of the book. The agent is there to advise you in these matters and then secure your aim to the best of their ability within the circumstances.

7. Contracts

There are many negotiable points in a publisher's contract. Some have financial implications, such as royalty rates and the way royalties are accounted. An agent's commission is based on all future income, so it is in their interest to take care over these matters. Many points are to do with authorial control over the book in the longer term, your obligations to the publisher in the overall life of the book and sometimes even your next book. Negotiating contracts is a very important part of an agent's duties, requiring willingness to fight a corner, attention to detail and not least patience to interpret the legalese to you insofar as you wish to be concerned.

8. Quality Control and Diplomacy

There are some areas that can't be definitively covered in a publishing contract but do need to be looked out for. It is in a publisher's interest to succeed with a book once they have committed to it, but every book will be published alongside a number of other books, and a publisher's time and overall resources are finite. There's rarely an exact science in the realms of publicity, advertising, marketing and promotions, and most authors find it difficult to press their own case even if they're confident that there's a case to be pressed. Indeed, it might be that your expectations are a little high; or that the publishing team as a whole is insufficiently behind your book; in these circumstances an agent may be able to step in and mediate, or contribute constructive support and ideas.

Most publishers will take an author's views into account in matters like the book's format, the cover design and the publication date, but these are ultimately the publisher's decision. This is as it should be, given the degree of specialist expertise arrayed within a publishing house, but even then it is sometimes necessary for an agent to help you get your point of view across and liaise for both parties.

Sometimes an agent has to stamp a foot on behalf of their client, but most of the time their relationship with publishers is not adversarial. The author doesn't necessarily know which things it is realistic to try to change, or how best to go about things if they have a complaint, so the agent's role is to take all that off their shoulders. They can hopefully pre-empt any communication breakdowns between author and publisher, thus keeping the creative channels clear in everyone's best interest.

9. Invoicing, Statement Processing and General Paperwork Relief

The agent will also invoice and check payments and statements for you. Aside from the advance payments, there are usually biannual royalty statements (and payments if the advance has been earned out). These statements can be complex and impenetrable to the layman.

There are also other bits of paperwork as you go forwards, such as when the publisher seeks consent to a sub-licence or to sell copies at a discount not allowed for in the original contract. The agent is there to advise you each time this happens, manage the paperwork and check that the receipts from these deals have been properly accounted for.

10. Career-Building

In the last 20 years or so, the role of agents has grown in importance and become better known. This is not just for all the reasons I have just outlined. Another major reason, at least if you have more than one book in mind, is that editors tend to move jobs a lot these days. They aren't looking out for your overall trajectory in the same way as an agent, who is often your most reliable industry constant and ally. In theory your career is the agent's career, so the agent is always thinking about your profile and taking care of it in the small world of publishing and the media.

In Summary

In all these ways and more, an agent earns his or her commission. If you are successful in securing an agent's attention, remember that the effort they commit is based on belief in you and your work. I would certainly advise against signing up with an agent without first meeting them in person. A good meeting provides opportunity for comfortable informal discussion, and of course it enables both you and the agent to establish whether you are likely to enjoy a happy working rapport together.

ACQUIRING FICTION

What an Editor is Looking For

Penelope Hoare

In my world, it is rare to *commission* fiction. Fiction is *acquired* – in other words, I read novels (when finished or almost finished), share them with colleagues and readers, assess them and get them costed. At every stage in this process, I examine the pros and cons thus far and might decide to reject. Occasionally, I suggest improvements and leave the door open for the author to make a second attempt. And sometimes, with all aspects considered, I make an offer to publish.

The Difference Between Fiction and Non-Fiction

Two strangers meet on a train. One is an editor. The other is a would-be author who tells the story of how the previous stranger he met on a train was an assassin and spymaster who took him on a journey of adventure and mayhem. If he chooses non-fiction as his medium, then his amazing experiences might – just might – amount to a bestseller for author and editor. But if he decides to tell the same story in the form of a fiction, and he isn't sufficiently talented as a *writer*, then no amount of adventure and mayhem will make his book into a first-class novel. This is as true of 'literature' as of 'popular' or 'commercial' fiction.

Contrary to the familiar cliché, not everyone has a novel in them. Getting a novel published is not a matter of selling an idea or a plotline. All depends on the *execution* – how cleverly that idea is explored and how thrillingly that story is told.

The Write Stuff

Getting a novel published also depends on making your approaches to the right publisher or agency.

Rule one is what I call 'horses for courses' – in other words *focus* or *branding*. Any novel that an editor acquires has to fit the profile of their publishing firm. More than that, it has to conform to the personal expertise of that editor – which can be a wide remit ('literary fiction') or a very narrow one ('crime novels translated from Norwegian').

Many an editor has lived to regret a rash foray into an unfamiliar world. I have acquired, in my day, science-fiction, only to discover that my choice happened to be a pale imitation of far better, already published SF novels – as any SF nerd could have told me.

A novel can be a splendid example of its kind, but unsuited to a particular imprint. Most imprints aspire to focus because it strengthens their powers of acquisition in their chosen fields, while branding maximizes their marketing and sales strategies.

Some imprints are rigid in their requirements – Mills & Boon, for example, used to be famous for laying down not only the subject area (doctors and nurses, Latin lovers, intrigue, historical romance) but also the precise number of words, and whether sex stopped at the bedroom door or was permitted to stray between the sheets. Other firms have a wide and eclectic range. But there is no point in sending raunchy adventure stories or perky chick lit to a publisher whose sole aspiration is to win the Booker or the Nobel Prize for Literature.

What I Look for When Acquiring Fiction

- **Originality above all.**
- **Dialogue and characterization:** if you can't do these well, you will never be a first-class novelist.
- **Storytelling:** as above – if you can't tell a gripping story, you will never be a first-class novelist.
- **Opportunities for sales and sales of rights:** hardback/trade paperback/mass-market paperback; book club; serialization and extract (including radio readings); sales in English all over the world, including America; sales in translation; etc.
- **Opportunities for publicity**, marketing, literary prizes and author promotion.
- **Style,** structure, set pieces, colour, wit and humour, denouement.
- **Metaphorical meaning, images and the 'under-text'** – i.e. what the novel is 'about', under the surface of narrative and action.

A good novel is more than an exciting plotline, a clever wheeze or a terrific idea. If I am at all tempted, I want to read the whole thing, including the all-important denouement. I want to judge the narrative drive and the trajectory, and to see the characters developing. I lay emphasis on 'reader satisfaction' – i.e. closing the book with a warm feeling that reading it has been a worthwhile experience, both fulfilling and enjoyable.

Having made a *value judgement* (it's good of its kind and I like it), I have to make a *commercial judgement* (will it sell? will it sell on my particular list?).

So from my side of the desk, for a novel to be publishable it has to be either a work of art or a work of commerce – or both. To get published it also has to fit in with a particular publisher's profile. From your side of the desk, the first hurdle is to persuade someone actually to *read* your submission.

The Truth About the Slush Pile

Unsolicited submissions (known as the slush pile) very often don't get over this first hurdle – i.e. no one reads them properly. This is for a variety of reasons, including:

Lack of gumption: my slush pile invariably contains submissions which are unsuited to me personally and unsuited to Chatto & Windus as an imprint. My instinctive reaction is that I can't be bothered to read the slush pile, because so many of these authors have failed even to find out where to send their material. (I don't, for example, ever publish any fiction for children – yet I am sent several children's novels a year.)

Lack of focus: in a lifetime in publishing, I have discovered about five wonderful books in the slush pile. It is because of this low hit-rate that some publishers refuse to look at unsolicited material at all. Even those who do accept it tend to treat it shabbily: unsolicited submissions gather dust on the shelf for three months, and then a junior spends ten minutes with each one, turns down about 97 per cent of them and passes three per cent to a reader or an editor for a more careful perusal and a second opinion.

Poor presentation: when I look at a covering letter which is prolix or incorrectly punctuated, I am immediately put off the accompanying submission. This is not because I am rigid about grammar, but because I am looking for *writers* – i.e. those who can use words and sentences to best effect.

Why Novelists Need Literary Agents

It is partly because the slush pile is a low priority for fiction editors and an inadequate conduit for novelists that literary agents wield power within British publishing.

Focus: literary agents are intensely familiar not only with imprints, but also with individual editors; they know about current lists and their specialities, and also about future lists and any planned changes of direction or policy.

When I receive a novel from an experienced agent (addressed to me by name and professionally presented in a colour-coded folder that I recognize), I know that an informed choice has been made, and that Chatto has been selected for this particular submission because a) it's the sort of thing we are looking for; b) we are likely to make a good job of publishing it, because it suits our profile; and c) I am quite likely to warm to it, because it chimes with both my personal taste and my professional brief.

Fine-mesh sieve: getting an agent to take you on as a client is just as difficult as getting your work published. Before an agented submission reaches an editor, it has already gone through a rigorous selection. The average agented submission is, therefore, of far better quality than the average unsolicited submission.

Doing business on a daily basis: editors deal with submissions from agents in a professional manner. If they fail to do so, they are in danger of missing out next time because the disgruntled agency will choose to submit its new bestseller to a different editor at a different firm.

Writing as the day-job: literary agents act for *writers*. If you are a celebrity chef, a violinist or a motor-racing driver, and you are invited to write a book as a sideline, you might prefer to consult a solicitor or an agent who specializes in your field. But if you aspire to be a novelist, you would be well advised to seek a literary agent (see *The Agent's View*, pages 73–78).

Submissions

Whether you are seeking an agent or seeking a publisher, the same common-sense advice applies. The most important part of a submission is the covering letter, so here are some key points to bear in mind:

- **Keep it short:** editors/agents won't read more than the first paragraph if your letter looks tedious.
- **Say *something!*** Some would-be authors think that a short covering letter means typing 'Please read the attached.' Editors/agents know full well that they are being invited to read the attached. The covering letter should tell them *why* they must read it, and should tempt and excite them into bothering to do so.
- **Don't be a bore:** I am quickly worn down, for example, by plot synopses of novels; unimpressed by showing off; irritated by naive claims about marketing and sales; and turned off by pretentiousness.
- **Remember that you are being judged as a *writer*:** all the skills of your novel should be displayed in your brief covering letter. My hard heart can be melted by a well-expressed joke, a well-told anecdote or a well-turned phrase.
- **Focus on your USPs** (Unique Selling Points) – i.e. what is special about *your* book. Put your most important one at the beginning of the letter.
- **Grab 'em quick:** the covering letter is your chance to catch the attention of the editor/agent. However, don't confuse making an instant impression with vulgarity – and don't pepper your presentation with exclamation marks.

The enclosures sent with your covering letter should include:

- a biographical note about yourself;
- a brief description of your book (what 'kind of an animal it is' – don't indulge in dozens of named characters and acres of plot);
- a sample chapter.

Don't submit bits and pieces from different chapters. Select either the first chapter or a representative section, preferably one which has a beginning, a middle and an end (i.e. a set piece) or one that finishes on a cliff-hanger. Make it clear that the completed novel is available, and that you will send it if the agent/editor requests.

Before submitting anything to anyone, do your homework:

- Never send a 'Dear Madam/Dear Sir' letter – always have the gumption to find out the name of an editor/agent who might be interested. Editorial categories in fiction are not as clear-cut as different kinds of non-fiction; but you can focus your submission according to such distinctions as literature/romance/children's fiction/crime/thrillers/historical fiction.
- Get an idea of who publishes what. Consult a reference book (such as this one), visit bookshops and browse the internet. If, for example, you are working on a graphic novel, it would take you less than ten minutes to learn that a leading publisher in this field is Jonathan Cape, and not much longer to find out that Jonathan Cape – like Chatto & Windus – is part of Random House.
- Find out who publishes/acts for whom. If you admire certain writers and perhaps compare your work to theirs, then think of sending your book to the firms that represent them. Editors and agents are susceptible: they support their stables of authors and they understand the importance building on their existing strengths.
- Keep abreast – if you want to be a contemporary novelist you should read contemporary fiction.

If your novel is a 'general' book – 'a work of fiction designed to appeal to everyone who likes reading' – you might think of approaching literary agents who handle a diverse range of different kinds of writing. But if your novel fits snugly into a slot – science-fiction, fantasy or horror, say, or indeed graphic novels – I suggest you first try the publishers that specialize in your chosen genre. The more focused the imprint, the more likely it is to employ editors and readers who are mind-bogglingly well-informed in these areas. And the more focused the slush pile, the higher its successful hit-rate.

Making the Approach

Again, there are some general rules, whether you are approaching a literary agent or going to a publishing house direct:

- Don't telephone, except to a main switchboard number to find out the name of the person you should write to. Editors and agents don't have time for self-serving calls.
- Email is used increasingly. It is the principal method of communication once contact has been made; and it will doubtless be the method of submission of the future.

It also has the advantage of going straight to the desk of the acquiring editor, without passing through the conduit of juniors or readers. But I find emailed unsolicited submissions shamefully easy to turn down. I read on screen the covering message and (unless it grabs me) am tempted to press the reply button and type 'Not for me, thanks' – without even opening any of the attachments, let alone printing them out.

- For a full-length novel the post is more appropriate. Many publishers and agents don't accept submissions by email simply because of the enormous cost in paper of printing them out to take home and read in comfort.
- You can send your material to more than one editor/agent at a time, as long as you make it clear that it's a multiple submission.
- Consider a chasing letter after six weeks and an email or telephone call after 12 weeks. The risk of chasing is that you 'bounce' the editor/agent into taking the easy route of saying 'Thanks, but no'. But a long silence is not a good sign, and you might do well to cut your losses and submit elsewhere, anyway, after six weeks.

Demonstrate Your Commitment

You can't expect an editor/agent to take the time to read your material if you don't take the time to present yourself as a professional.

Don't:
- **Expect your novel to get published unless you are both passionate and serious about writing:** you can get endless satisfaction from writing for your own delight – or for the pleasure of family and friends. But you can't be self-indulgent if you want to be published.
- **Expect to place your novel until it is finished:** it is common practice for an editor to acquire the rights in a work of non-fiction on the basis of a proposal and a sample chapter; but it is only occasionally that a novel by a first-time writer is commissioned – that is, bought by a publishing house before it is written. Indeed, even many well-established and successful authors finish their novels before they are offered for publication and before terms are agreed.
- **Expect to get away with sloppiness:** remember that you are a writer – words are your tools, so use them well.

There is no such thing as a cynical novelist: whether you write bodice-rippers or philosophical novels of ideas, political thrillers or Aga-sagas, you must believe in yourself, and you must persuade publishers and agents to believe in you too.

But remember, there are as many different opinions as there are editors and literary agents. If one of them rejects your novel, try someone else. Editors and agents have no magic answers. Indeed they make appalling mistakes – taking on books that fail, turning down books that are huge successes elsewhere. Have faith in yourself.

FIRST IMPRESSIONS

How to Ensure Your Submission Attracts Instant Attention

Hilary Johnson

'My novel came back exactly as I sent it. I don't think they even read it!'

How often have I heard these words from aspiring authors, the tone at once angry and disappointed. My immediate answer, I'm afraid, is harsh: 'They probably didn't need to.'

The Covering Letter

Where so many hopefuls appear to shoot themselves disastrously in the foot is with the covering letter. As a part of my service, I regularly assess these for clients, a job that is often time-consuming out of all proportion to the letter's length.

It is astonishing how often these sample letters contain careless errors of the most basic kind: mistakes in the spelling of the author's own name, address or title of his novel; typos, accidental omission of words; sloppy constructions and general evidence of a failure to proofread the letter before printing the final version. Errors of grammar, spelling and punctuation in a covering letter, especially when all three are present, do not inspire confidence in the author's ability to write a novel of publishable standard. Neither does extensive use of cliché or the repetition of words, phrases or ideas.

For these letters it's important to use the name of an individual rather than 'Dear Sir or Madam'. Extreme as it may sound, there are those who would be minded to reject on that alone. The phrase 'for your perusal' virtually guarantees rejection.

Indulgence in irrelevancies, extended explanations of the plot – pointless when a synopsis is included – and talking up your own book are all bad signs. Agents and editors don't want to be told how the novel should be marketed; it's amazing how often authors fail to credit these people with knowing their own business! Detailed CVs showing your personal history from primary school onwards are not a good idea, especially if they are so lengthy as to suggest a commensurate length of tooth. (Age is not necessarily a disadvantage, but, there's no need to bring it to the fore at the outset.)

For example, 'I was for a period PA to a Premier League football manager until he was sacked last year' gives less away – and will attract swifter attention – than 'I worked with the same company from leaving school until retirement five years ago.'

Unless anything different is specifically requested, stick to businesslike – but without business-speak, be it dated or modern jargon – courteous and correct. The aim is that the recipient will be keen to read the synopsis, and after that the actual novel, rather than becoming bogged down in a verbose and messy covering letter. A letter that indicates that you have a professional attitude and also shows true originality of thought and voice is, of course, one that instantly excites interest in a submission.

The Synopsis

Once the hurdle of the letter has been successfully surmounted, there then presents that most formidable of obstacles, the synopsis. The ability to write a strong synopsis is a vital part of the aspiring author's armoury. It is no good lamenting the difficulty of the task – and anyway, if the novel has already been written, boiling it down to its essence shouldn't be *that* hard!

Different agents and editors vary in their expectations of a synopsis, so it is always sensible to check these individually, but in the absence of specific guidelines, following these should result in a professional-looking synopsis:

For most adult fiction two A4 pages single spaced is the norm, but some editors ask for one page only. Begin with two or three sentences stating what kind of novel it is. Say what it is about, who it features and when and where it is set:

> *Girly Gang is a novel aimed at girls in their mid-teens. A contemporary story with a Tyneside setting, it shows how 15-year old Jess Curtis, seeking an exciting alternative to her drab and difficult home life, finds herself embroiled with a notorious girl gang. When her new friends' activities lead her into a world far scarier than she could have imagined, she discovers that leaving the gang is a lot harder than joining it.*

The remainder of the synopsis should encapsulate the *whole* story within the proverbial nutshell. There is nothing to be gained by including teasers or leaving the reader guessing as to the ending. The purpose of this piece of writing is to enable someone who is permanently inundated with stuff to read to absorb the gist of the story within a few minutes; it is not in any way the same as a jacket blurb, designed to whet the appetites of bookshop browsers.

Omit unimportant detail and minor subplots or characters. Make sure that the overall tone of your synopsis is lively, giving a sense of the narrative drive and resonating with your own individual voice. A flat retelling of the story will not help your cause. And crucially, avoid the temptation to include anything that may smack of personal opinion concerning the novel's qualities. Allow the agent/editor to make up his/her own mind as to these.

A good synopsis should create in the reader a strong desire to read the novel itself, or at any rate the first three chapters, which nowadays usually comprise the initial submission. A reasonable one might prompt a decision just to have a look. Either way, if you have begun your novel with a brilliant opening sentence, a marvellous first paragraph and two or three pages that draw the professional reader into the story almost without noticing and compelling him or her to read on, even if ultimately this novel is for some reason turned down, you will at least have the satisfaction of knowing that your typescript was indeed read. And, who knows, maybe it won't come back at all and you will be en route to publication, all because you took care to ensure a sequence of irresistible first impressions!

BEFORE YOU SEND ANYTHING

Basic Rules for Letters

- Include your name, address, phone number, email address and website, if you have one.
- Address a specific person, not 'Dear Sir or Madam', 'Dear Commissioning Editor' or anything else that suggests you haven't bothered to do your research.
- Limit your letter to one single-spaced page.
- Include a stamped self-addressed envelope with postal submissions and make sure it is the right size and has the right amount of postage on it.
- Use a standard format and typeface, such as Times New Roman in 10- or 12-point: don't use fancy fonts or 'clever' formatting. You're a writer, not a designer.
- Use block paragraph format – that is, leave a line between paragraphs rather than indenting the first line of each one.
- Thank the recipient for considering your submission.

Email Considerations

- An email is not the same as a letter. This may sound obvious, but when you are writing to a potential agent or publisher for the first time by email you should think carefully about the information you need to provide, simply because we all tend to treat email as a more informal form of communication.
- So, in your first email, you should include your full name, just as you would in a letter. Don't sign off simply with your given name, leaving the recipient with no idea what your family name is.
- In your first email, write as thoughtfully and formally as you would if it were a letter. Address the recipient as 'Dear First Name Last Name', rather than using just the first name – and certainly don't begin the first approach with 'Hi'.
- One of the foibles of email writing is that many of us use many more exclamation marks than we would in a letter. Don't do this – it won't be read as amusing. And don't litter your email with smiley faces.
- Make your subject line meaningful: no 'Hi Caroline' or 'Here's a Great Idea'. The recipient is likely to think it is spam and delete it without opening it. If what you are sending is a book proposal, why not say exactly that: 'Book Proposal for your Consideration'?
- Supposedly funny or cryptic email addresses are off-putting and make you less likely to be taken seriously. Always go for the most straightforward option.

ALWAYS JUDGE A BOOK BY ITS COVER

A Sales View

Dominic Brendon

The 64-million-dollar bookselling question is – what makes a bestseller or even a good seller? Over ten years of bookselling in various London locations followed by periods in the sales department of a small and then a large publishing house have, I hope, given me a little insight into this, which in turn might help you, the author or potential author, to understand what is going on in the minds of the people who are selling your book.

The terminology can be a bit confusing, because in this context the book buyer may also be the bookseller! For the purposes of this article, a book buyer is the person working in the book trade; when I'm talking about members of the public I'll call them customers.

I am starting from the standpoint that the publisher has decided to publish your book, for whatever reason. Trying to get into the mind of a commissioning editor is not something any sensible salesperson would do, but sometimes we think along the same lines and you may find that your editor has asked you a number of these questions before taking your book on. What I am giving here is a purely sales point of view – and if it sounds cynical, please remember that publishing and book retailing are businesses and are rarely altruistic.

- The first and most crucial question, whatever the book is about, is does it have a good cover? (The title of this article is only partly tongue in cheek.) Obviously the answer to this is subjective but it helps if a cover is eye-catching and the important words can be read from a distance. If the author is well known, his or her name will be the most important selling point and may well appear larger than the title (look at books by John Grisham, Jodi Picoult or Bill Bryson next time you are in a bookshop). If the title is quirky and likely to tempt the customer to pick the book up to find out more (*Why Don't Penguins Feet Freeze?*), those will be the words that stand out.
- Is it obvious what type of book it is and will it appeal to people who read this kind of book? The pastel colours and informal 'handwriting' typography that work so well with chick lit would look ridiculous on a macho SAS adventure title, just as the chunky, no-nonsense type of a Chris Ryan cover would be completely offputting to readers of Sophie Kinsella.
- Does the title compare favourably to others in its genre and is it a genre that is doing well at the moment? Popularity of genres fluctuates over the years and sometimes book chains announce that they are cutting back on one and expanding another. This happens more frequently in non-fiction than in fiction but, whatever your subject area, it's always a good idea to see what's happening in the market at any given time.

- Is it well written? It may be shocking to see this question coming so far down my list, but I did say that this was a sales point of view. The good news is that I do believe that if a book is well written it will usually do well, even if it takes time to establish a reputation.
- Does the author have a track record? Obviously if you are a brand name, a celebrity or a recognized authority in your field, this helps enormously. But if you are less well known, whether the book is a novel or a yoga manual, if the first bombed it makes the second very hard to sell. It's important for the publisher to repackage before trying again.
- Is the book being published at the right price? Some subject areas are very sensitive to price and format (that is, whether they are hardback or paperback and how big they are). First novels have a better chance as paperback originals as these tend to be cheaper than hardbacks and the customer is not taking so much of a risk. Supermarkets – which are an increasingly important sales channel – don't generally take fiction in hardback (unless it is written by a celebrity), but might take a chance on an inexpensive first novel.
- How wide is the book's appeal? The book buyer can judge this from the blurb on the back of a paperback or the jacket of a hardback, and also from any extra sales material the publisher has produced (proof copies, sample chapters etc.). This might seem obvious, but the more mainstream the book is, the more sales channels there are for the publisher to sell it to.

In the book trade, pretty much everything is pigeon-holed or likened to existing books – always successful ones, obviously – to help create a positive image in the buyers' minds. While this sounds bandwagonish, it really does help if it's immediately clear to the book buyer who is going to buy a particular book. Remember that this poor soul is seeing information about new titles all day every day and may have only a matter of seconds to absorb the information about each one. That's why there so many 'John Grisham mixed with Robert Harris' soundbites to place a title in the market. The book may bear only the slightest resemblance to either of those authors, but it tells the buyer on which shelf the book will go in his shop.

Publicity and Promotion

I've left these till last because they are so massively important and can fall under so many different headings. But it is important for novice authors to understand how they can help (or hinder) the sales of their book. In no particular order (and depending very much on the nature of the book):

- Is it likely to be reviewed? Unlikely with a first novel, but it does happen and can make a big difference.

- Is the book, or the author, controversial in any way at all? This is usually a guarantee of publicity.
- Is the author promotable? This can be a euphemism for attractive or funny, but it can also mean well connected. Publicity really does drive sales and who you know can be incredibly helpful in gaining newspaper or magazine features and reviews. If you know or are related to a celebrity there are slots in national newspapers like 'when we met' that are a good chance to plug your book. TV is the holy grail here and an appearance on *BBC Breakfast* is guaranteed to get the tills ringing. Some of the bigger authors spend weeks on publicity junkets – a necessary evil that can make a huge difference to sales. Lesser 'names' can help by having their own website and/or blog, and by making use of social-networking media. Publicity, publicity, publicity cannot be stressed enough.
- Is the book likely to sell on after it ceases to be new? Books promoted in chains tend to have a limited time on the tables at the front of the shop, but if they sell, they are likely to remain there longer, thus getting the opportunity to keep doing well. Most people are fairly time starved and often don't make it beyond the front of the shop, so will a book sell when it makes the move back to its 'home' section? Again, publicity is the key – if customers have read or heard about a book, they are more likely to come into a bookshop and ask about it, even if it isn't prominently displayed.
- Is it likely to sell better at certain times of year? For some titles, publishing at the right time is crucial to give them their best shot of being successful. Paperback fiction tends to sell most during the summer months to coincide with holiday reading.
- Lastly and maybe most importantly, is the publisher putting marketing money behind the book? Tube or bus billboard ads, proof copies, meet-and-greet dinners, postcards – the list is endless. Is the publisher putting aside money for bookshop or internet promotions, which are increasingly expensive but can be very influential? High-street chains and web-based bookselling sites charge anything £50 to £25,000 for varying levels of promotion, so it's important to discover if there is money set aside for this type of thing. The amount of money spent usually dictates the number of copies a bookseller will buy and can have a big effect on sales.

Many of these are questions over which you as the author have no control; with others you can help enormously by working as part of a team and helping your publisher to make your book a success. So here is a final thought. As an author, it's always good to be nice to salespeople in your publisher's office and to booksellers. The book industry, like many others, is a small world. Get a reputation for being difficult or rude and you could find your book does not even make it out of the stock room. Make it clear that you appreciate other people's efforts and we'll pull out all the stops for you.

IT'LL PROBABLY NEVER HAPPEN, BUT...

A Few Legal Issues

Caroline Taggart

At first glance a publisher's contract can look pretty daunting. Some run to 20 pages and include things that seem irrelevant (how likely is it that a literary first novel is going to be made into a strip cartoon?), but it is irresponsible not to understand it and take it seriously. Even if an agent negotiates the deal for you, it is your name on the contract, not theirs, and you are the one who will be liable if things go badly wrong.

Delivery and Acceptance

The first thing that might go wrong is that you fail to deliver what you have promised. The contract will detail the nature of the work – provisional title, approximately how many words it is and, if it hasn't been completed yet, when it is to be delivered. Few publishers will cancel a contract if you are a week or so late, but you should always keep them informed. More importantly, the contract will specify that the work must be of a *professional and publishable* standard and that it must be along the lines of the material they have already seen. If what you deliver doesn't meet these standards, the publisher may decline to publish and all your hard work will have been in vain.

Advance and Royalties

Once your work is accepted by a publisher, you should be offered an advance against royalties. The royalty may be a percentage of the book's published price or it may be based on the publisher's receipts, and the percentages will vary according to a number of factors: you will be offered a lower rate, for example, on books sold at a high discount for export or to a supermarket or Amazon. Some publishers offer a flat fee – which means that if the book is successful you have no share in the profits – so your agent will resist this if at all possible. If you are acting for yourself, this might be more difficult and you have to decide whether you are prepared to risk losing the deal in order to be properly paid. If you are a member of the Society of Authors (and you should consider joining, especially if you don't have an agent), they can help you.

An advance is a lump sum in advance of anything you may earn on sales of your book and you then have to 'earn it out' before you receive anything more. Say you are paid an advance of £5000 on a book that is going to sell for £10 and you are paid a royalty of 10 per cent of the cover price. That means that for every copy sold at a full royalty rate, you earn £1 (10 per cent of £10). In order to earn out, therefore, you have to sell 5000 copies

(5000 x £1 = £5000, the amount of the advance). Once you sell the 5001st copy, you start to make money. In real life, books are often sold at other than the full royalty rate (the high discounts already mentioned) and there may be other sources of income such as the sale of an extract to a newspaper, but that is the principle.

The good news is that this advance is non-refundable. If the book in our example fails to sell 5000 copies, you have what is called an 'unearned balance' in the publisher's accounts but that is the publisher's problem. It may make them less likely to buy another book from you but at least you don't have to pay anything back.

What About E-Books?

The question of who has the right to licence e-books and on what terms is, at the time of writing, *the* hot potato in the publishing world. Arguments for 'free access to all information' run directly counter to the concept of intellectual property – and authors' ability to make a living from their work. Keep up to date at www.thebookseller.com or www.societyofauthors.org.

Warranty

As author, you have to assure the publisher that your book has not previously been published in the territories covered by the agreement, that it is not an infringement of any existing copyright or licence, that it is not libellous, blasphemous or obscene, that anything purporting to be a fact is true and, if it contains recipes or formulae, that they are not likely to poison anyone or blow anyone up. This is not a clause to be taken lightly. Which brings us to…

Libel, Plagiarism and Breach of Copyright

In signing this warranty, you have taken on certain responsibilities *throughout the life of your book* (even if the contract with this particular publisher is terminated and even if, for whatever reason, you assign the copyright to the publisher or anyone else). Imagine if someone bought the book in a charity shop 20 years from now, thought they recognized themselves and decided to sue. Ignorance of the law is no excuse so, if you are in any doubt at all, warn your editor of your concerns and if needs be, seek professional advice.

Libel

It is your responsibility to ensure that you have not defamed any living person who is identifiable from what you have written (libel laws do not protect the dead). It is possible to libel someone – or something, such as a company or an institution, even if you change their name and even if you are writing about them in a novel – if their real identity is recognizable. Avoid expensive legal fees by being aware of the risks, doing your research thoroughly and keeping detailed and accurate records of your sources of information.

Plagiarism

There is no copyright in ideas but if you steal (or appear to steal) someone else's ideas, you can be sued for plagiarism. A few years ago the well-publicized case revolving round *The Da Vinci Code* cost the losing parties huge sums of money and you don't want to go there.

Plagiarism is a difficult area because we all consciously or unconsciously absorb ideas and even turns of phrase from everything we read and hear, but you can help your own cause by remembering the cynical maxim that taking ideas from one source is plagiarism, taking them from a number of sources is research. Don't base too much of your book on a single source and if you want to quote someone else's work acknowledge the fact (but see *Copyright*, below).

Copyright

Copyright is a complicated business but what it boils down to is that a creative work is the property of the person who created it and cannot be used by anyone else without their permission. For written work, under British and European law, copyright lasts for 70 years after the end of the year in which the author dies, so anyone who died in 1941 will come out of copyright on 1 January 2012 (good news for those who want to quote Virginia Woolf or James Joyce).

The law of copyright protects 'a substantial part' of a written work. If you want to quote a couple of lines from a 500-page history book, you would probably not be in breach of copyright (though you should always acknowledge your source); two lines of a haiku, a limerick or even a sonnet might actually involve fewer words but could still be considered 'a substantial part', simply because the 'whole' is so much smaller.

If quoting a substantial passage from a copyright work is essential to your novel, you must seek permission. Your first approach should be to the publisher of the work in question, who may then refer you to the author's agent or estate, or to the author himself. The right to grant permission to quote from a song probably lies with the music publisher: unless you are an industry insider, Google is as good a place as any to start tracking them down. You will probably have to pay a fee, which will vary according to the length of the passage you want to quote, the fame of the author and the policy or whim of the copyright holder.

Dealing with copyright issues can be frustrating, so leave yourself plenty of time. You may find that the UK publisher can grant UK and Commonwealth rights only, so if the contract for your book covers the entire English-speaking world you will need to go to the US publisher too. Your urgent request may be the recipient's boring piece of admin and they may not reply for weeks. Or at all.

Disclaimers

You often see on the imprint page of a book (or at the end of the acknowledgements) a statement to the effect that 'the author and publishers have made every effort to trace copyright holders; they apologize in advance for any omissions and will be pleased to make due acknowledgement in any future editions of this book'. Would this stand up in court? It might. If there is any doubt, you and your editor should jointly make a decision as to whether or not to include the material. Your parents' wedding photo is probably OK; the lyric of a recent pop song whose copyright holder you can't trace (or who hasn't bothered to reply to your request) is more dodgy ground. It may break your heart to leave it out, but this might be preferable to breaking the bank because of a legal claim.

*

A lot of this article may sound like scaremongering and indeed the vast majority of the things I have told you to be careful about will never happen. But publishing contracts are founded in common sense and aim to protect the interests of everyone concerned. Read yours carefully, make sure you understand it and are prepared to commit to it, sign it and get on with the exciting business of publishing your book.

THE PUBLISHING PROCESS

How Your Manuscript is Turned Into a Book

Caroline Taggart

Congratulations. You've written your book and you've got a publisher. An enormous amount of the hard work that goes into being a published author is behind you. An enormous amount. But not all of it. Not understanding the publishing process is a cause of woe for a lot of first-time authors, so here is a rough guide to what happens after you have delivered your manuscript.

Editing

You and your book will be assigned to an editor who will steer you through the production process and be your main point of contact with the company. At least one person is now going to read your book very closely and ask you questions and make comments about it. There are likely to be two levels of queries and they may come from two different people. Broadly speaking:

- A commissioning editor, senior editor or project editor cares about the structure and content of the book. She will tell you that the action takes too long to get going and you should drop Chapter 2 altogether, that Chapter 4 would be better if it came after Chapter 7, or that your hero simply isn't romantic enough. So you may be asked to add, subtract, rewrite or shuffle. (With fiction this is likely to happen before they offer to publish, but even so you should be prepared for further suggestions.)
- A copy editor, line editor or desk editor (who in many cases will be a freelancer employed on a project-by-project basis) cares about consistency, spelling, grammar, punctuation and repetition. Her job is to notice that you spell 'organisation' with an s but 'realize' with a z, or that you have told that anecdote about your heroine's first day at work three times. A lot of this will seem like nitpicking, but that is what a copy editor is paid for. Good publishers believe in 'getting it right' and that includes putting the apostrophes in the right place and not saying 'imply' when you mean 'infer'.
- Either or both of these will care about factual accuracy, copyright issues and potential libel problems. Copyright and libel are dealt with in more detail on pages 92–93. Accuracy, of course, means 'getting it right' again, and it's just as important in historical novels as it would be in non-fiction. If you are old enough to remember the 1960s film *El Cid*, you probably know that at one point the 11th-century heroine, played by Sophia Loren, is seen wearing a dress with a zip, a device that was patented in 1851. It may well be the only thing you know about the film – a sad reflection on what was probably several years' work for hundreds of people. Don't let that sort of carelessness spoil your own opus.

How you deal with editorial queries is a matter of give and take. Obviously, the more personal your book, the more sensitive you are going to feel but remember that it is in the editor's interests to make you look good by making the book as good as it can possibly be. If she says a section is boring (she may phrase it differently but you will know what she means), look at it again. Is there anything you can take out? Can you add to it to make it more appealing? If you really want to dig your heels in, consider giving way on some other point that is less important to you.

The Jacket/Cover

While you and your editor are busy getting the text right, the salespeople are starting to think about selling the book, and to that end they will prepare a jacket (for a hardback) or cover (for a paperback) many months in advance of publication. Your contract will probably say that you will be consulted about jacket/cover design, but consulting means just that: the publisher has the final say and publishers vary enormously in their attitude to author input.

If they produce something you don't like or weren't expecting, try to be objective about it. You should certainly point out if they have got the concept of the book wrong e.g. if it is aimed at teenagers and the cover is more likely to appeal to seven-year-olds, or if you have written a work of literary fiction and they have made it look like a thriller. But otherwise, imagine that you are a book buyer for a large chain store, seeing a million covers a day and spending perhaps ten seconds considering each one. Would this cover attract you and make you want to stock the book in your shops? Put a colour print-out of the cover on a shelf or mantelpiece, with a couple of other books alongside it, and look at it from the other side of the room. Does it leap out at you? Can you read the words? Does it make you want to pick it up? If so, it is doing its job.

The blurb – the bit designed to whet the buyer's appetite, which appears on the front flap of a hardback jacket or on the back cover of a paperback – has to be written at this stage. Your editor may ask you if would like to write your own. Some authors are brilliant at this, but many feel uncomfortable writing effusively about their own book and are happier leaving it to the editor. That's fine. She should send it to you for approval and you can alter it as you see fit. But remember that this is a selling tool, not a summary of the plot or a table of contents. It has to grab the reader in the first sentence and keep him grabbed.

You will probably also be asked to provide a brief autobiography. This is in my experience harder (and more embarrassing) than it sounds, so be prepared. Don't produce a full CV – no one cares that you were captain of netball at school unless your book is about netball. Do mention anything that shows you are the ideal person to have written this book (you have a degree in archaeology and your novel is set in ancient Greece) or that is quirky, heart-warming or otherwise likely to appeal to your particular type of reader.

Design and Production

When you have a text that everyone is happy with, you start making it into a book. The page size will be decided (you are unlikely to have much say in this). Then someone will mark up the type, which means that they will choose the typeface (font) to be used, the type size, the number and length of lines on a page, what the chapter openers will look like and a myriad of other things of this kind. The book will now be typeset and in due course you will be sent page proofs to read.

Proofreading

Your editor should warn you when proofs are due and when you need to return them. This is not an invitation to rewrite, just to get it right. The publisher will employ a professional proofreader to do a final check, so in addition to any spelling or grammar mistakes that may have slipped through you should be looking out for things that only you will notice, such as errors of fact.

Mark any corrections on the pages you have been given in something bold like black felt tip or red pen. Timid pencil marks are easy to overlook. Write your corrections clearly, accurately and completely. Don't leave the person who is typing in your amendments to guess at what you mean or to finish your sentences for you.

And Then...

...there is a pause, of weeks or even months while the book is printed and bound. And *then*, something very wonderful happens. The phone rings and it is your editor saying, 'I've got a copy of your book in my hand.' If she is really kind and you live within half a mile, she'll courier a copy over to you. If not, you'll have to wait till tomorrow's post, but suddenly you have the physical, almost living proof that all this work has been worth it. At this point, it is OK to cry. There is no feeling quite like it.

Part 3 Directory Listings

UK & IRISH BOOK PUBLISHERS

Abbey Press

✉ Courtenay Hill, Newry, Co. Down, BT34 2ED
☎ T 028 3026 3142
F 028 3026 2514
✎ E adrianrice@earthlink.net
W www.abbeypressbooks.com

Contact Co-Founder/Editor, Adrian Rice;
Co-Founder/Administrator, Mel McMahon

Established 1997

Insider Info Publishes three titles per year.
Receives approximately 200 queries and 100
manuscripts per year. 20 per cent of books
published are from first-time authors, and 75
per cent are from unagented authors. Does not
publish author subsidy books. Authors paid by
small fee, plus free books. Average lead time is
seven months. Does not accept simultaneous
submissions. Submissions accompanied by SAE
will be returned. Aims to respond to queries,
proposals and manuscript submissions within
four months. Catalogue available online, or via
email. Author guidelines available by sending
SAE, online, or via email.

Publishes Historical and Literary Fiction titles.

Submission Guidelines Accepts query with SAE.
Submit proposal package (including outline,
one sample chapter, your publishing history,
author biography and SAE.) Does not review
artwork/photographs.

Recent Title(s) *Whereabouts*, Mark Roper
(Paperback)

Tips Abbey's target audience is literary or
academic readers with an interest in either
poetry or history.

Accent Press

✉ The Old School, Upper High Street, Bedlinog,
Mid Glamorgan, CF46 6RY
☎ T 01443 710930
F 01443 710940
✎ E info@accentpress.co.uk
W www.accentpress.co.uk

Contact Managing Director, Hazel Cushion

Established 2003

Imprint(s) Curriculum Concepts UK Ltd,
Xcite Books

Insider Info Publishes roughly 36 titles per
year. Receives approximately 500 queries and
750 manuscripts per year. Three per cent of
books published are from first-time authors
and ten per cent of books published are from
unagented authors. Payment is via royalty (on
retail price) with 0.1 (per £) maximum. Average
lead time is six months, with simultaneous
submissions not accepted. Submissions
accompanied by SAE will be returned. Aims to
respond to queries, proposals and manuscripts
within six months, and all other enquiries within
twelve months. A catalogue is free on request
and available online.

Publishes Erotica, Historical, Literary
Mainstream/Contemporary, Romance,
Crime and Thriller titles.

* Check the published titles catalogue to see
what kind of fiction is of interest.

Submission Guidelines Accepts proposal
package (including outline, with three
sample chapters).

Recent Title(s) *The Judgement Book*, Simon Hall
(Crime)

Tips Accent Press has a mainstream and mass-
market readership.

Allison & Busby Ltd

13 Charlotte Mews, London, W1T 4EJ
T 020 7580 1080
F 020 7580 1180
E susie@allisonandbusby.com
W www.allisonandbusby.co.uk

Established 1969

Insider Info Catalogue is available online.

Publishes Literary, Mainstream/Contemporary, Science-Fiction, Fantasy and Crime Fiction titles.

Submission Guidelines Accepts agented submissions only.

Recent Title(s) Above the Bright Blue Sky, Margaret Thornton

Alma Books Ltd

London House, 243–253 Lower Mortlake Road, Richmond, Surrey, TW9 2LL
T 020 8948 9550
F 020 8948 5599
E info@almabooks.com
W www.almabooks.com

Contact Publisher, Alessandro Gallenzi

Established 2005

Imprint(s) Herla Publishing

Insider Info Publishes 25 titles per year. Receives 500 queries and 400 manuscripts per year. 30 per cent of books published are from first-time authors and 20 per cent are from unagented authors. Payment is via royalty (on retail price) with 0.1 (per £) minimum and 0.12 (per £) maximum. Advance offered is from £1,000–£5,000. Average lead time is 12 months, with simultaneous submissions accepted. Submissions accompanied by SAE will be returned. Aims to respond to queries within one day, proposals within one week and manuscripts within one month. Catalogue is free on request, and available online or via email. Manuscript guidelines are available online.

Publishes Humour, Literary, Mainstream/Contemporary and Translation titles.

Submission Guidelines Accepts query with SAE or proposal package (including outline, two sample chapters).

Recent Title(s) Remainder, Tom McCarthy (Literary Fiction); The Water Theatre, Lindsay Clarke (Literary Fiction)

Anova Books Company Ltd

The Old Magistrates Court, 10 Southcombe Street, London, W14 0RA
T 020 7605 1400
F 020 7605 1401
E customerservices@anovabooks.com
W www.anovabooks.com

Contact Senior Editor, Emily Preece-Morrison; Commissioing Editor, Michelle Lo (Craft); Commissioning Editor, Victoria Alers-Hankey (Reference, Health); Commissioning Editor, Barbara Phelan (Biography, Popular Culture); Senior Editor, Nicola Birtwisle; Editor, Kristy Richardson

Established 2005

Publishes Erotica, Fantasy, Military/War, Spiritual and Sports titles.

Submission Guidelines Accepts proposal package (including outline and one sample chapter).

Apex Publishing Ltd

PO Box 7086, Clacton on Sea, Essex, CO15 5WN
T 01255 428500
E mail@apexpublishing.co.uk
W www.apexpublishing.co.uk

Contact Production and Publishing Manager, Chris Cowlin; Marketing Manager, Jackie Bright

Established 2002

Insider Info Publishes 30 titles per year. Receives approximately 500 queries and 500 manuscripts per year. 60 per cent of books published are from first-time authors, and 90 per cent of books published are from unagented authors. 50 per cent of books published are author subsidy published, based on potential sales. Payment is via royalty (on retail price). Average lead time is nine months, with simultaneous submissions accepted. Submissions accompanied by SAE will be returned. Aims to respond to queries within seven days, proposals within 14 days, manuscripts within 21 days, and any other enquiry within seven days. Catalogue and manuscript guidelines are free on request, and available online or by email.

Publishes Erotica, Fantasy, Horror, Humour, Regional, Science-Fiction, Children's and General Fiction titles.

Submission Guidelines Accepts query with SAE, or completed manuscript (including publishing history, clips, author biography and SAE).

Arcadia Books

✉ 15–16 Nassau Street, London, W1W 7AB
☎ **T** 020 7436 9898
F 020 7436 9898
✐ **E** info@arcadiabooks.co.uk
W www.arcadiabooks.co.uk

Contact Managing Director, Gary Pulsifer; Associate Publisher, Daniela de Groote

Established 1996

Imprint(s) BlackAmber, Bliss Books, EuroCrime

Insider Info Catalogue available online.

Publishes Ethnic, Gay/Lesbian, Literary, Mainstream/Contemporary, Multicultural, Suspense, Translation and European Crime-Writing titles.

Submission Guidelines Accepts agented submissions only.

Recent Title(s) *The Envoy*, Edward Wilson

Tips Of the different imprints, Arcadia publishes fiction, translated world fiction and gay fiction. BlackAmber publishes multicultural literary fiction and translations. Bliss publishes popular bestsellers, including biography and autobiography. EuroCrime publishes European crime writing. Arcadia Books does not consider children's, teenage, science-fiction, fantasy, horror or romance titles.

Arris Books

✉ 12 Main Street, Adlestrop, Moreton in Marsh, Gloucestershire, GL56 0YN

☎ **T** 01608 659328
F 01608 659345
✐ **E** info@arrisbooks.com
W www.arrisbooks.com

Contact Publishing Director, Victoria Huxley

Established 2003

Insider Info Submissions accompanied by SAE will be returned. Catalogue and manuscript guidelines available online.

Publishes Multicultural and Translated Fiction titles.

Submission Guidelines Accepts query with SAE and proposal package (including outline and one sample chapter). Do not email submissions.

Recent Title(s) *Everything Good Will Come*, Sefi Atta

Tips Titles aimed at travellers interested in world culture, not tourism. All submissions should reflect this principle.

Arrow

✉ Random House, 20 Vauxhall Bridge Road, London, SW1V 2SA
☎ **T** 020 7840 8518
F 020 7233 6127
✐ **E** arroweditorial@randomhouse.co.uk
W www.randomhouse.co.uk

Parent Company The Random House Group Ltd

Contact Publishing Director, Kate Elton

Insider Info Catalogue available online.

Publishes Mass-market paperback Fiction titles.

Submission Guidelines Accepts agented submissions only.

Recent Title(s) *Flora's Lot*, Katie Fforde, *A Mistletoe Kiss*, Katie Flynn

Tips Writers are recommended to get a literary agent, as Arrow will not accept unagented submissions.

Atlantic Books

Ormond House, 26–27 Boswell Street,
London, WC1N 3JZ
T 020 7269 1610
F 020 7430 0916
E enquiries@atlantic-books.co.uk
W www.atlantic-books.co.uk

Parent Company Grove/Atlantic Inc

Contact Chairman and Publisher, Toby Mundy;
Managing Director, Daniel Scott; Editor-in-Chief,
Ravi Mirchandani

Established 2000

Insider Info Publishes roughly 90 titles per year.

Publishes Crime and Literary Fiction titles.

Recent Title(s) *In a Strange Room*,
Damon Galgut

Tips No unsolicited submissions. Accepts
agented submissions only.

Aurora Metro

67 Grove Avenue, Twickenham, TW1 4HX
T 020 3261 0000
F 020 8898 0735
E info@aurorametro.com; submissions@
aurorametro.com
W www.aurorametro.com;

Contact Publisher, Cheryl Robson

Established 1989

Imprint(s) Amp Books

Insider Info Publishes eight titles per year.
Receives approximately 100 queries and 25
manuscripts per year. Ten per cent of books
published are from first-time authors and 50 per
cent of books published are from unagented
authors. 20 per cent of books published are
author-subsidy published, based on funding
available from the Arts Council. Payment is via
royalty (on retail price), or outright purchase.
Average lead time is one year, with simultaneous
submissions accepted. Submissions will not be
returned. Aims to respond to queries within
ten days, proposals within four months, and
manuscripts within six months. Catalogue is
free on request, or available by email.

Publishes Adventure, Erotica, Ethnic,
Experimental, Fantasy, Feminist, Gay/Lesbian,
Gothic, Historical, Horror, Humour, Children's
Literary, Mainstream/Contemporary,
Multicultural, Mystery, Romance, Science-
Fiction, Suspense, Translation and Young
Adult titles.

Submission Guidelines Accepts proposal
package (including outline, synopsis, three
sample chapters, author biography and reviews).

Recent Title(s) *Sobiber*, Jean Molla
(Young Adult)

Tips Aurora Metro often seeks subsidies from
the Arts Council for projects that fall within
their funding criteria, such as translations.

Authentic Media

9 Holden Avenue, Bletchley, Milton Keynes,
MK1 1QR
T 01908 364213
F 01908 648952
E editorial@authenticmedia.co.uk
W www.authenticmedia.co.uk

Contact Publishing Co-ordinator, Kath Williams
(Authentic); Robin Parry, Commissioning Editor
(Paternoster)

Established 1962

Imprint(s) Authentic, Paternoster Press

Insider Info Publishes roughly 50 titles per year.
Catalogue available online.

Publishes Young Adult titles.

Tips Publishes Christian books to help all types
of Christians, as well as music and other media
content. Welcomes unsolicited manuscripts or
synopsis submissions, sent by post or email to
the editor.

AVON

77–85 Fulham Palace Road, Hammersmith,
London, W6 8JB
T 020 8741 7070
F 020 8307 4440
E enquiries@harpercollins.co.uk
W www.avon-books.co.uk

Parent Company HarperCollins Publishers Ltd – General Books Division

Contact Publishing Director, Michael Doggart

Established 2007

Insider Info Catalogue available online.

Publishes Women's Fiction titles.

Submission Guidelines Accepts agented submissions only.

Recent Title(s) *Down to Earth*, Melanie Rose, *Mother's Ruin*, Kitty Neale

Tips AVON publishes a wide range of debut and established authors, both British and International, and aims to fast-track them to bestseller status.

Bantam Press

61–63 Uxbridge Road, London, W5 5SA
T 020 8579 2652
F 020 8579 5479
E info@transworld-publishers.co.uk
W www.booksattransworld.co.uk

Parent Company Transworld Publishers

Insider Info Catalogue available online. Manuscript guidelines not available.

Publishes Historical, Mainstream/Contemporary, Military/War, Mystery, Romance and Suspense titles.

Submission Guidelines Agented submissions only.

Recent Title(s) *Twelve*, Jasper Kent

Tips Bantam Press publishes hardbacks only.

Barny Books

The Cottage, Hough on the Hill, Grantham, Lincolnshire, NG32 2HL
T 01400 250246
E info@barnybooks.biz
W www.barnybooks.biz

Contact Managing Director, Molly Burkett

Established 1980

Insider Info Catalogue available online. Too small to accept unsolicited manuscripts. Manuscript guidelines not available.

Publishes Historical, Children's, Military/War and Young Adult titles.

Submission Guidelines Accepts query with SAE.

Tips Barny Books offers professional critiquing and editing services, as well as some self-publishing facilities. This process can also include translation when the author's first language is not English, and help for those who are dyslexic, disabled or elderly. Be advised that services are fee-based and the minimum order for book printing is 300 copies.

Beautiful Books

36–38 Glasshouse Street, London, W1B 5DL
T 020 7734 4448
F 020 3070 0764
E office@beautiful-books.co.uk
W www.beautiful-books.co.uk

Contact Publisher, Simon Petherick

Established 2005

Imprint(s) Bloody Books, Burning House

Insider Info Published 15 titles per year. Receives 500 queries and 300 manuscripts per year. 30 per cent of books published are from first-time authors and 30 per cent of books published are from unagented authors. Payment via royalty (on wholesale price) with 0.15 (per £) minimum and 0.20 (per £) maximum, or outright purchase. Advance offered is from £1–1,000. Average lead time is eight months, with simultaneous submissions accepted. Submissions accompanied by SAE will be returned. Aims to respond to queries within seven days, proposals within 18 days and manuscripts within two months. Catalogue is free on request, and available online, or by email. Manuscript guidelines are available online.

Publishes Confession, Erotica, Gay/Lesbian, Horror, Humour, Literary, Mainstream/Contemporary and Translation titles. *Horror fiction is published under the Bloody Books imprint, while contemporary fiction is published under the Burning House imprint.

Submission Guidelines Accepts query with SAE or via email. Submission details to: submission@beautiful-books.co.uk

Recent Title(s) *Will*, Christopher Rush (Literary Fiction); *Redress*, Adele Hartley (Psychological Thriller)

Tips When submitting to Beautiful Books be clear and patient, and give as much information about yourself as you can.

Birlinn Ltd

West Newington House, 10 Newington Road, Edinburgh, EI I9 1QS
T 0131 668 4371
F 0131 668 4466
E info@birlinn.co.uk
W www.birlinn.co.uk

Contact Managing Editor, Hugh Andrew

Established 1992

Imprint(s) Birlinn, Birlinn Limited Editions, John Donald, Mercat Press, Polygon

Insider Info Publishes 90 titles per year. Receives approximately 50 queries and 24 manuscripts per year. Average lead time is 12 months, with simultaneous submissions accepted. Catalogue is available online.

Publishes Adventure, Crime/Detective, Historical, Humour, Military/War, Scottish and Gaelic Fiction titles.

Submission Guidelines Accepts unsolicited submissions. Submission details to: submission@birlinn.co.uk

Recent Title(s) *Capital Caricatures*, Sheila Szatkowski (History/Scottish); *Shadow of the Serpent*, David Ashton (Fiction/Crime)

Tips Birlinn publishes a range of books of Scottish interest, including books on history, archaeology, customs and traditions, travel and folklore, and modern and classic Scottish poetry and fiction. Ideas or synopses for fiction are welcomed, providing they relate to Scottish interest.

Biscuit Publishing

PO Box 123, Washington, Newcastle upon Tyne, NE37 2YW
E info@biscuitpublishing.com
W www.biscuitpublishing.com

Contact Managing Director, Brian Lister

Established 2000

Insider Info Catalogue is available online.

Publishes Adventure, Historical and Literary titles and Short Story Collections.

Recent Title(s) *Sky Light*, Peter Bromley; *Knife on the Edge*, Asit Maitra

Tips All publications are by Biscuit prize winners, or by selected authors approached and commissioned by Biscuit. Therefore, it is best to enter one of Biscuit's many writing competitions, rather than sending unsolicited submissions.

Bitter Lemon Press

37 Arundel Gardens, London, W11 2LW
T 020 7727 7927
F 020 7460 2164
E books@bitterlemonpress.com
W www.bitterlemonpress.com

Contact Managing Editors, Laurence Colchester and François von Hurte

Established 2003

Insider Info Publishes six to eight titles per year. Catalogue and manuscript guidelines are available online.

Publishes Crime, Thriller and Noir/Roman Noir titles. *Must be foreign writers/fiction from abroad.

Submission Guidelines Accepts agented submissions only. Submission details to: books@bitterlemonpress.com

Recent Title(s) *A Walk in the Dark*, Gianrico Carofiglio

Tips Bitter Lemon Press aims to bring readers high-quality thrillers and other contemporary fiction from abroad. The publisher is dedicated to the crime genre and publishes dark, sexy and often humorous novels that expose the seamier side of society. Bitter Lemon Press is pleased to receive submissions in the literary crime and thriller area, though submissions should be through a literary agent. Please include a synopsis and a sample chapter in the first submission.

Black & White Publishing

29 Ocean Drive, Edinburgh, EH6 6JL
T 0131 625 4500
E mail@blackandwhitepublishing.com
W www.blackandwhitepublishing.com

Contact Managing Director, Campbell Brown

Established 1990

Imprint(s) Itchy Coo

Insider Info Submissions accompanied with SAE will be returned, but submissions by email are preferred. Aims to respond to queries and manuscript queries within three months. Catalogue and manuscript guidelines are available online.

Publishes General Fiction, Historical, Children's, Crime, Children's Scottish Language and Scottish Interest titles.

Submission Guidelines Accepts query with SAE/proposal package (including outline, sample chapter(s), 30 pages maximum, contact details and SAE). Submission by email preferred.

Recent Title(s) *Villains*, Paul Ferris and Reg McKay (Fiction).

Tips Titles are aimed at anyone, especially children and Scottish language speakers. Unsolicited manuscripts are accepted, but please do not send complete manuscripts.

Black Ace Books

PO Box 7547, Perth, Scotland, PH2 1AU
T 01821 64282
F 01821 642101
W www.blackacebooks.com

Contact Publisher, Hunter Steele

Insider Info Catalogue and manuscript guidelines are available online.

Publishes Mainstream/Contemporary and Scottish Interest titles.

Recent Title(s) *The Broken Lyre*, Lorn Macintyre

Tips Black Ace Books are not currently accepting submissions from new authors. They also offer some self-publishing services, although they do not recommend this route for fiction titles.

Black Amber

15–16 Nassau Street, London, W1W 7AB
T 020 7436 9898
E info@arcadiabooks.co.uk
W www.arcadiabooks.co.uk

Parent Company Arcadia Books

Contact Commissioning Editor, Rosemary Hudson

Insider Info Catalogue is available online.

Publishes Literary and Translation titles.

Submission Guidelines Accepts agented submissions only.

Recent Title(s) *Brixton Rock*, Alex Wheatle

Tips Black Amber places strong emphasis on multicultural literary fiction.

Black Spring Press

Curtain House, 134–146 Curtain Road, London, EC2A 3AR
T 020 7613 3066
F 020 7613 0028
E enquiries@blackspringpress.co.uk
W www.blackspringpress.co.uk

Parent Company Dexter Haven Associates

Contact Publisher, Robert Hastings

Established 1985

Insider Info Publishes five titles per year. Receives approximately 100 queries and 80 manuscripts per year. 20 per cent of published books are from first-time authors and ten per cent of published books are from unagented authors. Payment is via royalty (on wholesale price). Average lead time is eight months, with simultaneous submissions accepted. Submission accompanied by SAE will be returned. Aims to respond to queries within two weeks, proposals and manuscripts within three months, and all other enquiries within five weeks. Catalogue is available online.

Publishes Mainstream/Contemporary and Classic Fiction titles.

Tips Specializes in contemporary, cutting-edge literature as well as reviving classic works.

Blackstaff Press

4c Heron Wharf, Sydenham Business Park, Belfast, BT3 9LE
T 028 9045 5006
F 028 9046 6237
E info@blackstaffpress.com
W www.blackstaffpress.com

Contact Managing Editor, Patsy Horton

Established 1971

Imprint(s) Beeline

Insider Info Publishes roughly 20 titles per year. Receives over 1,000 queries per year. Aims to respond to submissions within six months. Submissions accompanied by SAE will be returned. Catalogue is available online.

Publishes Erotica, Romance and Irish Fiction titles.

Submission Guidelines Accepts proposals package (including outline, synopsis and three sample chapters) by post with SAE.

Recent Title(s) *Where No Storms Come*, John F Deane

Tips The publisher is always on the lookout for good new writing, but will consider submissions of Northern Ireland/Irish interest only.

Black Swan

61–63 Uxbridge Road, London, W5 5SA
T 020 8579 2652
F 020 8579 5479
E info@transworld-publishers.co.uk
W www.booksattransworld.co.uk

Parent Company Transworld Publishers

Insider Info Catalogue is available online. Manuscript guidelines are not available.

Publishes Historical, Humour, Mainstream/Contemporary, Mystery, Romance, and Suspense titles.

Submission Guidelines Accepts agented submissions only.

Recent Title(s) *The White King*, Gyorgy Dragoman (Modern Fiction)

Tips Do not send any unsolicited manuscripts.

Bloody Books

36–38 Glasshouse Street, London, W1B 5DL
T 020 7734 4448
F 020 3070 0764
E office@beautiful-books.co.uk
W www.beautiful-books.co.uk

Parent Company Beautiful Books

Contact Publisher, Simon Petherick

Established 2006

Insider Info Publishes four titles per year. Catalogue is available online.

Publishes Horror Fiction titles.

Submission Guidelines Check website for latest submission guidelines.

Recent Title(s) *Dracula*, Luis Scafati: *Meat*, Joseph D'Lacey

Tips A proposal package should generally consist of a synopsis and the first three chapters.

Bloomsbury Publishing Plc

36 Soho Square, London, W1D 3QY
T 020 7494 2111
F 020 7434 0151
E csm@bloomsbury.com
W www.bloomsbury.com

Contact Chairman/Chief Executive, Nigel Newton; Publishing Director (Book Division), Liz Calder (Fiction); Editorial Director, Sarah Odedina (Children's Books); Editor in Chief, Alexandra Pringle

Established 1986

Insider Info Payment is via royalties. Aims to respond to proposals within three months. Catalogue and manuscript guidelines are available online.

Publishes Children's, Literary, Mainstream/Contemporary, Translation, Young Adult and Classics titles.

Submission Guidelines No unsolicited submissions.

Recent Title(s) *Soloman's Oak*, Jo-Ann Mapson; *Angelica Lost and Found*, Russell Hoban

Tips Bloomsbury, and its various divisions, publishes a wide range of adult and children's books. Bloomsbury is not currently accepting unsolicited submissions. Aside from its UK imprints, Bloomsbury also has a division in America and owns the American publisher Walker & Company and the German company Berlin Verlag GmbH.

Blue Door

77–85 Fulham Palace Road, Hammersmith, London, W6 8JB
T 020 8741 7070
F 020 8307 4440
E enquiries@harpercollins.co.uk
W www.harpercollins.co.uk

Parent Company HarperCollins Publishers Ltd – Press Books Division

Contact Publisher, Patrick Janson-Smith

Established 2008

Insider Info Publishes between 12 and 20 titles per year. Catalogue available online.

Publishes Commercial and Literary Fiction titles.

Submission Guidelines Accepts agented submissions only.

Recent Title(s) *The Hungry Ghosts*, Anne Berry (Family Saga); *Dead Spy Running*, Jon Stock (Thriller)

Tips Blue Door is a recently established imprint headed up by former Transworld publisher Patrick Janson-Smith, focusing primarily on fiction.

Book Guild Publishing Ltd

Pavilion View, 19 New Road, Brighton, East Sussex, BN1 1UF
T 01273 720900
F 01273 723122
E info@bookguild.co.uk
W www.bookguild.co.uk

Contact Managing Director, Carol Biss; Managing Editor, Joanna Bentley

Insider Info Offers a variety of publishing options for authors, businesses and charities, including conventional publishing, 'Partnership Publishing' and production options. Publishes approximately 100 titles per year.

Publishes Mainstream and Contemporary Fiction titles.

Submission Guidelines Ideas and manuscripts welcome. Initially send a synopsis, covering letter and CV. Submission details are available on the website.

Tips Book Guild offers a range of different publishing options, including subsidy publishing. Research all fees carefully before you commit to anything.

Brandon/Mount Eagle Publications

PO Box 32, Cooleen, Dingle, Co. Kerry, Republic of Ireland
T 00353 66 915 1463
F 00353 66 915 1234
W www.brandonbooks.com

Contact Publisher, Steve MacDonogh

Established 1982

Insider Info Publishes around 15 titles per year. Receives approximately 200 queries and 200 manuscripts per year. Submissions accompanied by SAE will be returned. Catalogue and manuscript guidelines are available online.

Publishes Crime/Thriller, Regional and Irish Fiction titles.

Submission Guidelines Accepts query with SAE with proposal package (including outline, synopsis and 40 sample pages, review quotes, author biography). No submissions by fax or email.

Recent Title(s) *Bloodstorm*, Sam Millar (Crime); *The Dramatist*, Ken Bruen (Thriller)

Tips Titles are aimed at a wide readership, generally with an Irish focus.

Brewin Books Ltd

Doric House, 56 Alcester Road, Studley, Warwickshire, B80 7LG
T 01527 854228
F 01527 852746
E admin@brewinbooks.com
W www.brewinbooks.com

Contact Managing Director, Alan Brewin (Non-Fiction); Editor, Alistair Brewin (Regional History Magazines)

Established 1976

Imprint(s) History Into Print, Brewin Junior

Insider Info Publishes 30 titles per year. Receives approximately 50 queries and 95 manuscripts per year. Payment is via royalty (on retail price). Average lead time is six months, with simultaneous submissions not accepted. Submissions accompanied by SAE will be returned. Catalogue is available online or by email. Manuscript guidelines are available free on request.

Publishes Regional (Midlands) titles.

Submission Guidelines Accepts proposal package (including outline, sample chapters, your publishing history, author biography and SAE).

Recent Title(s) *Adrift in Paradise*, Shirley Thompson

Tips Brewin Books publishes books with mass-market appeal for a general readership.

Brown, Son & Ferguson Ltd

4–10 Darnley Street, Glasgow, G41 2SD
T 0141 429 1234
F 0141 420 1694
E info@skipper.co.uk
W www.skipper.co.uk

Contact Managing Director, L Ingram-Brown

Established 1832

Insider Info Catalogue available online.

Publishes Regional Interest titles.

Recent Title(s) *Back From the Brink*, Jamie Webster and Russel Walker

Tips Brown, Son & Ferguson have been nautical publishers, printers and ships' stationers since 1832. Their list ranges from nautical textbooks, both technical and non-technical, books about the sea, historical books, information on old sailing ships, and how to build model ships. Brown, Son & Ferguson publishes anything related to sailing or other nautical themes, plus Scottish interest plays and non-fiction.

Brown Skin Books

PO Box 57421, London, E5 0ZD
T 020 8986 1115
E info@brownskinbooks.co.uk
W www.brownskinbooks.co.uk

Contact Managing Director, Vastiana Belfon

Established 2002

Insider Info Publishes roughly seven titles per year. 75 per cent of books published are from first-time authors and 80 per cent are from unagented authors. Payment is via royalty (on retail price), with £1,500 advance (for novels). Average lead time is ten months, with simultaneous submissions accepted. Submissions accompanied by SAE will be returned. Aims to respond to proposals and manuscripts within two months. Catalogue available online. Manuscript guidelines available online, by post or via email.

Publishes Erotica novels.

Submission Guidelines Accepts query with proposal package (including outline, one sample chapter and SAE). Novels should be between 75,000 and 90,000 words.

Recent Title(s) *Sorcerer*, Tamzin Hall (Erotic Novel)

Tips Titles are primarily aimed at women of colour aged 18–50, living in the US, Canada, Europe, Africa and the Caribbean. There is a dedicated 'hints and tips' section published on the website that writers should read before submitting. Also, make sure there is a strong story with believable characters, as this is just as important as the sex in Brown Skin Books' publications.

Bryntirion Press

- Bryntirion, Bridgend, CF31 4DX
- T 01656 655886
- F 01656 665919
- E office@emw.org.uk
- W www.emw.org.uk

Contact Press Manager, Huw Kinsey

Established 1955

Publishes Religious titles.

Recent Title(s) *On the Wings of the Dove*, Noel Gibbard (Religion/History)

Tips Titles aimed at the Evangelical/Welsh markets. Also publishes Christian books and magazines in the Welsh language. Welsh-language writers are in demand.

Burning House

- 36–38 Glasshouse Street, London, W1B 5DL
- T 020 7734 4448
- F 020 3070 0764
- E office@beautiful-books.co.uk
- W www.beautiful-books.co.uk

Parent Company Beautiful Books

Contact Publisher, Simon Petherick

Established 2007

Publishes Contemporary Fiction titles.

Submission Guidelines Accepts query with SAE or via email. Submission details to: submissions@beautiful-books.co.uk

Recent Title(s) *The Turkish Diplomat's Daughter*, Deniz Goran

Tips Burning House focuses entirely on contemporary fiction.

Canongate Books Ltd

- 14 High Street, Edinburgh, EH1 1TE
- T 0131 557 5111
- F 0131 557 5211
- E info@canongate.co.uk
- W www.canongate.net

Contact Publisher, Jamie Byng; Managing Director, David Graham

Established 1973

Imprint(s) Canongate Classics, Canongate Crime, Canongate International

Insider Info Aims to respond to proposal within three months. Catalogue and manuscript guidelines available online.

Publishes Contemporary, Literary, Regional, Religious, Crime and Scottish titles.

Submission Guidelines Accepts proposal package (including outline, sample chapters and an SAE) by post only.

Recent Title(s) *Eunoia*, Christian Bök (Contemporary Fiction)

Tips With a distinctly international outlook, Canongate Books continues to nurture and publish new talent from around the world, while retaining the essence of the Scottish Canon. They have no specific agenda other than to promote and publish challenging, quality work from as broad a perspective as possible.

Cardiff Academic Press

- St Fagans Road, Fairwater, Cardiff, CF5 3AE
- T 029 2056 0333
- E enquiries@cardiffacademicpress.com
- W www.cardiffacademicpress.com

Parent Company Drake Group

Publishes Literary titles.

Catholic Truth Society

- 40–46 Harleyford Road, London, SE11 5AY
- T 020 7640 0042
- F 020 7640 0046
- E p.finaldi@acts-online.org.uk
- W www.cts-online.org.uk

Contact Publisher, Fergal Martin; Commissioning Editor, Pierpaolo Finaldi

Established 1868

Insider Info Catalogue is available online.

Publishes Religious titles.

Tips Publications appeal to many different age groups, to Catholic parishes and schools, and to the wider Christian community, as well as to a wide range of other enquirers. The principal goal of CTS publications is to explain the Catholic faith.

Century

Random House, 20 Vauxhall Bridge Road, London, SW1V 2SA
T 020 7840 8554
F 020 7233 6127
E centuryeditorial@randomhouse.co.uk
W www.randomhouse.co.uk

Parent Company The Random House Group Ltd

Contact Publishing Director, Mark Booth

Insider Info Catalogue is available online.

Publishes Mystery, Romance, Suspense, General Fiction and Chick Lit titles.

Submission Guidelines Accepts agented submissions only.

Recent Title(s) The Confession, John Grisham (Crime Fiction)

Tips View the Century section of the main Random House catalogue for examples of publishing lists.

Chatto & Windus

Random House, 20 Vauxhall Bridge Road, London, SW1V 2SA
T 020 7840 8745
F 020 7233 6117
E chattoeditorial@randomhouse.co.uk
W www.randomhouse.co.uk

Parent Company The Random House Group Ltd

Contact Publishing Director, Alison Samuel

Established Founded in the 19th Century, part of The Random House Group since 1987.

Insider Info Catalogue is available online.

Publishes Literary, Mainstream/Contemporary and Translation titles.

Submission Guidelines Accepts agented submissions only.

Recent Title(s) Once on a Moonless Night, Dai Sijie (Literary Fiction)

Tips Look at the Chatto & Windus section of the Random House catalogue to get a feel for the list before submitting.

Chimera

Sheraton House, Castle Park, Cambridge, CB3 0AX
T 01223 370012
F 01223 370040
E editors@pegasuspublishers.com
W www.pegasuspublishers.com

Parent Company Pegasus Elliot MacKenzie Ltd

Inside Info Catalogue and manuscript details are available online.

Publishes Contemporary, Futuristic, Historical and Relationship Erotica titles.

Submission Guidelines Accepts proposal package (including outline and two sample chapters).

Tips Chimera publishes adult erotic fiction for over 18s and specializes in the work of 'previously unpublished first-time authors from all over the world who have a good spanking tale to tell.' Chimera accepts submissions of erotic fiction from any author over the age of 18 as long as the content does not 'contravene the law of the land or international law.'

Cinnamon Press

Ty Meirion, Glan yr afon, Tanygrisiau, Blaenau Ffestiniog, Gwynedd, LL41 3SU
T 01766 832112
E jan@cinnamonpress.com
W www.cinnamonpress.com

Contact Jan Fortune-Wood (Editorial)

Insider Info Catalogue and manuscript guidelines are available online.

Publishes All genres except Erotica, Crime and Horror. *Wants full-length novels that are unique and affecting. No children's novels, although well-written work for older teenagers will be considered.

Not currently accepting submissions. Check website for when submissions are being taken.

Tips Books should have a wide audience appeal and the publishers state that they are particularly interested in authors who can demonstrate a willingness to actively promote their work to the widest possible audience, particularly through local and national media. Submissions queries by email. Cinnamon Press publish authors from around the world, and also strongly promote the voice of Welsh writers.

Cois Life

62 Páirc na Rós, Ascaill na Cille, Dún Laoghaire, Co. Dublin, Republic of Ireland
T 00353 1 280 7951
F 00353 1 280 7951
E eolas@coislife.ie
W www.coislife.ie

Contact Directors, Dr Caoilfhionn Nic Pháidín and Dr Seán Ó Cearnaigh

Established 1995

Insider Info Catalogue available online.

Publishes Irish-Language Fiction titles.

Recent Title(s) *Canary Wharf*, Orna Ní Choileáin (Fiction)

Tips Cois Life aims to publish literary and research works in the Irish language, for both young readers and learners of Irish.

Constable & Robinson Ltd

3 The Lanchesters, 162 Fulham Palace Road, London, W6 9ER
T 020 8741 3663
F 020 8748 7562
E enquiries@constablerobinson.com
W www.constablerobinson.com

Contact Publisher and Managing Director, Nick Robinson

Insider Info Publishes 160 titles per year. Receives approximately 3,000 queries and 1,000 manuscripts per year. Payment is via royalty and advance is offered. Average lead time is one year, with simultaneous submissions accepted. Aims to respond to proposals within one month and queries within three months. Catalogue is free on request.

Publishes Mainstream/Contemporary, Mystery, Suspense and Crime Fiction titles.

Submission Guidelines Accepts query with SAE, or proposal package (including outline, one sample chapter).

Tips Constable & Robinson does not accept email submissions, and does not accept children's fiction or any adult fiction other than crime.

Contact Publishing

1 Rosemont Road, London, NW3 6NG
T 020 7193 1782
E info@contact-publishing.com
W www.contact-publishing.com

Contact Publisher, Anne Mortensen

Established 2003

Insider Info Aims to respond to proposals and manuscripts within one month. Catalogue and manuscript guidelines are available online.

Publishes Literary and General Fiction titles.

Submission Guidelines Accepts query with SAE/proposal package (including outline, three sample chapters, author biography and SAE) or via email to: submission@contact-publishing.com

Recent Title(s) *Sayonara, Dream-eater*, Ethne Ashizawa (Novel)

Corgi

61–63 Uxbridge Road, London, W5 5SA
T 020 8579 265
F 020 8579 5479
E info@transworld-publishers.co.uk
W www.booksattransworld.co.uk

Parent Company Transworld Publishers

Insider Info Catalogue is available online. Manuscript guidelines are not available.

Publishes Historical, Humour, Mainstream/ Contemporary, Mystery, Romance and Suspense titles.

Submission Guidelines Accepts agented submissions only.

Recent Title(s) *The Survivor,* Tom Cain (Crime & Mystery)

Tips Do not send unsolicited submissions.

Crème de la Crime

PO Box 523, Chesterfield, S40 9AT

T 01246 520835

E info@cremedelacrime.com

W www.cremedelacrime.com

Contact Managing Director (Debut Crime Fiction), Lynne Patrick

Established 2003

Insider Info Publishes six titles per year. Receives approximately 500 queries and 300 manuscripts per year. 60 per cent of books published are from first-time authors, 90 per cent of books published are from unagented authors. Payment is via royalty (on wholesale price). Average lead time is one year, with simultaneous submissions not accepted. Submissions accompanied by SAE will be returned. Aims to respond to queries within ten days and manuscripts within eight weeks. Catalogue is available online. Manuscript guidelines are available online, or by post for the cost of £2.50, with an A4 envelope and three first-class stamps.

Publishes Crime, Mystery, Suspense and Thriller titles. *Crème de la Crime publishes crime fiction from both debut authors, and from a small stable of authors they have previously nurtured. All titles are 70–80,000 words.

Submission Guidelines Crème de la Crime are currently not accepting submissions.

Recent Title(s) *Dead Woman's Shoes,* Kaye C Hill (Crime Fiction)

Tips Crème de la Crime stipulates that all prospective authors must follow the submission guidelines, available on the website, carefully when preparing a proposal.

Doubleday

61–63 Uxbridge Road, London, W5 5SA

T 020 8579 2652

F 020 8579 5479

E info@transworld-publishers.co.uk

W www.booksattransworld.co.uk

Parent Company Transworld Publishers

Publishes Ethnic, Historical, Humour, Literary, Mainstream/Contemporary and Multicultural titles.

Submission Guidelines No unsolicited manuscripts, agented submissions only.

Recent Title(s) *The Spiders of Allah,* James Hider (Military/True Life)

Egg Box Publishing

25 Brian Avenue, Norwich, NR1 2PH

T 01603 470191

E mail@eggboxpublishing.com

W www.eggboxpublishing.com

Contact Managing Editor, Nathan Hamilton; Founder, Gordon Smith

Established 2001

Insider Info Receives approximately 5,000 manuscripts per year. Authors are paid around 30 per cent of the profits from their book.

Publishes Fiction by unpublished writers only.

Submission Guidelines Accepts postal submissions only.

Recent Title(s) *Donjong Heights,* Ben Borek

Tips Egg Box Publishing is completely self funded, and allows new writers the chance to be published and possibly picked up by a more mainstream publisher. Authors must not have had any novels previously published anywhere. There are no guidelines for manuscripts as the ethos of the company is to encourage writing outside the usual constraints of mainstream publishing.

Eilish Press

4 Collegiate Crescent, Broomhall Park, Sheffield, S10 2BA
T 07973 353964
E eilishpress@hotmail.co.uk
W http://eilishpress.tripod.com

Contact Dr Suzi Kapadia (Women's Issues, Human Rights, Anti-Racism)

Established 2006

Insider Info Publishes five titles per year. Receives approximately 30 queries and five manuscripts per year. 100 per cent of books published are from unagented authors. Payment is via royalty (on wholesale price) or outright purchase. Catalogue available online or by email.

Publishes Ethnic, Feminist, Historical, Multicultural and Young Adult titles. *All Children's Fiction proposals must contain human rights or anti-racism themes.

Recent Title(s) *Conception Diary: Thinking About Pregnancy & Childbirth*, Dr Susan Hogan (Polemical Feminist, Humour)

Tips Eilish Press only publishes non-sexist, non-racist literature with humanitarian themes for children, or books on women's studies and childcare.

Elliott & Thompson

27 John Street, London, WC1N 2BX
T 020 7831 5013
F 020 7831 5011
E mark@eandtbooks.com
W www.eandtbooks.com

Contact Publishers, Mark Searle and Lorne Forsythe

Established 2001

Imprint(s) Gold Edition, Spitfire, Spitfire Originals, Young Spitfire

Insider Info Catalogue is available online. Manuscript guidelines are available online.

Publishes Literary and Classic Male Writers titles.

Submission Guidelines Elliott & Thompson are currently not accepting fiction submissions.

Recent Title(s) *Dance to Your Daddy*, Gail Levy (Novel)

Tips Elliott & Thompson publishes within a specific area of writing, once classified by the more traditional bookshops as 'belles-lettres'.

Enitharmon Press

26b Caversham Road, London, NW5 2DU
T 020 7482 5967
F 020 7284 1787
E info@enitharmon.co.uk
W www.enitharmon.co.uk

Contact Director, Stephen Stuart-Smith

Established 1967

Imprint(s) Enitharmon Editions

Insider Info Catalogue is available online.

Publishes Literary Collections.

Submission Guidelines No unsolicited submissions.

Recent Title(s) *A Voice Through a Cloud*, Denton Welch

Tips Enitharmon commissions collaborations between distinguished artists and writers. These 'artists' books' have earned an international reputation for their exceptional quality.

EuroCrime

15–16 Nassau Street, London, W1W 7AB
T 020 7436 9898
F 020 7436 9898
E info@arcadiabooks.co.uk
W www.arcadiabooks.co.uk

Parent Company Arcadia Books

Insider Info Catalogue available online.

Publishes Crime Fiction titles.

Submission Guidelines Accepts agented submissions only.

Recent Title(s) *Priest of Evil*, Matti Joensuu (Crime)

Tips Publishes European crime writing only (excluding the UK).

Faber & Faber Ltd

Bloomsbury House, 74–77 Great Russell Street,
London, WC1B 3DA
T 020 7927 3800
F 020 7927 3801
E gapublicity@faber.co.uk
W www.faber.co.uk

Contact Chief Executive, Stephen Page;
Publishing Director (Fiction), Lee Brackstone;
Editor (Crime), Angus Cargill; Editorial Director
(Children's), Julia Wells

Established 1929

Insider Info Publishes roughly 300 titles per
year. Payment is via royalty, along with varying
advances. Submissions accompanied by SAE will
be returned. Aims to respond to manuscripts
within 12 weeks. Catalogue is available online
and via email to: gacatalogue@faber.co.uk

Publishes Adventure, Ethnic, Experimental,
Historical, Literary, Mystery, Plays, Sports,
Suspense, Young Adult, and Children's
Fiction titles.

Submission Guidelines Accepts agented
submissions only.

Recent Title(s) *The Museum of Innocence*, Orhan
Pamuk; *Private Life*, Jane Smiley

Fal Publications

PO Box 74, Truro, Cornwall, TR1 1XS
T 07887 560018
E editor@falpublications.co.uk
W www.falpublications.co.uk

Contact Publisher, Victoria Field (Poetry,
Cornish Interest)

Established 2004

Insider Info Publishes three titles per year.
Receives approximately 12 queries per year. 50
per cent of books published are from first-time
authors, 80 per cent of books published are
from unagented authors. Payment is via royalty
(on wholesale price). Simultaneous submissions
not accepted. Submissions accompanied by SAE
will be returned. Aims to respond to queries
within seven days. Catalogue available online.

Publishes Cornwall-related Fiction titles.

Submission Guidelines Accepts query by email.

Recent Title(s) *The Gift*, Victoria Field
(Illustrated story about Cornwall); *Knights
of Love*, Jane Tozer

Tips Publishes general fiction aimed at those
interested in Cornwall.

Fig Tree

80 Strand, London, WC2R 0RL
T 020 7010 3000
F 020 7010 6060
E customer.service@penguin.co.uk
W www.penguin.co.uk

Parent Company Penguin General

Contact Publishing Director, Juliet Annan

Established 2006

Insider Info Catalogue is available online.

Publishes Literary titles.

Submission Guidelines Accepts agented
submissions only.

Recent Title(s) *22 Britannia Road*, Amanda
Hodgkinson

Tips Fig Tree is a Penguin imprint that specializes
in literary books with commercial appeal. Titles
aim to be fresh, distinct, well written, clever,
entertaining and sometimes funny.

Flambard Press

Holy Jesus Hospital, City Road, Newcastle
upon Tyne, NE1 2AS
T 0191 233 3865
F 01434 674178
E editor@flambardpress.co.uk
W www.flambardpress.co.uk

Contact Managing Editor, Peter Lewis

Established 1990

Insider Info Publishes five titles per year. Authors
are paid royalties. Catalogue and manuscript
guidelines are available online.

Publishes Literary titles. *No Genre Fiction.

Submission Guidelines Accepts query with

SAE/proposal package (including synopsis and opening chapters).

Recent Title(s) *The Sweet Track*, Avril Joy (Novel)

Tips Flambard Press is a small, independent publisher that aims to offer opportunities to new and neglected writers, especially in the North of England. Flambard is keen to nourish developing talent. Poetry is the backbone of the list, but Flambard now publishes a small amount of fiction as well. Authors are very carefully selected. Children's books, science-fiction, fantasy, romance, westerns, and horror are not published.

Flicking Lizard

T 020 8761 1536
E flickliz@googlemail.com
W www.flickinglizard.co.uk

Contact Publisher, Mark Boccalatte

Established 2007

Insider Info Aims to publish ten books per year. Accepts unagented submissions. Payment is via royalty (of net) with 0.1 (per £) minimum. Offers an advance. Aims to respond within three months for manuscripts.

Publishes Contemporary Fiction titles.

Submission Guidelines Accepts proposal package (including synopsis and first 40 pages) by email. No postal submissions.

Tips Flicking Lizard seeks fresh contemporary writing from quality authors that are often overlooked by the big publishing houses. They aim to give writers the opportunity to make themselves known to the public without having to resort to spending their own money on self-publishing or the vanity press.

Flipped Eye
Publishing Limited

PO Box 43771, Suite 13, London, W14 8ZY
T 0845 652 9517
F 0845 652 9574
E newwork@flippedeye.net
W www.flippedeye.net

Contact Editor (Literary Fiction), Sally Strong

Established 2001

Imprint(s) Lubin & Kleyner, Waterways, Mouthmark Poetry

Insider Info Publishes roughly ten titles per year. Receives approximately 200 queries and 140 manuscripts per year. 90 per cent of books published are from first-time authors, 95 per cent of books published are from unagented authors. Payment is via royalty (on retail price). Advance offered is from £50 to £1,000. Average lead time is nine months, with simultaneous submissions not accepted. Submissions will not be returned. Aims to respond to queries and proposals within three months, manuscripts within six months and all other enquiries within 14 days. Catalogue is free on request and available online. Manuscript guidelines are available online.

Publishes Erotica, Fantasy, Literary, Mainstream/Contemporary, Multicultural and Translation titles and Short Story Collections.

Submission Guidelines Accepts query by post with proposal package (including outline, three sample chapters and your publishing history). Or by email to: newwork@flippedeye.net

Recent Title(s) *29 Ways to Drown*, Niki Aguirre

Floris Books

15 Harrison Gardens, Edinburgh, EH11 1SH
T 0131 337 2372
F 0131 347 9919
E floris@florisbooks.co.uk
W www.florisbooks.co.uk

Contact Managing Director, Christian Maclean; Editors, Gale Winskill and Christopher Moore

Established 1977

Imprint(s) Flyways (Young Adult's Fiction), Kelpies (Scottish Children's Fiction)

Insider Info Payment via royalties. Catalogue and manuscript guidelines are available online.

Publishes Historical, Children's, Young Adult, Regional and Scottish titles.

Submission Guidelines Accepts query with

SAE/proposal package (including outline, three sample chapters, author biography and SAE). No email submissions. No simultaneous submissions. Allow three months for a response.

Recent Title(s) *Hox*, Annemarie Allan (Children's)

Tips Floris Books publishes books for children, in which the subject matter is predominantly Scottish. Floris primarily seeks books encompassing modern settings, with contemporary situations and characters to which today's children can relate. This does not rule out historical fiction, but more modern titles will be prioritized.

Fourth Estate

✉ 77–85 Fulham Palace Road, Hammersmith, London, W6 8JB
☎ T 020 8741 7070
F 020 8307 4440
✎ E enquiries@harpercollins.co.uk
W www.4thestate.co.uk

Parent Company HarperCollins Publishers Ltd – Press Books Division

Contact Publishing Director, Nick Pearson

Insider Info Catalogue available online.

Publishes Literary and Mainstream/Contemporary titles.

Submission Guidelines Accepts agented submissions only.

Recent Title(s) *The Shipping News, 25th Anniversary Edition*, Annie Proulx (Novel)

Tips Fourth Estate publishes cutting-edge non-fiction and fiction, often with a controversial flavour. Editors accept submissions only from literary agents or previously published authors, but may consider submissions that are accompanied by a positive assessment from a manuscript assessment agency.

The Friday Project

✉ 77–85 Fulham Palace Road, Hammersmith, London, W6 8JB
☎ T 020 8741 7070
F 020 8307 4440
✎ E enquiries@harpercollins.co.uk
W www.thefridayproject.co.uk

Parent Company HarperCollins Publishers Ltd – Press Books Division

Contact Managing Director, Clare Christian (Non-Fiction, Humour, Literary Fiction); Publisher, Scott Pack (Fiction, Humour, Non-Fiction); Managing Editor, Heather Smith

Established 2005

Insider Info Catalogue is available online.

Publishes Confession, Experimental, Gothic, Historical, Humour, Literary and Mainstream/Contemporary titles.

Submission Guidelines Accepts proposal package via email (including outline, sample chapters, your publishing history and author biography). Submission details to: authors@thefridayproject.co.uk

Tips The Friday Project develops much of its publishing programme from the most exciting and innovative websites, properties and content already in existence, as well as from submissions.

Gerald Duckworth & Co. Ltd

✉ 90–93 Cowcross Street, London, EC1M 6BF
☎ T 020 7490 7300
F 020 7490 0080
✎ E info@duckworth-publishers.co.uk
W www.ducknet.co.uk

Established 1898

Imprint(s) Ardis, Bristol Classical Press, Duckworth Adademic, The Overlook Press

Insider Info Aims to respond to proposals within 12 weeks and manuscripts within 12 weeks. Catalogue and manuscript guidelines available online.

Publishes Literary and Commercial Fiction titles.

Submission Guidelines No unsolicited submissions.

Recent Title(s) *An Appeal to Reason*, Nigel Lawson; *Christopher's Ghosts*, Charles McCarry

Tips Gerald Duckworth is an independent publisher with a general trade and academic list. Duckworth generally publishes literary and commercial fiction and non-fiction, including history, biography and memoir. They do not accept phone calls, or email submissions.

Gollancz

✉ Orion House, 5 Upper St Martin's Lane, London, WC2H 9EA
☎ T 020 7240 3444
F 020 7240 4822
✎ E info@orionbooks.co.uk
W www.orionbooks.co.uk

Parent Company Orion Publishing Group Ltd

Contact Editorial Directors, Simon Spanton and Jo Fletcher

Established 1927 (incorporated into Orion in 1998)

Imprint(s) Gollancz Manga

Insider Info Catalogue available online (as a downloadable pdf or via the online catalogue request form).

Publishes Fantasy, Science-Fiction and Manga titles. *Gollancz specializes in Fantasy and Science-Fiction, and also publishes the Masterworks series of reprints of Fantasy and Science-Fiction classics.

Submission Guidelines Accepts agented submissions only.

Recent Title(s) *Absolution Gap*, Alastair Reynolds (Science-Fiction); *Orcs, Bad Blood: Weapons of Magical Destruction*, Stan Nicholls (Fantasy)

Gomer Press/Gwasg Gomer

✉ Llandysul Enterprise Park, Llandysul, Ceredigion, SA44 4JL
☎ T 01559 363090
F 01559 363758
✎ E gwasg@gomer.co.uk
W www.gomer.co.uk

Contact Managing Director, Jonathan Lewis; Head of Publishing, Dylan Williams

Established 1892

Imprint(s) Gomer, Pont Books

Insider Info Publishes 120 titles per year. Aims to respond to proposals and manuscripts within one month. Catalogue and manuscript guidelines available online.

Publishes Children's, Young Adult and Welsh titles.

Submission Guidelines Accepts query with SAE, or via email, with proposal package (including outline, one sample chapter and your author biography). See website for email submissions addresses.

Recent Title(s) *Here Comes the Doctor*, Viv Sayer (Illustrated Children's Fiction)

Tips Gomer Press is Wales' largest independent publisher, specializing in books from Wales, about Wales. They work in Welsh and English language, for children and adults. Do not send whole manuscripts to an editor, a sample chapter and a synopsis will be sufficient at first. It would also be useful to include a CV and an outline of the sales strengths of the proposal. As the publisher receives a large number of manuscripts for consideration every week, they advise authors to be patient. They aim to send an acknowledgement of receipt for manuscripts within one month.

Granta Books

✉ 12 Addison Avenue, London, W11 4QR
☎ T 020 7605 1360
F 020 7605 1361
✎ E info@granta.com
W www.granta.com

Parent Company Granta Publications

Contact Publisher, Philip Gwyn Jones; Publishing Director, Sara Holloway

Established 1989

Insider Info Publishes 25 titles a year. Payment is via royalties. Catalogue and manuscript guidelines available online.

Publishes Literary titles. *No Genre Fiction.

Submission Guidelines Accepts query with SAE/proposal package (including outline, 50 pages, or two sample chapters).

Recent Title(s) *The Rowing Lessons*, Anne

Landsman (Novel)

Tips Granta Books is weighted more towards non-fiction publishing than fiction, with a ratio of about 70:30. Submissions should be made by post only. Granta does not accept faxes, emails or computer disc submissions. Due to the large number of submissions, it can take some time before they are able to respond.

Great Northern Publishing

✉ PO Box 202, Scarborough, North Yorkshire, YO11 3GE
☎ T 01723 581329
  F 01723 581329
✎ E books@greatnorthernpublishing.co.uk
  W www.greatnorthernpublishing.co.uk

Contact Production Manager, Mark Marsay

Established 1999

Insider Info Payment is via royalties. Catalogue and manuscript guidelines available via the website.

Publishes Erotica, Humour and Crime titles.

Submission Guidelines Do not accept unsolicited material from prospective authors. Accepts query with SAE.

Recent Title(s) *The Drowning Man*, Gary Mortimer (Crime)

Tips Great Northern Publishing is a wholly independent, family-owned, award-winning small publishing and production company, who produce the bi-monthly magazines *The Great War* and *The Second World War*, and the international erotic art and literature magazine *Jade*. Book production is mainly done on contract terms with other publishers and organizations.

Guildhall Press

✉ Unit 15, Rath Mor Business Park, Bligh's Lane, Creggan, Derry, BT48 0LZ
☎ T 028 7136 4413
  F 028 7137 2979
✎ E info@ghpress.com
  W www.ghpress.com

Contact Managing Editor, Paul Hippsley

Established 1979

Insider Info Catalogue available online.

Publishes Historical, Literary, Humour and Young Readers' Fiction titles.

Recent Title(s) *Derry: Days of Rain*, Chris Sheerin (Fiction); *Zoom Zang Alang*, Liam Black (Children's)

Tips Guildhall Press is one of Northern Ireland's leading independent publishers.

Gwasg Pantycelyn

✉ St Davids Road, Caernarfon, Gwynedd, LL55 1ER
☎ T 01286 672018
  F 01286 677823
✎ E gwasgpantycelyn@ukonline.co.uk

Publishes Welsh and English-Language Fiction titles.

Tips Gwasg Pantycelyn has previously published a collection of around 150 books for adults and children. The intended audience is general readers interested in a more analytical approach to literature, as well as readers interested in the culture and social history of Wales.

Hachette Ireland

✉ Unit 8 Castlecourt Centre, Castleknock, Dublin 15, Republic of Ireland
☎ T 00353 1 824 6288
✎ E info@hbgi.ie
  W www.hachette.ie

Parent Company Hachette UK

Contact Managing Director, Breda Purdue

Established 2002

Insider Info Catalogue and manuscript guidelines available online.

Publishes Literary and Mainstream/ Contemporary titles on the following subjects: Crime, Irish Writing.

Submission Guidelines Agented submissions only.

Tips Hachette Ireland is not currently accepting unsolicited fiction from previously unpublished authors. Submission details for published authors and general non-fiction titles are available from the website. Now reports directly to Hachette UK, following the closure of Hodder Headline.

Hachette Scotland

2a Christie Street, Paisley, PA1 1NB
T 0141 552 8082
E bob.mcdevitt@hodder.co.uk
W www.headline.co.uk

Parent Company Hachette UK

Contact Bob McDevitt

Insider Info Catalogue available from website on request.

Publishes Literary, Mainstream/Contemporary, Scottish Writing titles.

Submission Guidelines Accepts proposal package by post or email (including outline, first 50 pages, SAE if sending by post). Address to Bob McDevitt or email to: submissions@hachettescotland.co.uk

Tips Seeking new Scottish writing by Scottish writers.

Halban Publishers Ltd

22 Golden Square, London, W1F 9JW
T 020 7437 9300
F 020 7437 9512
E books@halbanpublishers.com
W www.halbanpublishers.com

Contact Directors, Peter and Martine Halban

Established 1986

Insider Info Publishes eight titles per year. Payment is via royalties. Catalogue available online.

Publishes Jewish Interest titles.

Submission Guidelines Accepts query with SAE.

Recent Title(s) *The Book of Q*, Jonathan Rabb (Thriller)

Tips All titles should reflect Jewish interest. Welcomes proposals, but approach by letter first.

Hamish Hamilton

80 Strand, London, EC2R 0RL
T 020 7010 3000
F 020 7010 6060
E customer.service@penguin.co.uk
W www.penguin.co.uk

Parent Company Penguin General

Contact Publishing Director, Simon Prosser

Established 1931

Insider Info Publishes no more than 20 titles per year. Catalogue is available online.

Publishes Literary Fiction titles.

Submission Guidelines Accepts agented submissions only.

Recent Title(s) *Moth Smoke*, Mohsin Hamid; *The Pinnacles*, Hari Kunzru

Tips The Hamish Hamilton list is a small section of the Penguin Group and focuses entirely on distinct, often unusual, literary fiction and non-fiction from an exciting and eclectic group of authors.

Harlequin Mills & Boon Ltd

Eton House, 18–24 Paradise Road, Richmond, TW9 1SR
T 020 8288 2800
F 020 8288 2899
E submissions@hmb.co.uk
W www.millsandboon.co.uk

Contact Executive Editor, Tessa Shapcott (Modern); Senior Editor, Joanne Grant (Romance); Senior Editor, Sheila Hodgson (Medical); Senior Editor, Linda Fildew (Historical); Senior Editor, Bryony Green (Modern Heat)

Established 1908

Imprint(s) Mills & Boon Modern Romance, Mills & Boon Romance, Mills & Boon Medical Romance, Mills & Boon Historical Romance, Modern Heat, MIRA, Silhouette, Harlequin

Insider Info Publishes 600 titles per year. Receives approximately 2,000 manuscripts per year. Payment is via royalties. Simultaneous submissions not accepted. Submissions accompanied by SAE will be returned. Aims to respond to manuscripts within three months. Catalogue and manuscript guidelines available online.

Publishes Erotica, Romance and Women's Fiction titles.

Submission Guidelines Accepts query by post with SAE or by email to submissions@hmb. co.uk. Submit proposal package (including outline and first three chapters).

Recent Title(s) *Count Maxime's Virgin*, Susan Stephens (Historical Romance); *Taken for Revenge, Bedded for Pleasure*, India Grey (Modern Romance)

Tips Harlequin Mills & Boon is a leading international publisher of romance fiction aimed at women. The Romance and Modern Romance imprints publish traditional romance novels, often set against a backdrop of luxury, wealth and international locations. Medical Romance publishes romance novels set in or around the medical professions. Historical Romance publishes romance novels set in historical eras and includes chivalrous knights, roguish rakes and rugged cattlemen as the main focus of interest. Other imprints such as Silhouette and MIRA – which publish racier romance fiction and general women's fiction respectively – are available in the other international editorial offices. Harlequin Mills & Boon accepts unsolicited submissions, and has substantial aspiring author information on the website, with detailed guidelines including word counts and proposal style guides, for each of their imprints.

HarperCollins Publishers Ltd

✉ 77–85 Fulham Palace Road, Hammersmith, London, W6 8JB
☎ T 020 8741 7070
F 020 8307 4440
✐ E enquiries@harpercollins.co.uk
W www.harpercollins.co.uk

Parent Company HarperCollins Worldwide (Division of News Corporation)

Contact CEO and Publisher, Victoria Barnsley; Publisher, Belinda Budge

Established 1819

Imprint(s) Collins (division), General Books (division), Press Books (division)

Insider Info Publishes around 1,500 titles per year. Catalogue and manuscript guidelines available online.

Publishes Adventure, Fantasy, Historical, Horror, Humour, Children's, Literary, Mainstream/Contemporary, Mystery, Romance, Science-Fiction, Suspense, Young Adult and Thriller titles.

Submission Guidelines Accepts agented submissions only.

Recent Title(s) *Dirty Game*, Jessie Keane (Thriller)

Tips HarperCollins Publishers UK is one of the leading English-language publishers in the world, and publishes the widest range of books of any of Britain's publishing groups, in a variety of different genres and styles. In addition it also publishes the complete works of JRR Tolkein, CS Lewis and Agatha Christie. HarperCollins accepts submissions only from literary agents or previously published authors, but may also consider submissions that are accompanied by a positive assessment from a manuscript assessment agency.

HarperCollins Publishers Ltd – General Books Division

✉ 77–85 Fulham Palace Road, Hammersmith, London, W6 8JB
☎ T 020 8741 7070
F 020 8307 4440
✐ E enquiries@harpercollins.co.uk
W www.harpercollins.co.uk

Parent Company HarperCollins Publishers Ltd

Contact Managing Director, Amanda Ridout

Imprint(s) AVON, HarperCollins Children's Books, HarperCollins Crime & Thrillers,

HarperEntertainment, HarperEstates, HarperFiction, HarperThorsons/HarperElement, HarperSport, HarperTrue, HarperVoyager

Insider Info Catalogues available online at: www.harpercollins.co.uk, www.voyager-books.co.uk, www.thorsens.com, www.harpercollinschildrensbooks.co.uk, www.collins-crime.co.uk and www.tolkien.co.uk

Publishes Fantasy, Children's, Mainstream/Contemporary, Science-Fiction, Young Adult, Crime, Thriller and Classic titles.

Submission Guidelines Accepts agented submissions only.

Tips The General Books division of HarperCollins Publishers Ltd publishes some of the most high profile writers around under the HarperFiction imprint – from Josephine Cox and Tony Parsons, to Sidney Sheldon and Tracey Chavalier. The Voyager imprint is the UK's leading science-fiction and fantasy imprint.

HarperCollins Publishers Ltd – Press Books Division

77–85 Fulham Palace Road, Hammersmith, London, W6 8JB
T 020 8741 7070
F 020 8307 4440
E enquiries@harpercollins.co.uk
W www.harpercollins.co.uk

Parent Company HarperCollins Publishers Ltd

Contact Managing Director, John Bond

Imprint(s) Blue Door, Fourth Estate, The Friday Project, HarperPerennial, HarperPress

Insider Info Catalogue available online.

Publishes Humour, Literary, Mainstream/Contemporary, Romance, Translation, Crime and Genre Fiction titles.

Submission Guidelines Accepts agented submissions only.

Tips HarperCollins has acquired some of the assets of The Friday Project, the only publishing company to specialize in sourcing the brightest talent from the web and developing it into great books, and also launched a new fiction imprint, Blue Door, in 2008. Press Books is a

large division within HarperCollins and it is best to direct enquiries to the relevant imprint, rather than to the division as a whole.

HarperCollins Crime & Thrillers

77–85 Fulham Palace Road, Hammersmith, London, W6 8JB
T 020 8741 7070
F 020 8307 4440
E enquiries@harpercollins.co.uk
W www.harpercollins.co.uk

Parent Company HarperCollins Publishers Ltd – General Books Division

Contact Publishing Director, Julia Wisdom

Insider Info Catalogue available online.

Publishes Mystery, Suspense, Crime and Thriller titles.

Submissions Guidelines Accepts agented submissions only.

Recent Title(s) *They Do it With Mirrors*, Agatha Christie (Crime)

Tips HarperCollins Crime & Thrillers publishes the best in modern crime fiction from popular writers such as Val McDermid, Reginald Hill and Robert Wilson.

HarperFiction

77–85 Fulham Palace Road, Hammersmith, London, W6 8JB
T 020 8741 7070
F 020 8307 4440
E enquiries@harpercollins.co.uk
W www.harpercollins.co.uk

Parent Company HarperCollins Publishers Ltd – General Books Division

Contact Publisher, Lynne Drew

Insider Info Catalogue available online.

Publishes Fantasy, Historical, Horror, Literary, Mainstream/Contemporary, Romance, Science-Fiction, Suspense, Women's Writing, and Crime/Thriller titles.

Submission Guidelines Agented submissions only.

Recent Title(s) *A Darker Domain*, Val McDermid (Crime)

Tips HarperFiction is the general fiction division under HarperCollins – General Books Division.

HarperPerennial

77–85 Fulham Palace Road, Hammersmith, London, W6 8JB
T 020 8741 7070
F 020 8307 4440
E enquiries@harpercollins.co.uk
W www.harpercollins.co.uk

Parent Company HarperCollins Publishers Ltd – Press Books Division

Contact Publishing Director, Paul Baggaley

Insider Info Catalogue available online.

Publishes Literary, Mainstream/Contemporary and Genre Fiction titles.

Submission Guidelines Accepts agented submissions only.

Recent Title(s) *The Cat Sanctuary*, Patrick Gale; *Out At Night*, Susan Arnout Smith

Tips HarperPerennial is the literary paperback imprint for all Press Books titles.

HarperPress

77–85 Fulham Palace Road, Hammersmith, London, W6 8JB
T 020 8741 7070
F 020 8307 4440
E enquiries@harpercollins.co.uk
W www.harpercollins.co.uk

Parent Company HarperCollins Publishers Ltd – Press Books Division

Contact Publishing Director, Michael Fishwick

Insider Info Catalogue available online.

Publishes Mainstream/Contemporary titles.

Submission Guidelines Accepts agented submissions only.

Recent Title(s) *The Book of Fires*, Jane Borodale (Novel)

Tips HarperPress publishes quality novels with real commercial potential.

HarperVoyager

77–85 Fulham Palace Road, Hammersmith, London, W6 8JB
T 020 8741 7070
F 020 8307 4440
E enquiries@harpercollins.co.uk
W www.harpercollins.co.uk

Parent Company HarperCollins Publishers Ltd – General Books Division

Contact Publishing Director, Jane Johnson

Insider Info Catalogue available online.

Publishes Fantasy, Gothic, Horror and Science-Fiction titles.

Submission Guidelines Accepts agented submissions only.

Recent Title(s) *The Painted Man*, Peter V Brett (Fantasy)

Tips HarperVoyager publishes modern fantasy, horror and science-fiction, with authors including Terry Goodkind, David Eddings, Raymond E. Feist, George RR Martin and Robin Hobb.

Headland Publications

York Avenue, West Kirby, Wirral, CH48 3JF
T 0151 625 9128
E headlandpublications@hotmail.co.uk
W www.headlandpublications.co.uk

Contact Director and Editor, Gladys-Mary Coles

Established 1969

Publishes Mainstream/Contemporary titles.

Submission Guidelines Accepts query with SAE. No unsolicited manuscripts.

Headline

338 Euston Road, London, NW1 3BH
T 020 7873 6000
F 020 7873 6024

E enquiries@headline.co.uk
W www.headline.co.uk

Parent Company Hachette UK

Contact Managing Director, Martin Neild; Publishing Director, Jane Morpeth (Fiction)

Established 1986

Insider Info Does not accept simultaneous submissions. Submissions accompanied by SAE will be returned. Aims to respond to proposals within six weeks. Catalogue and manuscript guidelines are available online on request.

Hesperus Press

4 Rickett Street, London, SW6 1RU
T 020 7610 3331
F 020 7610 3337
E info@hesperuspress.com
W www.hesperuspress.com

Contact Managing Editor, Ellie Robins

Established 2001

Insider Info Publishes 50 titles per year. Payment via royalties. Catalogue available online or by post upon request.

Publishes Literary, Translation and Classics titles.

Submission Guidelines Accepts query with SAE.

Recent Title(s) *The Maytrees*, Annie Dillard (Novel)

Tips Hesperus Press is committed to reprinting works that have been neglected or are simply little known in the English-speaking world – making them accessible through new translations and a completely fresh editorial approach. They don't generally accept proposals for new fiction, as they mainly publish classic literary fiction. If you're proposing a translation, send it to Ellie Robins by post or email, with as many details as possible.

Hilltop Press

4 Nowell Place, Almondbury, Huddersfield, HD5 8PD

Contact Steve Sneyd

Insider Info Catalogue available with SAE.

Publishes Fantasy, Horror and Science-Fiction titles.

Tips All material falls within the speculative fiction category, which includes fantasy, horror and science-fiction. As well as by mail, a list of publications is available at www.bbr-online.com

Hodder & Stoughton General

338 Euston Road, London, NW1 3BH
T 020 7873 6000
F 020 7873 6024
W www.hodder.co.uk

Parent Company Hachette UK

Contact CEO, Martin Neild; Managing Director, Jamie Hodder-Williams

Established 1868

Imprint(s) Coronet, Hodder Faith, Sceptre

Insider Info Catalogue available online.

Publishes Mainstream/Contemporary Fiction titles.

Submission Guidelines Accepts agented submissions only.

Recent Title(s) *Just After Sunset*, Stephen King (Fiction/Collection); *A Most Wanted Man*, John le Carré (Thriller)

Tips Hodder & Stoughton General publishes under three imprints: Hodder & Stoughton – which handles general fiction and non-fiction, including crime, thrillers and women's fiction; Hodder Faith – which publishes religious books for the general and Christian markets; and Sceptre – which publishes innovative non-fiction and prize-winning fiction authors, such as Melvyn Bragg, Keri Hulme and David Mitchell. They have also recently relaunched the Coronet imprint, an imprint of fiction and non-fiction with a venerable history that includes PG Wodehouse and Ian Fleming. Hodder & Stoughton General now reports directly to Hachette UK, following the closure of Hodder Headline.

Honeyglen Publishing Ltd

56 Durrels House, Warwick Gardens,
London, W14 8QB
T 020 7602 2876
F 020 7602 2876

Contact Director, NS Poderegin

Established 1983

Publishes Literary titles. *No Science-Fiction or
Children's Fiction titles.

Submission Guidelines Accepts query with SAE.
Submit completed manuscript.

Tips A small publishing house that handles
biography, history and philosophy of history,
as well as some literary fiction. Unsolicited
submissions are welcome, but due to the
small size of the publisher, output is usually
extremely limited.

Honno Welsh Women's Press

Unit 14, Creative Units, Aberystwyth Arts
Centre, Aberystwyth, SY23 3GL
T 01970 623150
F 01970 623150
E post@honno.co.uk
W www.honno.co.uk

Contact Publishing Manager, Lindsay Ashford;
Editor, Caroline Oakley

Established 1986

Insider Info Publishes eight titles per year.
Payment is via royalties. Aims to respond
to proposals and manuscripts within four
months. Catalogue available online on request.
Manuscript guidelines available online via
website.

Publishes Children's, Mainstream/
Contemporary, Regional, Translation, Young
Adult and Welsh Fiction titles.

Submission Guidelines Accepts proposal
package (including outline and 50 pages) by
post only.

Submission Guidelines Accepts queries with
complete manuscript.

Recent Title(s) *Not Funny Not Clever*, Jo Verity

Tips Honno is an independent cooperative
press run by women and committed to
publishing the best in Welsh women's
writing. Most of Honno's titles are novels,
autobiographies and short story anthologies in
English, but it also publishes poetry, children's
and teenage titles and books in Welsh. Honno
only considers for publication the work of
women who are Welsh, living in Wales, or have
a significant Welsh connection.

House of Lochar

Isle of Colonsay, Argyll, PA61 7YR
T 01951 200232
E sales@houseoflochar.com
W www.houseoflochar.com

Contact Chairman, Kevin Byrne; Managing
Director, Georgina Hobhouse

Established 1995

Imprint(s) Colonsay Books, West Highland
Series

Insider Info Payment via royalties. Catalogue
and manuscript guidelines available online.

Publishes Mainstream/Contemporary,
Children's, Regional and Scottish titles.

Submission Guidelines House of Lochar are not
currently seeking new titles.

Recent Title(s) *The Blood is Strong*, Richenda
Francis (Novel)

Tips House of Lochar is a specialist Scottish
publisher with a particular remit to print quality
books on a number of subjects, including
Scottish history, traditions and other titles of
general Scottish interest in both fiction and
non-fiction.

Hutchinson

Random House, 20 Vauxhall Bridge Road,
London, SW1V 2SA
T 020 7840 8564
F 020 7233 6127
E hutchinsoneditorial@randomhouse.co.uk
W www.randomhouse.co.uk

Parent Company The Random House
Group Ltd

Contact Publishing Director, Sue Freestone

Publishes General, Historical and Literary Fiction titles.

Submission Guidelines Accepts agented submissions only.

Recent Title(s) *Land of Marvels*, Barry Unsworth (Historical Fiction)

Ignotus Press

BCM-Writer, London, WC1N 3XX
T 0845 230 2980
E ignotuspress@eircom.net
W www.ignotuspress.com

Contact Commissioning Editor, Suzanne Ruthven

Established 1994

Imprint(s) Moonraker (Fiction), Past Tomes, Alphard (Lifestyle)

Insider Info Simultaneous submissions accepted. Submissions accompanied by SAE will be returned. Aims to respond to queries within seven days, proposals two weeks and manuscripts within one month. Book catalogue available online.

Publishes Fiction titles on the following subjects: Adventure, Gothic, Historical, Humour, Mystery, Occult, Regional and Spiritual.

*All fiction proposals must be metaphysically based to appeal to the target audience.

Submission Guidelines Accepts query with SAE.

Recent Title(s) *The Google Tantra*, Alan Richardson (Fiction)

Tips Ignotus Press titles are aimed at those with an alternative lifestyle and an interest in genuine pagan/new age/metaphysical writing. Any prospective author should study the guidelines thoroughly before submission.

Immanion Press

8 Rowley Grove, Stafford, ST17 9BJ
T 01785 613299
E editorial@immanion-press.com
W www.immanion-press.com

Contact Managing Director and Commissioning Editor, Storm Constantine

Established 2003

Imprint(s) Megalithica

Insider Info Authors paid by royalty. Manuscript guidelines available online.

Publishes Fantasy, Gothic, Horror, Science-Fiction and Slipstream titles.

Submission Guidelines Accepts query with SAE. Submit proposal package (including outline, synopsis, author biography and a sample of the first 30 pages).

Recent Title(s) *Angelglass*, David Barnett (Dark Fantasy)

Tips Publishes mainly speculative fiction such as horror, fantasy and science-fiction. Check the website for details submission guidelines before submitting by post or email.

IMP Fiction Ltd

PO Box 69, Church Stretton, Shropshire, SY6 6WZ
T 01694 720049
F 01694 720049
E info@impbooks.com
W www.impbooks.com

Parent Company Independent Music Press

Contact Managing Director, Kaye Roach

Established 1998

Insider Info Authors paid by royalty. Catalogue and author guidelines available online.

Publishes Mainstream/Contemporary Fiction titles. *Does not publish Science-Fiction, Horror, Crime or novels about bands/music.

Submission Guidelines Accepts query with SAE. Submit proposal package (including outline, three sample chapters and author biography). Does not accept email submissions.

Recent Title(s) *The Peacock Manifesto*, Stuart David

Tips IMP Fiction has a reputation for refreshing, innovative, cutting-edge and original storytelling.

Iron Press

5 Marden Terrace, Cullercoats, North Shields, Northumberland, NE30 4PD
T 0191 253 1901
E ironpress@blueyonder.co.uk
W www.ironpress.co.uk

Contact Pete Mortimer

Established 1973

Insider Info Submissions accompanied by SAE will be returned. Contact for catalogue.

Publishes Novels and Short Stories. *Iron Press aims to publish fiction it likes, regardless of market potential.

Submission Guidelines Query with Peter Mortimer before submission.

Tips Iron Press' policy is to seek new writers from the North of England, the rest of the country, and occasionally from overseas. It spurns literary competitions, prizes and mass-market fiction.

John Murray

338 Euston Road, London, NW1 3BH
T 020 7873 6000
F 020 7873 6446
W www.johnmurray.co.uk

Parent Company Hachette UK

Contact CEO, Martin Neild; Managing Director, Roland Philipps

Established 1768

Insider Info Catalogue available online.

Publishes Literary Fiction titles.

Submission Guidelines Accepts agented submissions only.

Tips A leading literary publisher. John Murray now reports directly to Hachette UK, following the closure of Hodder Headline.

Jonathan Cape

Random House, 20 Vauxhall Bridge Road, London, SW1V 2SA

T 020 7840 8576
F 020 7233 6117
E capeeditorial@randomhouse.co.uk
W www.randomhouse.co.uk

Parent Company The Random House Group Ltd

Contact Publishing Director, Dan Franklin

Established 1921

Insider Info Catalogue available online.

Publishes Literary and Children's Fiction titles.

Submission Guidelines Accepts agented submissions only.

Recent Title(s) The Rescue Man, Anthony Quinn (Literary Fiction)

Karnak House

300 Westbourne Park Road, London, W11 1EH
T 020 7243 3620
E karnakhouse@aol.com
W www.karnakhouse.co.uk

Contact Director, Amon Saba Saakana; Art Director, Seheri Sujai

Established 1979

Imprint(s) The Intef Institute

Insider Info Publishes seven titles per year. Receives approximately 30 queries and 20 manuscripts per year. 15 per cent of books published are from first-time authors, 100 per cent of books published are from unagented authors. Payment is via royalty (on wholesale price), with 0.08 (per £) minimum. Advance offered is from £200 to £500. Average lead time is more than 18 months, with simultaneous submissions accepted. Submissions accompanied by SAE will be returned. Aims to respond to queries within seven days, proposals within 14 days and manuscripts within four months. Catalogue is available online. Manuscript guidelines are available by email.

Publishes African/Caribbean and Children's Fiction titles.

Submission Guidelines Accepts query with SAE/proposal package (including outline, contents page, two sample chapters and SAE).

The Kates Hill Press

24 Fernhurst Drive, Brierley Hill,
West Midlands, DY5 4PU
T 01384 485034
E kateshillpress@blueyonder.co.uk
W www.kateshillpress.pwp.blueyonder.co.uk

Contact Greg Stokes

Established 1992

Insider Info Payment is via royalties.

Publishes Regional titles and Short Story
Collections on a West Midlands theme, or by
a West Midlands writer.

Submission Guidelines Accepts proposal
package (including sample chapter(s)).

Tips Any work submitted should also be
available in electronic format. Responses to
proposals may take a while as the press is a
part-time venture.

Kinglake Publishing

Office S4, Ashgrove House, Elland,
Calderdale, HX5 9JB
E info@kinglakepublishing.co.uk
W www.kinglakepublishing.co.uk

Contact Managing Editor, Harry Taylor;
Administrative Assistant, Jennifer Jackson

Established 2005

Imprint(s) Kinglake Non-Fiction, Kinglake
Religion, Kinglake Fiction

Insider Info Publishes roughly 30 titles per
year. Receives approximately 250 queries and
80 manuscripts per year. 30 per cent of books
published are from first-time authors. Accepts
work from unagented authors. Some books
are author subsidy published, based on an
estimation of market reach. Payment is via
annual royalty (on retail price), with 0.08 (per
£) minimum and 0.12 (per £) maximum. Does
not offer an advance. Catalogue is available with
SAE, or by email.

Publishes Novels in all genres. First novels
welcome for consideration. No Erotica
unless there is a good narrative drive. Teen
Fiction welcome.

Submission Guidelines Accepts initial queries by
email only (including outline and short letter).
Phone calls not welcome in the initial stages.

Tips Kinglake publishes books for a popular/
general readership, or a carefully worked-out
niche market.

Legend Press Ltd

2 London Wall Buildings, London, EC2M 5UU
T 020 7448 5137
E info@legend-paperbooks.co.uk
W www.legendpress.co.uk

Contact Managing Director, Tom Chalmers
(Contemporary Fiction); Publishing Executive,
Emma Howard (General Fiction)

Established 2005

Insider Info Publishes five titles per year.
Receives approximately 500 queries and 300
manuscripts per year. 80 per cent of books
published are from unagented authors. Payment
is via royalty (on wholesale price), with 0.08
(per £) minimum and 0.15 (per £) maximum,
or via royalty (on retail price), with 0.05 (per £)
minimum and 0.09 (per £) maximum. Advance
offered is from £1,000 to £5,000. Average
lead time is six months, with simultaneous
submissions accepted. Submissions will not be
returned. Aims to respond to queries within five
days, proposals within ten days and manuscripts
within six weeks. Catalogue is available with
an SAE, or by email. Manuscript guidelines are
available online or by email.

Publishes Literary and Mainstream/
Contemporary titles.

Submission Guidelines Accepts proposal
package (including outline, three to four sample
chapters and a full synopsis).

Recent Title(s) *Queer Fish In God's Waiting
Room*, Lee Henshaw (Contemporary Fiction)

Tips Submissions are judged on a book-by-book
basis, although they should generally be aimed
at the mainstream, modern reader.

The Lilliput Press Ltd

62–63 Sitric Road, Arbour Hill, Dublin 7,
Republic of Ireland
T 00353 1 671 1647
F 00353 1 671 1233
E info@lilliputpress.ie
W www.lilliputpress.ie

Contact Publisher/Editor in Chief, Antony Farrell

Established 1984

Insider Info Publishes 18 titles per year. Receives
approximately 300 queries and 200 manuscripts
per year. 50 per cent of books published are
from first-time authors and 50 per cent of books
published are from unagented authors. Ten per
cent of books are author subsidy published,
and these are determined by integrity of
subject and source of subvention. Payment is
via royalty on wholesale price, with 0.1 (per £)
minimum and 0.2 (per £) maximum, or royalty
on retail price with 0.05 (per £) minimum and
0.15 (per £) maximum. Advance offered is from
£300–£10,000. Simultaneous submissions are
accepted. Submissions accompanied by SAE
will be returned. Aims to respond to queries
within five days, proposals within eight days,
and manuscripts within ten months. Catalogue
is free on request, and available online. Author
guidelines are not available, although digital
work is preferred.

Publishes Erotica and Literary Fiction titles.

Submission Guidelines Accepts proposal
package (including outline, and two sample
chapters).

Tips Most work published has a broadly
Irish theme.

Little, Brown Book Group

100 Victoria Embankment, London, EC4Y 0DY
T 020 7911 8000
F 020 7911 8100
E info@littlebrown.co.uk
W www.littlebrown.co.uk

Parent Company Hachette UK

Contact CEO and Publisher, Ursula Mackenzie

Established 1988

Imprint(s) Abacus, Atom, Little Brown, Orbit,
Piatkus Books, Sphere, Virago Press

Insider Info Submissions accompanied by SAE
will be returned. Aims to respond to proposals
within eight weeks. Catalogue available online.

Publishes Mainstream/Contemporary and
General Fiction titles in most genres. *Publishes
Literary and Commercial Fiction titles across
various imprints.

Submission Guidelines Accepts query with
SAE/proposal package (including outline, three
sample chapters, covering letter and SAE).

Recent Title(s) *Testimony*, Anita Shreve (Novel)

Tips Formerly known as The Time Warner Book
Group, Little, Brown reverted to its original
name following purchase by Hachette UK. The
company publishes a wide range of paperback
and hardcover fiction across its many imprints.
See individual entries for more details.

Little Books Ltd

48 Catherine Place, London, SW1E 6HL
T 020 7792 7929
E info@littlebooks.net
W www.littlebooks.net

Contact Publishers, Margaret Little and
Max Hamilton Little

Established 2003

Imprint(s) Max Press

Insider Info Catalogue available online.

Publishes Historical and Mainstream/
Contemporary titles.

Recent Title(s) *Endgame*, Denise Roberston

Tips Little Books publishes concise books to
fit in pockets, by well-known writers. Their
philosophy is to bring books to those who are
juggling busy lives, but are still passionate about
reading, who want to be entertained as well
as informed, without needing to devote huge
chunks of time to reading. Each book needs to
be about something important, something that
makes the world a better place. Each is written
by the leading writer in their field.

Loki Books

39 Chalcot Crescent, London, NW1 8YD
T 020 7722 6718
E all@lokibooks.vianw.co.uk
W www.lokibooks.com

Established 1967

Publishes Full-length Fiction and Drama titles
in translation, and Short Story Collections.
*Often publishes work with women's voices
in minority languages.

Recent Title(s) *Blue China*, Bamboo Hirst
(Translation)

Tips One of Loki's main concerns is to promote
women writers, who are dedicated to peace and
the understanding of Arab-Israeli relations.

Luath Press Ltd

543/2 Castlehill, The Royal Mile, Edinburgh,
EH1 2ND
T 0131 225 4326
F 0131 225 4324
E gavin.macdougall@luath.co.uk
W www.luath.co.uk

Contact Director, Gavin MacDougall

Established 1981

Insider Info Publishes 30 titles per year.
Receives less than 1,000 queries and less than
1,000 manuscripts per year. 10–50 per cent of
books published are from first-time authors,
more than 90 per cent of books published
are from unagented authors. Payment is via
royalty. Submissions accompanied by SAE will
be returned. Catalogue is free on request and
available online. Manuscript guidelines are
available online.

Publishes Mainstream/Contemporary titles.

Submission Guidelines Accepts queries with
SAE and complete manuscripts (including your
publishing history, clips, author biography and
SAE).

Recent Title(s) *My Epileptic Lurcher*, Des
Dillon (Humour); *The Bower Bird*, Ann
Kelley (Children's)

Tips Most Luath Press books have a
Scottish connection.

Macmillan Publishers Ltd

The Macmillan Building, 4 Crinan Street,
London, N1 9XW
T 020 7833 4000
F 020 7843 4640
E fiction@macmillan.co.uk
W www.macmillan.com

Parent Company Verlagsgruppe Georg von
Holtzbrink GmbH

Contact CEO, Annette Thomas; Deputy
Chairman, Michael Barnard

Established 1843

Imprint(s) Macmillan Education (division);
Palgrave Macmillan (division); Pan Macmillan
Publishers (division); Nature Publishing
(subsidiary)

Publishes General Fiction from British and
international writers.

Submission Guidelines Does not accept
unsolicited or unagented submissions.

Tips The Macmillan Group and its divisions
cover education publishing, including English
language teaching (ELT), academic publishing,
including reference science, technological and
medical publishing, fiction and non-fiction
book publishing, and publishing services
including distribution and production. For more
information, see the individual division entries.
Authors should see the Macmillan New Writing
imprint, under Pan Macmillan, for information
about submitting manuscripts.

Macmillan New Writing

T 020 7014 6000
F 020 7014 6001
E Online form
W www.macmillannewwriting.com

Parent Company Pan Macmillan Publishers

Established 2006

Insider Info All books published are from first-
time authors. No advances paid; instead an
open-ended royalty deal at a relatively high
rate is offered.

Publishes General Fiction titles (all genres
considered).

Submission Guidelines All submissions must come through the website.

Recent Title(s) *The Hoard of Mhorrer*, MFW Curran (Supernatural)

Tips Macmillan New Writing is a fiction list set up specifically to publish first novels from new authors.

The Maia Press

15–16 Nassau Street, London, W1W 7AB
T 020 7436 9898
E info@arcadiabooks.co.uk
W www.maiapress.com

Contact Founders, Maggie Hamand and Jane Havell

Parent Company Arcadia Books

Established 2002

Insider Info Publishes six titles per year. Payment is via royalties. Aims to respond to proposals and manuscripts within six weeks. Catalogue and manuscript guidelines available online.

Publishes Literary and Mainstream/Contemporary titles.

*The Maia Press aims to publish works by writers from diverse backgrounds, including works in translation, giving priority to writers whose work is censored in their country of origin.

Submission Guidelines Maia Press are currently not accepting fiction submissions.

Recent Title(s) *The Resurrection of the Body*, Maggie Hamand (Novel)

Tips The Maia Press is a young publishing house, dedicated to publishing new and established authors. They publish only a small number of books each year.

Mam Tor

PO Box 6785, Derby, DE22 1XT
E info@mamtor.com
W www.mamtor.com

Contact Editor-in-Chief, Liam Sharp; Prose

Submissions Editor, Susan J Boulton; Art Submissions Editors: Liam Sharp, John Bamber and Jason Harris

Established 2004

Insider Info Does not offer an advance or guarantee any payment as a result of sales. Due to being a small company Mam Tor may not be able to respond to failed submissions.

Publishes Science-Fiction, Fantasy, Gothic/Horror and Comic content, in both prose and graphic novel format.

Recent Title(s) *The Enemy's Son*, James Johnson (Science-Fiction/Fantasy)

Tips Mam Tor is a small company created not as a commercial venture, but as a forum for subcultural, underground, science-fiction, horror or fantasy writers and artists. There are no fees for the work produced, nor are there the usual editorial restrictions.

Mandrake of Oxford

PO Box 250, Oxford, OX1 1AP
T 01865 243671
E mandrake@mandrake.uk.net
W www.mandrake.uk.net

Contact Directors, Mogg Morgan and Kym Morgan

Established 1986

Insider Info Catalogue and manuscript guidelines are available online.

Publishes Crime, Occult and Spiritual Fiction titles.

Submission Guidelines Accepts query with SAE. Submit proposal package (including outline, one sample chapter and SAE).

Recent Title(s) *Gateway to Hell*, Margaret Bingley (Occult)

Tips Mandrake of Oxford is a specialist independent press that is always happy to look at ideas for new books. The publishers urge that before potential authors submit their work they look at the catalogue, and a book in a similar category, to gauge whether a proposal fits their list.

Mango Publishing

✉ PO Box 13378, London, SE27 0ZN
☎ T 020 8480 7771
F 020 8480 7771
✎ E info@mangoprint.com
W www.mangoprint.com

Established 1995

Insider Info Catalogue available online.

Publishes Mainstream/Contemporary, Translation, Black African/Caribbean and Latin American titles and Short Story Collections.

Recent Title(s) *Havana: Between the Sky and Heaven*, Rusell Piñeiro (Novel)

Tips Mango Publishing is committed to promoting and publishing the work of quality first-time and established writers. They focus on publishing and promoting literary works by writers from African, Caribbean, and Latin American literary traditions. The list includes translations of important works not originally written in English.

Marion Boyars Publishers Ltd

✉ 24 Lacy Road, London, SW15 1NL
☎ T 020 8788 9522
F 020 8789 8122
✎ E catheryn@marionboyars.com
W www.marionboyars.co.uk

Contact Director, Catheryn Kilgarriff; Editor, Rebecca Gillieron (Fiction)

Established 1960s

Insider Info Catalogue and manuscript guidelines available online.

Publishes Literary, Mainstream/Contemporary, Translation, Black Writing and Women's titles.

Submission Guidelines Accepts agented submissions only. Would prefer a synopsis and sample chapter in the first instance.

Recent Title(s) *Stolen Time*, Vangelis Hatziyannidis (Translation/Novel)

Tips Fiction submissions must be sent through an agent. Does not accept submissions by email.

Methuen Publishing Ltd

✉ 8 Artillery Road, London, SW1P 1RZ
☎ T 020 7798 1600
F 020 7828 1244
✎ E sales@methuen.co.uk
W www.methuen.co.uk

Contact Managing Director, Peter Tummons

Established 1889

Imprint(s) Politico's Publishing

Insider Info Publishes 60 titles per year. Receives approximately 200 queries and 100 manuscripts per year. Ten per cent of books published are from first-time authors, five per cent are from unagented authors and ten per cent are author subsidy published. Catalogue is available online.

Publishes Literary, Drama and Stage Play titles and Short Story Collections.

Submission Guidelines Accepts query with SAE with proposal package (including synopsis). Prefers agented submissions.

Recent Title(s) *One Hundred Days: One Hundred Nights*, Christopher Bigsby

Tips Does not encourage unagented submissions. Do not send any material via email.

Michael Joseph

✉ 80 Strand, London, WC2R 0RL
☎ T 020 7010 3000
F 020 7010 6060
✎ E customer.service@penguin.co.uk
W www.penguin.co.uk

Parent Company Penguin General

Contact Managing Director, Louise Moore; Editorial Director, Harriet Evans

Insider Info Catalogue is available online or by email.

Publishes Crime, Humour, Mainstream/Contemporary, Romance, Suspense, Thriller and Women's Interest titles.

Submission Guidelines Accepts agented submissions only.

Recent Title(s) *Bleeding Heart Square*, Andrew Taylor (Crime)

Tips Michael Joseph publishes market-focused popular fiction and non-fiction, and is primarily focused on top-ten bestsellers from authors such as Tom Clancy and Clive Cussler.

Morning Star

19 Off Quay Building, Foundry Lane, Byker, Newcastle upon Tyne, NE6 1AF
T 0191 265 6699
E alecfinlay@yahoo.com
W www.alecfinlay.com

Contact Alec Finlay

Established 1990

Insider Info Catalogue available online.

Publishes Regional titles.

Tips Often co-publishes innovative projects that have included pocketbooks, folios and a small press series, combining local accounts with art in unusual ways.

Myriad Editions

59 Lansdowne Place, Brighton, BN3 1FL
T 01273 720000
F 01273 720000
E info@myriadeditions.com
W www.myriadeditions.com

Contact Rights Manager, Sadie Mayne

Established 1993

Insider Info Catalogue available online.

Publishes Literary Fiction and Graphic titles.

Recent Title(s) *The Cloths of Heaven*, Sue Eckstein (Fiction)

Tips Myriad Editions is committed to making global issues accessible for general readers, students and professionals alike. They aim to combine clear analysis with creative graphics in order to illustrate human development and social concerns. Myriad has expanded its publishing programme to include edgy literary fiction, innovative non-fiction and documentary comic books.

New Beacon Books Ltd

76 Stroud Green Road, Finsbury Park, London, N4 3EN
T 020 7272 4889
F 020 7281 4662
E newbeaconbooks@btconnect.com
W www.newbeaconbooks.co.uk

Contact Editor-in-Chief, John La Rose; Managing Director, Sarah White

Established 1966

Insider Info Payment is via royalties.

Publishes Black Literature titles.

Submission Guidelines No unsolicited material.

Tips New Beacon Books specializes in books that highlight black life in Britain and their links in Europe, the Caribbean, Africa and African America.

New Island

2 Brookside, Dundrum Road, Dublin 14, Republic of Ireland
T 00353 1 2989937
F 00353 1 2982783
E Online form
W www.newisland.ie

Contact Publisher, Edwin Higel; Editorial Manager, Deidre O'Neill

Insider Info Catalogue free on request online.

Publishes Mainstream/Contemporary titles.

Tips New Island also publishes the Open Doors series of fiction novellas aimed at adults with literacy problems. Open Doors authors are advised to avoid sentences with multiple clauses, to keep vocabulary simple, using common and straightforward words, but to allow the occasional challenging word (where useful).

No Exit Press

PO Box 394, Harpenden, AL5 1XJ
T 01582 766348
F 01582 766348

E Online form
W www.noexit.co.uk

Parent Company Oldcastle Books

Contact Managing Director, Ion Mills

Publishes Crime titles.

Submission Guidelines No unsolicited material. May not return unsolicited manuscripts.

Recent Title(s) *The Spare Change*, Robert B Parker (Crime)

Oldcastle Books

PO Box 394, Harpenden, AL5 1XJ
T 01582 766348
F 01582 766348
E Online form
W www.oldcastlebooks.co.uk

Imprint(s) No Exit Press, Pocket Essentials, High Stakes Publishing

Publishes Suspense and Crime titles.

Recent Title(s) *Luca Antara*, Martin Edmond

Tips See separate imprint entries for more information.

Onlywomen Press

40d St Lawrence Terrace, London, W10 5ST
T 020 8354 0796
E Online form
W www.onlywomenpress.com

Contact Lilian Mohin

Established 1974

Insider Info Publishes roughly four titles per year. 98 per cent of books published are from first-time authors, 100 per cent of books published are from unagented authors. Payment is via royalty (on retail price). Average lead time is one year, with simultaneous submissions not accepted. Submissions accompanied by SAE will be returned. Aims to respond to queries within one month and proposals and manuscripts within three months. Catalogue is free on request. Manuscript guidelines are available with SAE, or available online or by email.

Publishes Adventure, Children's, Fantasy, Feminist, Lesbian, Literary, Multicultural, Mystery, Science-Fiction and Young Adult titles.

Submission Guidelines Accepts proposals package (including outline, first 60 pages, your publishing history, author biography and SAE).

Tips Onlywomen Press publishes feminist fiction and non-fiction from female authors only. They will accept postal submissions only and tend to give priority to lesbian authors.

Orbit

100 Victoria Embankment, London, EC4Y 0DY
T 020 7911 8000
F 020 7911 8100
E orbit@littlebrown.co.uk
W www.orbitbooks.net

Parent Company Little, Brown Book Group

Contact Publishing Director, Tim Holman

Insider Info Submissions accompanied by SAE will be returned. Aims to respond to proposals within 12 weeks. Catalogue available online.

Publishes Fantasy and Science-Fiction titles. *Full-length novels only.

Submission Guidelines Accepts outline of up to 30 pages of double-spaced text.

Recent Title(s) *The Riven Kingdom*, Karen Miller (Fantasy); *Orphan's Journey*, Robert Buettner (Science-Fiction)

Tips Orbit is the UK's leading science-fiction and fantasy imprint, with a market share twice that of any other publisher. Orbit does not accept emailed submissions and prefers submissions from agented writers, although they will occasionally accept unsolicited material.

Original Plus

17 High Street, Maryport, Cumbria, CA15 6BQ
T 01900 812194
E smithsssj@aol.com
W www.freewebs.com/thesamsmith

Contact Publisher/Editor, Sam Smith

Established 1995

Insider Info Publishes two titles per year. Receives approximately 100 queries and 12 manuscripts per year. 50 per cent of books published are from first-time authors, 100 per cent of books published are from unagented authors. Payment is via an agreed percentage of books for resale. Average lead time is one year, with simultaneous submissions not accepted. Submissions accompanied by SAE will be returned. Aims to respond to queries within two days and proposals and manuscripts within four weeks. Manuscript guidelines available with SAE, and available online or by email.

Publishes Literary Fiction titles.

Recent Title(s) *Days of Fire and Flood*, Chrissy Banks

Orion Publishing Group Ltd

Orion House, 5 Upper St Martin's Lane, London, WC2H 9EA
T 020 7240 3444
F 020 7240 4822
W www.orionbooks.co.uk

Parent Company Hachette UK

Contact Chairman, Armand Nourry; Chief Executive, Peter Roche

Established 1992

Imprint(s) Everyman Classics, Orion, Gollancz, Weidenfeld & Nicholson

Insider Info Catalogue available online via downloadable pdf, online catalogue request form, or via email on request.

Publishes Fantasy, Humour, Children's, Literary, Mainstream/Contemporary, Science-Fiction, Crime, Thriller and Classics titles.

Submission Guidelines Accepts agented submissions only.

Orion

Orion House, 5 Upper St Martin's Lane, London, WC2H 9EA
T 020 7240 3444
F 020 7240 4822
W www.orionbooks.co.uk

Parent Company Orion Publishing Group Ltd

Contact Managing Director, Lisa Milton; Managing Director (Orion Paperback Division), Susan Lamb

Established 1992

Imprint(s) Orion Children's Books, Orion Paperback (division)

Insider Info Catalogue available online, download a pdf or use online request form. Also available via email on request.

Publishes Crime and Thriller titles.

Submission Guidelines Accepts agented submissions only.

Recent Title(s) *Dexter by Design*, Jeff Lindsay (Crime/Thriller)

Orion Paperbacks

Orion House, 5 Upper St Martin's Lane, London, WC2H 9EA
T 020 7240 3444
F 020 7240 4822
W www.orionbooks.co.uk

Parent Company Orion

Established 1993

Imprint(s) Phoenix, Everyman Classics

Insider Info Catalogue available online.

Publishes A variety of Fiction titles.

Submission Guidelines Accepts agented submissions only.

Tips All books are published in paperback. Everyman Classics' list is made up entirely of reprints.

Palladour Books

23 Eldon Street, Southsea, Hampshire, PO5 4BS
T 023 9282 6935
F 023 9282 6395
E jeremy.powell@ntlworld.com

Contact Managing Editors, Anne Powell and Jeremy Powell

Established 1986

Publishes Military/War, World War(s) titles.

Tips Palladour Books specializes in secondhand and out-of-print books on the literature and poetry of the First World War. They produce catalogues twice a year in May and November. Unsolicited manuscripts or proposals are not accepted.

Pan

20 New Wharf Road, London, N1 9RR
T 020 7014 6000
F 020 7014 6001
E fiction@macmillan.co.uk
W www.panmacmillan.com

Parent Company Pan Macmillan Publishers

Established 1944

Insider Info Catalogue is available online.

Publishes Mainstream/Contemporary and Popular Fiction titles.

Submission Guidelines Accepts agented submissions only.

Recent Title(s) *Life on the Refrigerator Door*, Alice Kuipers (Contemporary Fiction)

Tips Publishes work by new writers, but will not accept unsolicited manuscripts.

Pan Macmillan Publishers

20 New Wharf Road, London, N1 9RR
T 020 7014 6000
F 020 7014 6001
E fiction@macmillan.co.uk
W www.panmacmillan.com

Parent Company Macmillan Publishers Ltd

Contact Managing Director, Anthony Forbes Watson

Established 1843

Imprint(s) Boxtree, Campbell Books, Kingfisher Publications Plc, Macmillan Children's Books, Macmillan New Writing, Pan, Picador, Sidgwick & Jackson, Think Books, Tor, Young Picador

Insider Info Catalogue available online via downloadable pdf.

Publishes Fantasy, Historical, Humour, Mainstream/Contemporary, Mystery, Romance, Science-Fiction, Suspense, Sagas, Thrillers, Anthologies, Children's, Young Adult and General Fiction titles.

Submission Guidelines Accepts agented submissions only.

Recent Title(s) *The Cradle Snatcher*, Tess Stimson (Thriller); *The Princess Diaries: Ten Out of Ten*, Meg Cabot (Young Adult)

Tips Although Pan Macmillan does not accept unsolicited/unagented manuscripts there is still a good deal of information for aspiring authors on the website. See the separate entry for the Macmillan New Writing imprint, which does accept unsolicited manuscripts, or go to: www.macmillannewwriting.com.

PaperBooks Publishing

2 London Wall Buildings, London, EC2M 5UU
T 01799 544657
F 01799 541747
E info@legend-paperbooks.co.uk
W www.legendpress.co.uk

Parent Company Legend Books

Contact Keirston Clark

Established 2006

Insider Info Publishes roughly three titles per year. Catalogue available online. Manuscript guidelines available online.

Publishes Mainstream/Contemporary titles.

Submission Guidelines Accepts query with SAE/proposal package (including three sample chapters, one-page synopsis and a marketing brief detailing who the target reader is, a list of any authors similar in style, and any previous publishing history that may be relevant). Alternatively, email submissions to: submissions@legend-paperbooks.co.uk. Will attempt to respond within 16 weeks from the date the submission is received but due to extremely high levels of submissions this is often not realistic.

Recent Title(s) *Friday at the Nobody Inn*, Mark Hayhurst (Novel)

Tips PaperBooks is a small independent press, dedicated to promoting and enlivening the independent book publishing world.

Paradise Press

Unit 2, 9 Golden Square, London, W1F 9HZ
T 020 7734 4880
E enquiries@paradisepress.org.uk
W www.paradisepress.org.uk

Parent Company Gay Authors Workshop

Established 1995

Insider Info Catalogue available online. Manuscript guidelines available online via website.

Publishes Gay/Lesbian Fiction titles and Short Story Collections.

Submission Guidelines Submissions form Gay Authors Workshop only. For membership details email eandk2@btinternet.com or write to GAW, BM 5700, London, WC1N 3XX

Recent Title(s) Rid England of This Plague, Rex Batten (Novel)

Tips Paradise Press is the publishing arm of Gay Authors Workshop, a collective of lesbian and gay writers. Work is only published by members of this group after a process of collective discussion and review. To submit work, first read the guidelines on the website.

Parthian

The Old Surgery, Napier Street, Aberteifi, Cardigan, SA43 1ED
T 01239 612059
F 01239 612059
E info@parthianbooks.co.uk
W www.parthianbooks.co.uk

Contact Publishing Director, Richard Davies (Fiction)

Established 1993

Insider Info Payment by royalties. Aims to respond to proposals and manuscripts within 12 weeks. Catalogue available online. Manuscript guidelines available online via the website.

Publishes Literary, Mainstream/Contemporary, Translation and Welsh writing in English titles.

Submission Guidelines Accepts query with SAE and proposal package (including outline and sample chapter(s)).

Recent Title(s) Just Another Mzungu Passing Through, Jim Bowen

Tips Publishes a range of new writing and is always available to read new material in the relevant subject areas.

Peepal Tree Press

17 King's Avenue, Leeds, LS6 1QS
T 0113 2451703
E contact@peepaltreepress.com
W www.peepaltreepress.com

Contact Founder and Managing Editor, Jeremy Poynting; Editor, Kwame Dawes

Established 1985

Insider Info Publishes roughly 15 titles per year.

Publishes Multicultural titles on the following subjects: Caribbean, Black British and South Asian Writing.

Recent Title(s) The Hangman's Game, Karen King Aribisala (Novel)

Tips Peepal Tree Press publishes challenging and inspiring literature from the Caribbean and Black Britain. Its books aim to express the popular resources of transplanted and transforming cultures.

Pegasus

Sheraton House, Castle Park, Cambridge, CB3 0AX
T 01223 370012
F 01223 370040
E Online form
W www.pegasuspublishers.com

Parent Company Pegasus Elliot MacKenzie Publishers Ltd

Insider Info Catalogue available online. Manuscript guidelines available online via website.

Publishes Literary and Mainstream/ Contemporary titles.

Submission Guidelines Accepts query with SAE.

Tips Pegasus publishes fiction, non-fiction and educational books from writers, agents and educationalists. They very rarely accept submissions from unknown or unpublished writers, but will sometimes offer an advance for accepted work.

Penguin Group (UK)

✉ 80 Strand, London, WC2R 0RL
☎ T 020 7010 3000
   F 020 7010 6060
✐ E customer.service@penguin.co.uk
   W www.penguin.co.uk

Parent Company Pearson Plc

Contact Group Chairman & Chief Executive, John Makinson; Managing Director, Helen Fraser

Established 1936

Imprint(s) BBC Children's Books, Penguin General (division), Penguin Press (division), Penguin Ireland, Penguin Audiobooks, ePenguin, Dorling Kindersley, Puffin, Ladybird Books, Rough Guides, Warne

Insider Info Publishes approximately 4,000 titles per year. Catalogue is available online.

Publishes Children's, Young Adult, Crime and Thriller, Classics, General Fiction and Popular Fiction titles.

Submission Guidelines Accepts agented submissions only.

Tips Although the Penguin Group does not accept unagented submissions, it does have some good information for authors on its website, including advice for aspiring adult fiction and children's fiction authors. For all other imprints, see individual entries.

Penguin General

✉ 80 Strand, London, WC2R 0RL
☎ T 020 7010 3000
   F 020 7010 6060

✐ E customer.service@penguin.co.uk
   W www.penguin.co.uk

Parent Company Penguin Group (UK)

Contact Managing Director, Tom Weldon

Imprint(s) Penguin Paperbacks, Fig Tree, Hamish Hamilton, Michael Joseph, Viking

Insider Info Catalogue is available online.

Publishes Crime, Experimental, Humour, Literary, Mainstream/Contemporary, Romance, Thriller and Women's Interest titles.

Submission Guidelines Accepts agented submissions only.

Penguin Ireland

✉ 25 St Stephen's Green, Dublin 2, Republic of Ireland
☎ T 00353 1 661 7695
   F 00353 1 661 7696
✐ E info@penguin.ie
   W www.penguin.ie

Parent Company Penguin Group (UK)

Contact Editorial Officer, Patricia McVeigh

Established 2002

Insider Info Aims to respond to proposals within three months. Catalogue is available online.

Publishes Literary and Mainstream/ Contemporary titles.

Submission Guidelines Accepts proposal package (including outline, 20–40 sample pages and SAE).

Recent Title(s) *Mr S and the Secrets of Andorra's Box*, Ross O'Carroll Kelly (Humour)

Tips Penguin Ireland welcomes unsolicited manuscripts and proposals. They're looking for passion and excellence from their authors, with books that are 'pitched towards that vast middle ground between popular literature and high literature,' and that get under the skin of contemporary Ireland. Accepts typewritten manuscripts only. Does not accept proposals or manuscripts by email.

Penguin Paperbacks

80 Strand, London, WC2R 0RL
T 020 7010 3000
F 020 7010 6060
E customer.service@penguin.co.uk
W www.penguin.co.uk

Parent Company Penguin General

Contact Publishing Director, Venetia Butterfield

Established 1935

Insider Info Catalogue is available online.

Publishes Literary and Mainstream/Contemporary titles.

Submission Guidelines Accepts agented submissions only.

Recent Title(s) *A New Earth*, Eckhart Tolle

Tips Penguin Paperbacks range from Booker Prize-winning contemporary authors, to mass-market bestsellers.

Peter Owen Publishers

20 Holland Park Avenue, London, W11 3QU
T 020 7373 5628
F 020 7221 0931
E admin@peterowen.com
W www.peterowen.com

Contact Editorial Director, Antonia Owen (Non-Fiction and Literary Fiction)

Established 1951

Insider Info Publishes roughly 25 titles per year. Receives thousands of queries and several hundred manuscripts per year. 20 per cent of books published are from first-time authors, 50 per cent of books published are from unagented authors. Payment via royalty (on retail price). Average lead time is one year, with simultaneous submissions accepted. Submissions accompanied with SAE will be returned. Aims to respond to queries within four weeks, proposals within six weeks and manuscripts within eight weeks. Catalogue is free on request and available online. Manuscript guidelines are available online or by email.

Publishes Literary Fiction and Translation titles.
*Peter Owen publishes only four or five Fiction titles per year and hardly ever publishes first novels.

Submission Guidelines Accepts queries with SAE or proposal package (including outline and one to three sample chapters) ideally by email. Submission details to: admin@peterowen.com

Recent Title(s) *Loving Mephistopheles*, Miranda Miller (Literary Fantasy)

Tips Peter Own specializes in international literary fiction. They very rarely publish memoirs or fiction from previously unpublished authors, and prefer submissions through a literary agent.

Phoenix

Orion House, 5 Upper St Martin's Lane, London, WC2H 9EA
T 020 7240 3444
F 020 7240 4822
W www.orionbooks.co.uk

Parent Company Orion Paperbacks (Orion Publishing Group Ltd)

Insider Info Catalogue available online.

Publishes Mainstream/Contemporary titles.
*Publishes in paperback only.

Submission Guidelines Accepts agented submissions only.

Recent Title(s) *Broken Bodies*, June Hampson (Crime/Thriller)

Tips Does not accept any unsolicited submissions.

Piatkus Books

Little, Brown Book Group, 100 Victoria Embankment, London, EC4Y 0DY
T 020 7911 8000
E info@littlebrown.co.uk
W www.piatkus.co.uk

Parent Company Little, Brown Book Group

Contact Publishing Director, Antonia Hodgson

Established 1979

Imprint(s) Piatkus, Portrait

Insider Info Publishes 150 titles per year. Payment is via royalties. Aims to respond to proposals and manuscripts within 12 weeks. Catalogue and manuscript guidelines available online.

Publishes Mainstream/Contemporary titles.

Submission Guidelines Does not accept unsolicited proposals.

Recent Title(s) *Deadly Desire*, Keri Arthur

Picador

20 New Wharf Road, London, N1 9RR
T 020 7014 6000
F 020 7014 6001
W www.picador.com

Parent Company Pan Macmillan Publishers

Contact Publisher, Paul Baggaley; Editorial Director, Kate Harvey

Established 1972

Insider Info Catalogue available online as a downloadable pdf.

Publishes General Fiction, Mainstream/Contemporary and Literary titles.

Submission Guidelines Accepts agented submissions only.

Recent Title(s) *A Beautiful Place to Die*, Malla Nunn (Crime)

Tips Picador has a particular reputation for ground-breaking non-fiction, reportage, literary biography and memoir, as well as poetry. Does not accept unsolicited manuscripts.

Pigasus Press

13 Hazely Combe, Arreton, Isle of Wight, PO30 3AJ
T 01983 865668
E mail@pigasuspress.co.uk
W www.pigasuspress.co.uk

Contact Editor (Science-Fiction, Fantasy, Horror), Tony Lee

Established 1989

Insider Info Publishes roughly two titles per year. Simultaneous submissions are not accepted. Submissions accompanied by SAE will be returned. Aims to respond to queries within seven days, proposals within ten days, and manuscripts and all other enquiries within six months. Catalogue and manuscript guidelines are available with SAE, or online.

Publishes Experimental, Fantasy, Horror, Literary (Genre), Mystery and Science-Fiction titles.

Submission Guidelines Accepts queries with SAE, or complete manuscripts.

Tips Pigasus Press is a genre publisher that specializes in speculative fiction of all kinds. They also publish Premonitions magazine which offers further publishing possibilities. Pigasus Press will not accept sword and sorcery fantasy submissions, or explicitly gory horror submissions.

Pipers' Ash Ltd

Church Road, Christian Malford, Chippenham, Wiltshire, SN15 4BW
T 01249 720563
E pipersash@supamasu.com
W www.supamasu.com

Contact The Manuscript Evaluation Desk (all subjects)

Established 1976

Insider Info Publishes roughly 15 titles per year. Receives 1,200 queries and 800 manuscripts per year. 90 per cent of books published are from first-time authors and 100 per cent are from unagented authors. Payment is via royalty (on retail price) of 0.1 (per £). No advance is offered. Average lead time is six months, with simultaneous submissions not accepted. Submissions accompanied by SAE will be returned. Aims to respond to queries within seven days, proposals within five weeks, and manuscripts within two months. Catalogue and manuscript guidelines available online.

Planet

PO Box 44, Aberystwyth, Ceredigion, SY23 3ZZ
T 01970 611255

E planet.enquiries@planetmagazine.org.uk
W www.planetmagazine.org.uk

Contact Managing Editor, John Barnie

Established 1970

Insider Info Payment is via royalties. Catalogue and manuscript guidelines (for the magazine only) are available online.

Publishes Mainstream/Contemporary, Translation, Welsh Fiction and World Writing titles.

Recent Title(s) *O For A Gun*, Nigel Jenkins (Haiku)

Tips Planet mainly focuses on the arts and current affairs magazine *Planet: The Welsh Internationalist*. It expanded into book publishing in 1995, mostly of Welsh poetry and fiction, and also some translated fiction from around the world.

Pocket Books

1st Floor, 222 Gray's Inn Road, London, WC1X 8HB
T 020 7316 1900
F 020 7316 0332
E enquiries@simonandschuster.co.uk
W www.simonandschuster.co.uk

Parent Company Simon & Schuster UK Ltd

Insider Info Catalogue available online.

Publishes Fantasy, Science-Fiction, Suspense, General Mass-Market Fiction and Television Tie-In titles.

Submission Guidelines Accepts agented submissions only.

Recent Title(s) *Beautiful Boy*, David Sheff (Novel)

Tips Pocket Books is Simon & Schuster's mass-market fiction and non-fiction imprint. All books are published in paperback.

Politico's Publishing

215 Vauxhall Bridge Road, London, SW1V 1EJ
T 020 7798 1600
F 020 7828 2098

E methuenpubltd@btinternet.com
W www.politicospublishing.co.uk

Parent Company Methuen Publishing Limited

Contact Chairman/Managing Director, Peter Tummons; Publishing Director, Alan Gordon-Walker

Established 1998 (acquired by Methuen in 2003)

Insider Info Catalogue available online.

Publishes Political Fiction titles.

Submission Guidelines Accepts query with SAE/proposal package (including synopsis). Prefers agented submissions.

Tips Specialists in political publishing, particularly to do with Britain, Europe, USA and the Middle East. Unagented submissions are not encouraged. No submissions by email.

Pomegranate Press

Dolphin House, 51 St Nicholas Lane, Lewes, Sussex, BN7 2JZ
T 01273 470100
F 01273 470100
E pomegranatepress@aol.com
W www.pomegranate-press.co.uk

Contact Dave Arscott (Self-Publishing; Sussex Themes)

Established 1992

Insider Info Publishes several titles per year, about half by first-time authors. Average lead time is three months. Aims to respond to queries and manuscripts within ten days. Catalogue available on the website.

Publishes Fiction for self-publishing authors.

Submission Guidelines Accepts query with SAE or via email.

Recent Title(s) *Sandies in the Beach Huts*, Cathy Watts (author) and Emma Ball (illustrator) (Children's Fiction)

Tips Pomegranate are a self-publishing company, with author/publisher David Arscott offering a one-to-one service.

Poolbeg Press

123 Grange Hill, Baldoyle, Dublin 13,
Republic of Ireland
T 00353 1 832 1477
F 00353 1 832 1430
E info@poolbeg.com
W www.poolbeg.com

Contact Publishing Director, Paula Campbell;
Managing Director, Kieran Devlin

Established 1976

Insider Info Catalogue available online.

Publishes Children's, Literary, Mainstream/
Contemporary, Romance, Young Adult and Irish
Interest titles.

Recent Title(s) *Nobody's Child*, Cora Coleman
(Memoir)

Tips Poolbeg is Ireland's premier popular fiction
publishing company and mainly publishes new
Irish writers.

Portobello Books Ltd

12 Addison Avenue, London, W11 4QR
T 020 7605 1380
F 020 7605 1361
E mail@portobellobooks.com
W www.portobellobooks.com

Established 2005

Insider Info Publishes 20 titles per year.
Catalogue is free on request.

Publishes Literary Fiction and Fiction in
Translation titles.

Submission Guidelines Accepts emailed queries.

Tips As an independent publisher, Portobello
is able to take more risks with unusual or
new work than is common in contemporary
publishing. Portobello does not consider
unsolicited manuscripts and will only accept
queries by email.

PS Avalon

PS Avalon, Box 1865, Glastonbury, Somerset,
BA6 8YR
T 01458 833864

E will@willparfitt.com
W www.psavalon.com

Contact Director, Will Parfitt

Established 2003

Insider Info Publishes roughly four titles per year.
Receives approximately 50 queries per year. 50
per cent of books published are from first-time
authors, 90 per cent of books published are
from unagented authors. Payment is via royalty
(on retail price), with 0.1 (per £) minimum
and 0.25 (per £) maximum. Average lead time
is six months, with simultaneous submissions
accepted. Submissions accompanied by SAE will
be returned. Aims to respond to queries and
proposals within seven days and manuscripts
within 28 days. Catalogue is free on request
and available online. Manuscript guidelines are
available online.

Publishes Occult, Religious and Spiritual titles.

Submission Guidelines Accepts query with SAE,
or by email.

Tips PS Avalon publishes for a general
readership.

Quartet Books

27 Goodge Street, London, W1T 2LD
T 020 7636 3992
F 020 7637 1866
E info@quartetbooks.co.uk
W www.quartetbooks.co.uk

Contact Managing Director, Jeremy Beale;
Publishing Director, Stella Kane

Established 1972

Insider Info Authors paid by royalty.

Publishes Literary, Mainstream/Contemporary
and Translation titles.

Submission Guidelines Accepts query with SAE
including a one-page synopsis, one-page author
biography and information on any previously
published work and the first three chapters, or
30 pages of manuscript. Submissions via email
or on disk are not considered.

Tips No genre fiction is accepted.

Quercus Publishing Plc

21 Bloomsbury Square, London, WC1A 2NS
T 020 7291 7200
E mail@quercusbooks.co.uk
W www.quercusbooks.co.uk

Contact CEO/Managing Director, Mark Smith;
Publishing Director, Wayne Davies; Consulting
Editor, Otto Penzler (Crime Fiction)

Established 2004

Imprint(s) Quercus Editions (contract
publishing), Quercus Books Limited (trade
publishing)

Insider Info Catalogue available online.

Publishes Crime and Women's Fiction titles.

Submission Guidelines Quercus do not accept
unsolicited manuscripts.

Recent Title(s) *The Girl with the Dragon Tattoo*,
Stieg Larsson

Tips Quercus has both trade and contract
publishing arms and is still largely driven by
contract publishing, especially in the non-fiction
areas. Their policy is to re-publish successful
contract titles in trade editions, and establish
a fiction list building on this trade presence.

The Random House Group Ltd

Random House, 20 Vauxhall Bridge Road,
London, SW1V 2SA
T 020 7840 8400
F 020 7840 8778
E emarketing@randomhouse.co.uk
W www.randomhouse.co.uk

Parent Company Random House Inc US
(Bertelsmann AG)

Contact Chief Executive, Gail Rebuck

Imprint(s) Arrow, BBC Books, Century, Chatto
& Windus, Ebury Press, Everyman, Fodor, Harvill
Secker, Hutchinson, Jonathan Cape, Mainstream,
Pimlico, Rider, Time Out Guides Ltd, Vermilion,
Vintage, William Heinemann, Yellow Jersey,
Random House Business Books, Random
House Children's Books (division), Transworld
Publishers (division)

Insider Info Catalogue is available online (to
search the catalogues of individual imprints
go to 'advanced search').

Publishes Mainstream/Contemporary, Literary
and Classic Fiction titles across its imprints.

Submission Guidelines Accepts agented
submissions only.

Recent Title(s) *Heliopolis*, James Scudamore
(Contemporary Fiction)

Tips Random House is one of the largest
general book publishing companies in the
UK and has some of the world's best-known
authors on its lists. The Random House Group
is an independently managed subsidiary of
Bertelsmann AG. Will not accept unsolicited
submissions, all submissions must come
through a literary agent.

Revenge Ink

1 Roger Close, Rommely, Stockport,
Cheshire, SK6 3DJ
E Online form
W www.revengeink.com

Contact Founders: Amita Mukerjee and
Gopal Mukerjee

Established 2008

Insider Info Aims to respond within six to
eight weeks.

Recent Title(s) *Ugly Duckling*, Amita Mukerjee;
The Armageddon Mandala, Gopal Mukerjee

Tips Prospective authors may submit proposals
by email, using the online forum, or by post.
If submitting by post ensure that you use the
alternative postal address listed on the website.

Reverb

PO Box 615, Oxford, OX1 9AL
E mail@readreverb.com
W www.readreverb.com

Parent Company Osiris Press Ltd

Insider Info Catalogue available online.

Publishes Mainstream/Contemporary and
Literary Fiction titles.

Submission Guidelines Does not accept unsolicited submissions.

Recent Title(s) *Who Needs Cleopatra?*, Steve Redwood

Tips Reverb publishes contemporary literary fiction with an edge and is committed to publishing new writers (and supporting independent bookshops). The Reverb website contains an informative writer's guide for prospective authors.

Robert Hale Ltd

 Clerkenwell House, 45–47 Clerkenwell Green, London, EC1R 0HT
T 020 7251 2661
F 020 7490 4958
E submissions@halebooks.com
W www.halebooks.com

Contact Managing Director, John Hale

Established 1936

Imprint(s) JA Allen, NAG Press

Insider Info Publishes roughly 250 titles per year. Receives approximately 3,000 queries and 1,000 manuscripts per year. 15 per cent of books published are from first-time authors and 15 per cent are from unagented authors. Payment is via royalty (on retail price). Average lead time is 12 months, with simultaneous submissions accepted. Aims to respond to queries within seven days, proposals within ten days, and manuscripts within two weeks. Catalogue is free on request. Manuscript guidelines are not available.

Publishes Adventure, Historical, Literary, Mainstream/Contemporary, Military/War, Mystery, Crime, Regional, Romance, Suspense and Western titles.

Submission Guidelines Accepts query with SAE/proposal package (including outline, and three sample chapters).

Recent Title(s) *The Cat Trap*, KT McCaffrey (Crime)

Tips Robert Hale specializes in general hardcover fiction. See the website for submission guidelines, and details of subjects they are currently looking to receive submissions on.

Sangam Books Ltd

 57 London Fruit Exchange, Brushfield Street, London, E1 6EP
T 020 7377 6399
F 020 7375 1230
E sangambks@aol.com

Contact Executive Director, Anthony de Souza

Publishes Literary and Mainstream/Contemporary titles.

Tips Sangam Books specializes in school and college textbooks and other educational publishing. They also publish fiction and non-fiction titles on technology, science, medicine, India, social sciences, art and religion.

Saqi Books

 26 Westbourne Grove, London, W2 5RH
T 020 7221 9347
F 020 7229 7492
E enquiries@saqibooks.com
W www.saqibooks.com

Contact Publisher, Andre Gaspard; Editorial Manager, Lara Frankena

Established 1981

Insider Info Publishes 20 titles per year. Payment is via royalties. Aims to respond to manuscripts within ten weeks. Catalogue available online and free on request. Manuscript guidelines available online and via the website.

Publishes Literary and Mainstream/Contemporary titles.

Submission Guidelines Accepts query with SAE/proposal package (including outline and two sample chapters).

Tips Saqi books does not accept submissions by fax, email or on disk. Never send the original photographs or manuscript.

Scottish Cultural Press & Scottish Children's Press

Unit 6, Newbattle Abbey Business Park, Newbattle Road, Dalkeith, EH22 3LJ
T 0131 660 6366
F 0131 660 4666

E info@scottishbooks.com
W www.scottishbooks.com

Contact Directors, Avril Gray and Brian Pugh

Established 1992

Insider Info Payment is via royalties. Aims to respond to proposals within six months. Catalogue and manuscript guidelines are available online.

Publishes Literary and Mainstream/Contemporary titles.

Submission Guidelines No unsolicited manuscripts.

Recent Title(s) *Moray the Dolphin's Adventure in Loch Ness*, Marit Brunskill (Picture Book)

Tips Scottish Cultural Press is one of the foremost publishers in Scotland, specializing in quality books with a Scottish interest. Scottish Children's Press publishes quality Scottish interest books for children of all ages, from graded readers to young fiction. Titles are written for, about, and by Scottish children and they aim to encompass Scots, English and Gaelic. As the publishers receive a great quantity of manuscripts, they recommend that prospective authors should phone first to discuss the suitability of the manuscript before sending any work.

Scribner

1st Floor, 222 Gray's Inn Road, London, WC1X 8HB
T 020 7316 1900
F 020 7316 0332
E enquiries@simonandschuster.co.uk
W http://imprints.simonandschuster.biz/scribner

Parent Company Simon & Schuster UK Ltd

Established 1999

Publishes Contemporary and Literary titles.

Submission Guidelines Accepts agented submissions only.

Tips Scribner is designed specifically to be Simon & Schuster's 'literary' imprint, publishing high-quality non-fiction and literary fiction.

Seafarer Books Ltd

102 Redwald Road, Rendlesham, Woodbridge, Suffolk, IP12 2TE
T 01394 420789
F 01394 461314
E info@seafarerbooks.com
W www.seafarerbooks.com

Contact Managing Director, Patricia Eve

Established 1998

Insider Info Publishes four titles per year. Receives approximately 100 queries and 200 manuscripts per year. Ten per cent of books published are from first-time authors and 90 per cent are from unagented authors. Payment is via royalty (on retail price).

Publishes General and Classic Maritime titles.

Recent Title(s) *Walking on Water*, Geoff Holt

Seren

57 Nolton Street, Bridgend, CF31 3AE
T 01656 663018
F 01656 649226
E seren@serenbooks.com
W www.serenbooks.com

Contact Chairman, Cary Archard; Publisher, Mick Felton; Fiction Editor, Penny Thomas

Established 1981

Insider Info Publishes roughly 25 titles per year. Payment is via royalties. Catalogue and manuscript guidelines available online.

Publishes Literary, Mainstream/Contemporary, Translation and Welsh Writing titles. *Seren publishes only around five works of fiction a year.

Submission Guidelines Accepts query with SAE/proposal package (including outline and three sample chapters).

Recent Title(s) *Blue Sky July*, Nia Wyn (Novel)

Tips Seren specializes in English-language writing from Wales. Authors considering submitting manuscripts should be aware that fiction lists are often full at least two years in advance.

Serif

✉ 47 Strahan Road, London, E3 5DA
☎ T 020 8981 3990
F 020 8981 3990
🖱 E info@serifbooks.co.uk
W www.serifbooks.co.uk

Contact Managing Editor, Stephen Hayward

Established 1993

Insider Info Payment is via royalties. Catalogue available online.

Publishes Literary and Mainstream/Contemporary titles. Does not publish new Fiction titles.

Submission Guidelines Accepts query with SAE.

Tips Serif welcomes ideas and proposals for non-fiction publications, but does not accept unsolicited manuscripts.

Serpent's Tail

✉ 3A Exmouth House, Pine Street, London, EC1R 0JH
☎ T 020 7841 6300
🖱 E info@serpentstail.com
W www.serpentstail.com

Parent Company Profile Books Ltd

Established 1987

Insider Info Catalogue available online.

Publishes Translation, Women's Writing, Classics, Debuts, Crime Fiction and Anthology titles.

Submission Guidelines Accepts agented submissions only.

Recent Title(s) *Old Devil Moon*, Christopher Fowler (Horror)

Tips Serpent's Tail is a renowned publisher of international fiction and non-fiction, founded with a commitment to publishing authors 'neglected by the mainstream'.

Severn House Publishers Ltd

✉ 9–15 High Street, Sutton, Surrey, SM1 1DF
☎ T 020 8770 3930
F 020 8770 3850
🖱 E sales@severnhouse.com
W www.severnhouse.com

Contact Chairman, Edwin Buckhalter; Editorial, Amanda Stewart

Established 1974

Insider Info Publishes roughly 150 titles per year. Payment is via royalties. Catalogue and manuscript guidelines available online.

Publishes Historical, Horror, Literary, Mainstream/Contemporary, Military/War, Mystery, Romance, Science-Fiction, Suspense and Crime titles. *Severn House publishes various kinds of genre and general fiction in large and regular print sizes. Most books are hardback and aimed at fiction libraries, however some titles are produced as paperbacks.

Submission Guidelines Accepts agented submissions only. Will not accept unsolicited manuscripts.

Recent Title(s) *Fathers and Sins*, Jo Bannister (Crime)

Tips As publications are aimed at the UK and US fiction library markets, they are unable to add authors to the list who do not have a significant background in this market.

Simon & Schuster UK Ltd

✉ 1st Floor, 222 Gray's Inn Road, London, WC1X 8HB
☎ T 020 7316 1900
F 020 7316 0332
🖱 E enquiries@simonandschuster.co.uk
W www.simonandschuster.co.uk

Contact CEO/Managing Director, Ian Stewart Chapman

Established 1924

Imprint(s) Free Press, Martin Books, Pocket Books, Scribner, Simon & Schuster Children's Books (division)

Insider Info Catalogue available online.

Publishes Fantasy, Historical, Horror, Humour, Children's, Mainstream/Contemporary, Mystery, Romance, Science-Fiction, Spiritual, Sports, Suspense and Translation titles.

Submission Guidelines Accepts agented submissions only.

Recent Title(s) *The Thirteen Treasures*, Michelle Harrison (Young Adult)

Tips Simon & Schuster publishes a broad range of non-fiction and fiction, from popular bestsellers, to heavyweight literary titles. No unsolicited manuscripts are accepted.

Snowbooks Ltd

120 Pentonville Road, London, N1 9JN
T 020 7837 6482
F 020 7837 6348
E info@snowbooks.com
W www.snowbooks.com

Contact Director, Rob Jones, Managing Director, Emma Barnes; Publisher, James Bridle; Publisher (Memoir, Handicrafts), Anna Torborg; Publisher, Gilly Barnard

Established 2003

Insider Info Publishes ten titles per year. Payment is via royalties. Catalogue and manuscript guidelines available online.

Publishes Mainstream/Contemporary, Thrillers and Women's Fiction titles.

Submission Guidelines Accepts proposals package (including outline and sample chapter(s)). Submissions must be emailed to: manuscripts@snowbooks.com. The subject line should read: Snowbooks Submission: [Author Name] [Book Title].

Recent Title(s) *God's End: The Fall*, Michael McBride (Modern Fiction)

Tips Snowbooks are happy to look at excellent works of fiction. They do not specify particular genres as they believe it is the writing that matters, not the category. Prospective authors must email submissions straight away (there is no need to send an initial email to check if the novel is appropriate). Postal submissions will not be accepted.

Souvenir Press Ltd

43 Great Russell Street, London, WC1B 3PD
T 020 7580 9307
F 020 7580 5064
E sp.trade@ukonline.co.uk

Contact Managing Director, Ernest Hecht

Imprint(s) Condor

Insider Info Publishes 50 titles per year. Payment is via royalties. Catalogue available free on request and via email.

Publishes Humour, Literary, Mainstream/Contemporary and Crime titles.

Submission Guidelines Accepts query with SAE/proposal package (including outline and two sample chapters).

Tips Souvenir Press covers a wide range of academic and general non-fiction topics, specializing in spiritual and mystical titles. Fiction lists are limited in comparison to the non-fiction list.

Sphere

100 Victoria Embankment, London, EC4Y 0DY
T 020 7911 8000
F 020 7911 8100
E info@littlebrown.co.uk
W www.littlebrown.co.uk

Parent Company Little, Brown Book Group

Contact Publishing Director, Antonia Hodgson (Commercial); Publishing Director, David Shelley (Digital)

Insider Info Submissions accompanied by SAE will be returned. Aims to respond to proposals within eight weeks. Catalogue available online.

Publishes Humour, Mainstream/Contemporary, Romance and Commercial Fiction titles.

Submission Guidelines Accepts query with SAE/proposal package (including outline, three sample chapters and covering letter). No email submissions are accepted.

Stacey International

128 Kensington Church Street,
London, W8 4BH

T 020 7221 7166
F 020 7792 9288
E info@stacey-international.co.uk
W www.stacey-international.co.uk

Contact Editor, Christopher Ind

Established 1973

Insider Info Catalogue available online.

Publishes Mainstream/Contemporary titles.

Submission Guidelines Accepts proposal
package via post or email (including sample
chapter, covering letter, market research,
intended book specifications and proposed
schedule and SAE).

Tips Titles are orientated towards a niche
readership and must fulfil a specific practical use.

Superscript

The Publishing House, 404 Robin Square,
Newtown, Powys, SY16 1HP

T 01686 610883
E drjbford@yahoo.co.uk
W www.dubsolution.org

Contact Editor-in-Chief, Max Fuller; Dr Bronwen
Martin (Literary Fiction)

Established 2002

Insider Info Publishes roughly four titles per
year. Receives approximately 85 queries and ten
manuscripts per year. Ten per cent of books
published are from first-time authors, 100
per cent are from unagented authors and 20
per cent are author subsidy publishes. These
are decided by a system where each title is
assessed by the Editorial Board who vote on
three ways forward: will not publish, will subsidy
publish, or will publish traditionally. The eight
members base their decision on the proposal
and the comparative state of the company's
and author's finances at the time the contract is
negotiated. Payment is via royalty (on retail price)
with 0.1 (per £) standard. Average lead time is
nine months, with simultaneous submissions
accepted. Submissions accompanied by SAE
will be returned. Aims to respond to queries

within two days, proposals within five days and
manuscripts within 21 days. Catalogue is free
on request. Manuscript guidelines are available
via email.

Publishes Ethnic, Experimental, Historical,
Literary, Mainstream/Contemporary,
Multicultural, Mystery, Science-Fiction,
Suspense, Political, Faction (20th Century), Spy
Fiction titles. *Books should not include racism,
sexism or vengeance as themes. The question
must be asked of all proposals, 'What is the
point of this book?'

Submission Guidelines Accepts query with SAE,
or via email.

Tips Titles are aimed at a readership that is
university education and/or streetwise. Potential
authors should realize that the company aims
to spread excellent ideas, not to make writers
famous or rich.

Tartarus Press

Coverley House, Carlton, Leyburn, North
Yorkshire, DL8 4AY

T 01969 640399
F 01969 640399
E tartarus@pavilion.co.uk
W www.tartaruspress.com

Contact Manager, Raymond Russell;
Editor, Rosalie Parker

Established 1987

Insider Info Publishes 12 titles per year.
Catalogue and manuscript guidelines
available online.

Publishes Reprints of Classic texts and
Fantasy, Gothic, Horror, Mystery, Occult
and Supernatural titles.

*Tartarus titles cross various genres and are
often of an unusual nature, meaning that they
may have been overlooked by mainstream
publishers. All should evoke a sense of wonder
at the supernatural, in well-written prose.

Submission Guidelines Accepts query via email
with a synopsis.

Recent Title(s) *The Triumph of Night*, Edith
Wharton (Reprint)

Tips Authors or editors who wish to submit a typescript should make sure that the subject matter of the book is relevant before emailing a synopsis. The manuscript, or sample of it, may then be requested.

Telegram Books

26 Westbourne Grove, London, W2 5RH
T 020 7229 2911
F 020 7229 7492
E editorial@telegrambooks.com
W www.telegrambooks.com

Contact Publisher, André Gaspard; Director Mai Ghoussoub; Commissioning Editor, Rebecca O'Connor

Established 2005

Insider Info Aims to respond to proposals and manuscripts within ten weeks. Catalogue is free on request and available online or via email to catalogues@telegrambooks.com. Manuscript guidelines are available online.

Publishes Mainstream/Contemporary, Translation, and International Fiction titles.

Submission Guidelines Accepts query with SAE, or via email, with proposal package (including outline and two sample chapters). Aims to respond in three to six months.

Recent Title(s) *Cairo Stories*, Anne-Marie Drosso

Tips Telegram Books publishes new international writing, in the areas of fiction and literary memoir. Telegram does not accept manuscripts via fax, email or on disk.

Timewell Press

10 Porchester Terrace, London, W2 3TL
T 0870 760 5250
F 0870 760 5250
E Online form
W www.timewellpress.com

Contact Andreas Campomar

Insider Info Catalogue available online.

Publishes Literary and Mainstream/Contemporary titles and Short Story Collections.

Recent Title(s) *Happy Hair Days*, Philip Kingsley

Tips Timewell Press specializes in contemporary life writing and cultural writing, either concerning current affairs, or popular celebrities. Queries are welcome using the online form on the website.

Tindal Street Press Ltd

217 The Custard Factory, Gibb Street, Birmingham, B9 4AA
T 0121 773 8157
F 0121 693 5525
E info@tindalstreet.co.uk
W www.tindalstreet.co.uk

Contact Managing Editor, Emma Hargrave; Assistant Editor, Luke Brown; Publishing Director, Alan Mahar

Established 1998

Insider Info Publishes six titles per year. Payment is via royalties. Catalogue and manuscript guidelines available online.

Publishes Mainstream/Contemporary and Regional titles.

Submission Guidelines Accepts query with SAE. Submit proposal package (including outline and three sample chapters). Submission details to: emma@tindalstreet.co.uk

Recent Title(s) *What Was Lost*, Catherine O'Flynn (Novel)

Tips Tindal Street Press publishes contemporary fiction from the English regions – which means the manuscripts that interest them mostly have a centre of gravity outside of London and the South East. They welcome unsolicited manuscripts, but will not consider children's, teenage, science-fiction, fantasy or romance.

Transworld Publishers

61–63 Uxbridge Road, London, W5 5SA
T 020 8579 2652
F 020 8579 5479
E info@transworld-publishers.co.uk
W www.booksattransworld.co.uk

Parent Company The Random House Group Ltd

Contact Publisher, Bill Scott-Kerr

Established 1950

Imprint(s) Bantam Press, Black Swan, Channel 4 Books, Corgi, Doubleday

Insider Info Catalogue available online. Imprints do not have individual websites; for imprint catalogues go to 'search catalogue by imprint'.

Publishes Crime, Fantasy, Historical, Literary, Mainstream/Contemporary, Mystery, Romance, Science-Fiction and Suspense titles.

Submission Guidelines Accepts agented submissions only.

Recent Title(s) *Dragon Harper*, Anne & Todd McCaffrey (Fantasy)

Tips Does not accept unsolicited manuscripts. Hardbacks are published under the Doubleday or Bantam Press imprints. Paperbacks are published by Black Swan, Bantam and Corgi.

Trident Press Ltd

 175 Piccadilly, Mayfair, London, W1J 9TB
T 020 7491 8770
F 020 7491 8664
E Online form
W www.tridentpress.com

Contact Managing Director, Peter Vine

Established 1997

Imprint(s) Trident Media

Insider Info Payment via royalties. Catalogue available online.

Publishes Irish Interest titles.

Tips Trident Press publishes a wide range of languages, including French and Arabic. Trident Media is a sister company based in Ireland that handles all the pre-press work for the main press. Trident Press will not accept unsolicited submissions, but will respond to brief email or phone contact.

Twenty First Century Publishers Ltd

Braunton Barn, Kiln Lane, Isfield, TN22 5UE
T 01892 522802

 E tfcp@btinternet.com
W www.twentyfirstcenturypublishers.com

Contact Chairman, Fred Piechoczek

Established 2002

Insider Info Payment is via royalties. Catalogue and manuscript guidelines available online.

Publishes Literary, Mainstream/Contemporary and Financial Thriller titles.

Submission Guidelines Accepts proposal package (including outline and three sample chapters) by email. Send fictional writing in English, French or German. The outline should be in the body of the email and the manuscript, or sample chapters should be sent as a file attachment.

Recent Title(s) *Celebrate Myself*, James Buckley (Novel)

Tips TFCP concentrates on developing new authors whom they wish to bring to the market, and uses the latest technology, including e-books, to achieve publication in minimum times. The company publishes general fiction, plot-driven original works and knowledgeably written financial thrillers.

UKUnpublished

 11a Spa Road, Hockley, Essex, SS5 4AZ
T 01702 204636
E info@ukunpublished.co.uk
W www.ukunpublished.co.uk

Contact Proprietor, David Buttle

Insider Info UKUnpublished is a publisher looking to offer the benefits of both Traditional and self-publishing – full publishing, printing, and distribution throughout the UK and the US, but paying up to 44 per cent higher royalties. Editing/proofreading services are not available. Will publish all categories of books, from Children's Fiction to Adult/Erotica, and Technical Non-Fiction to Cookery. Aims to respond to queries and manuscripts within six weeks, however this is considered to be an outside timescale. Visit the website to find out more about the service, or email/write to request a brochure. Prefers to deal directly with the author, instead of through an agent.

Publishes all Fiction genres, including Children's and Adult titles.

Submission Guidelines Visit the website to find out full details about the service and the company, and email David Buttle directly to ask any questions you may have.

Tips UKUnpublished is dedicated to giving as many authors as possible an outlet, to 'let the world share your imagination', while providing a quality and personal service. UKUnpublished also offers accounting and tax services provided by qualified accountants, ensuring that you can concentrate on writing. All royalties are paid regularly.

Vanguard Press

Sheraton House, Castle Park, Cambridge, CB3 0AX
T 01223 370012
F 01223 370040
E Online form
W www.pegasuspublishers.com

Parent Company Pegasus Elliot MacKenzie Publishers Ltd

Insider Info Catalogue and manuscript guidelines available online.

Publishes Adventure, Historical, Humour, Mainstream/Contemporary, Romance, Science-Fiction and Crime titles.

Submission Guidelines Accepts proposal package (including outline, two sample chapters).

Tips Vanguard Press encourages submissions from new and untested authors.

Viking

80 Strand, London, WC2R 0RL
T 020 7010 3000
F 020 7010 6060
E customer.service@penguin.co.uk
W www.penguin.co.uk

Parent Company Penguin General

Contact Publisher, Venetia Butterfield; Editorial Director, Joel Rickett

Insider Info Catalogue is available online.

Publishes Experimental, Literary and Mainstream/Contemporary titles.

Submission Guidelines Accepts agented submissions only.

Tips Viking publishes the widest possible range of literary fiction and non-fiction. This varies from the highly literary and sometimes experimental, to more commercial titles.

Vintage

Random House, 20 Vauxhall Bridge Road, London, SW1V 2SA
T 020 7840 8608
F 020 7233 6117
E vintageeditorial@randomhouse.co.uk
W www.vintage-books.co.uk

Parent Company The Random House Group Ltd

Contact Publisher, Rachel Cugnoni

Established 1990

Imprint(s) Vintage Books, Vintage Classics, Vintage Originals

Insider Info Catalogue available online.

Publishes Literary and Mainstream/Contemporary titles and Classics.

Submission Guidelines Accepts agented submissions only.

Recent Title(s) *Revolutionary Road*, Richard Yates (Novel/Film Tie-In)

Tips Vintage publishes entirely in paperback and places itself at the cutting edge of contemporary fiction. Vintage Classics publishes reprints of 'classic books that changed the world'.

Virago Press

100 Victoria Embankment, London, EC4Y 0DY
T 020 7911 8000
F 020 7911 8100
E virago.press@littlebrown.co.uk
W www.virago.co.uk

Parent Company Little, Brown Book Group

Contact Publishing Director, Lennie Goodings

Established 1973

Insider Info Catalogue available online.

Submission Guidelines Agented submissions are preferred.

Recent Title(s) *Apology for the Woman Writing*, Jenny Diski (Novel)

Tips Virago, founded by Carmen Callil, has grown into the largest women's imprint in the world. The Virago VS list publishes the best young female writers with an eclectic mix of subject matter and style. Virago Modern Classics incorporates a large backlist of female fiction. They are not currently accepting unsolicited manuscripts.

Virgin Books Ltd

Random House, 20 Vauxhall Bridge Road, London, SW1V 2SA
T 020 7840 8400
F 020 7840 8406
E editorial@virgin-books.co.uk
W www.virginbooks.com

Parent Company Ebury Press, a division of the Random House Group

Established 1991 (following a merger with publisher WH Allen)

Imprint(s) Black Lace, Nexus, Cheek, Virgin

Insider Info Catalogue available online.

Publishes Erotica, Romance and General Adult Fiction titles.

The Waywiser Press

Bench House, 82 London Road, Chipping Norton, Oxfordshire, OX7 5FN
T 01608 644755
E waywiserpress@aol.com
W www.waywiser-press.com

Contact Dr Philip Hoy (Poetry, Fiction, Memoir, Criticism)

Established 2001

Imprint(s) Between The Lines

Insider Info Publishes five or six titles per year. Receives approximately 500 queries and 1,000 manuscripts per year. 40 per cent of books published are from first-time authors, 85 per cent of books published are from unagented authors. Payment is via royalty. Average lead time is nine months, with simultaneous submissions accepted. Aims to respond to queries and proposals within two weeks and manuscripts within twelve weeks. Catalogue and manuscript guidelines are available online.

Publishes Novels.

Submission Guidelines Accepts proposal package (including outline, one to two sample chapters, author biography and SAE). For full details, see www.waywiser-press.com/authors.html.

Recent Title(s) *Bundle o' Tinder*, Rose Kelleher; *Shuffle and Breakdown*, Cody Walker; *Identity Theft*, Joseph Harrison; *A Most Marvellous Piece of Luck*, Greg Williamson

Tips Waywiser Press titles are aimed at a general literary readership. The press is currently seeking submissions for fiction. See the website for further details.

Weidenfeld & Nicholson

Orion House, 5 Upper St Martin's Lane, London, WC2H 9EA
T 020 7240 3444
F 020 7240 4822
W www.orionbooks.co.uk

Parent Company Orion Publishing Group Ltd

Contact Managing Director, Malcolm Edwards; Publisher, Alan Samson

Established 1949

Imprint(s) Weidenfeld Illustrated, Weidenfeld General, Weidenfeld Fiction, Cassell Reference

Insider Info Catalogue available online, or via an online form.

Publishes Literary, Mainstream/Contemporary and Translation titles.

Submission Guidelines Agented submissions only.

Tips Weidenfeld & Nicholson publishes a range

of titles under its various imprints: Weidenfeld Fiction publishes a range of literary and commercial fiction.

William Heinemann

✉ Random House, 20 Vauxhall Bridge Road, London, SW1V 2SA
☎ T 020 7840 8707
F 020 7233 6127
✎ E heinemanneditorial@randhomhouse.co.uk
W www.randomhouse.co.uk

Parent Company The Random House Group Ltd

Contact Publishing Director, Ravi Mirchandani

Insider Info Catalogue available online.

Publishes General, Women's Fiction, Crime and Thriller titles.

Submission Guidelines Accepts agented submissions only.

Recent Title(s) *The Last Watch*, Sergei Lukyanenko (Novel)

Willow Bank Publishers Ltd

✉ E-Space North, 181 Wisbech Road, Littleport, Ely, CB6 1RA
☎ T 01353 687934
✎ E editorial@willowbankpublishers.co.uk
W www.willowbankpublishers.co.uk

Contact Christopher Sims

Imprint(s) Willow Books, Derringer Books, Butterfly Books, Fen Books

Insider Info Payment is via royalties. Catalogue and manuscript guidelines available online.

Publishes Children's, Mainstream/Contemporary, Mystery and Crime titles.

Submission Guidelines Accepts query with SAE. Submit proposal package (including outline and two sample chapters).

Recent Title(s) *White Roads to Akyab*, James Meridew

Tips Willow Bank publishes general fiction and non-fiction, as well as crime fiction under their Derringer imprint. The Butterfly Books imprint publishes children's non-fiction, fiction and poetry. The Fen Books imprint is a mainstream publisher of literary fiction from authors with a proven writing history. Any book accepted by Fen Books will be funded entirely by the company and may also receive an advance. Willow Bank Publishers may choose to offer either a traditional or author-funded publishing agreement for authors whose work meets the required standard set by their publishing panel, but whose commercial viability is not quite strong enough.

The Women's Press

✉ 27 Goodge Street, London, W1T 2LD
☎ T 020 7636 3992
F 020 7637 1866
✎ E david@the-womens-press.com
W www.the-womens-press.com

Contact Managing Director, Stella Kane

Established 1978

Imprint(s) Women's Press Classics, Livewire Books for Teenagers

Insider Info Publishes 50 titles per year. Payment is via royalties. Catalogue available online.

Publishes Literary, Mainstream/Contemporary and Young Adult titles.

Submission Guidelines Accepts agented submissions only.

Recent Title(s) *Soul Kiss*, Shay Youngblood; *Mud Puppy*, Erica Wooff

Tips The Women's Press is dedicated to publishing incisive feminist fiction and non-fiction by outstanding women writers from all round the world. They will only publish books written by women and even then, only if there is a female protagonist (for fiction) or the book details with women's issues (for non-fiction). A series of up-front, contemporary, issue-driven works of fiction and non-fiction for young women are published in the Livewire list. A series of classic work by women are published through the Women's Press Classics list.

Wordsonthestreet

Six San Antonio Park, Salthill, Co. Galway, Republic of Ireland
E publisher@wordsonthestreet,com
W www.wordsonthestreet.com

Contact Directors, Geraldine Burke and Tony O'Dwyer; Editorial Assistant, Judith Gannon

Imprint(s) 6th House

Insider Info Catalogue available online. Author guidelines available online. Member of CLÉ, The Irish Book Publishers' Association.

Publishes Novels/Novellas.

Submission Guidelines Accepts proposal package (including synopsis, author biography and three sample chapters) by post only. For collections include three sample short stories.

Recent Title(s) *Eclipsed*, Patricia Burke Brogan

Tips Accepts submissions by post only, but include an email address for reply.

Wrecking Ball Press

24 Cavendish Square, Hull, East Yorkshire, HU3 1SS
E editor@wreckingballpress.com
W www.wreckingballpress.com

Contact Managing Director, Shane Rhodes

Insider Info Catalogue and manuscript guidelines available online.

Publishes Mainstream/Contemporary titles.

Submission Guidelines Submit completed manuscript.

Recent Title(s) *Digging the Vein*, Tony O'Neill (Novel)

Tips Wrecking Ball Press is an independent press specializing in poetry and contemporary fiction. If possible all submissions should be on a disk, as well as paper.

Xcite Books

Suite 11769, 2nd Floor, 145–147 St John Street, London, EC1V 4PY

T 020 7858 1024
E Online form
W www.xcitebooks.com

Parent Company Accent Press

Insider Info Catalogue is free on request, and available online. Manuscript guidelines are available online.

Publishes Erotica titles.

Submission Guidelines Submission guidelines available online.

Recent Title(s) *The First Deadly Sin*, Gwen Masters

The X Press

PO Box 25694, London, N17 6FP
T 020 8801 2100
F 020 8885 1322
E vibes@xpress.co.uk
W www.xpress.co.uk

Contact Editorial Director, Dotun Adebayo; Publisher, Steve Pope

Established 1992

Imprint(s) Black Classics, Nia, 20/20

Insider Info Publishes 25 titles per year. Catalogue available online.

Publishes Children's/Teenage, Literary, Mainstream/Contemporary and Black Interest titles.

Submission Guidelines Submit completed manuscript.

Recent Title(s) *Black Rising Star*, Peter Kalu (Novel)

Tips The X Press has grown into Europe's largest publisher of black interest books. The Nia imprint publishes literary black fiction, 20/20 publishes contemporary black fiction, and the Black Classics series reprints classic novels by black writers. The X Press also publishes general black fiction aimed at a younger audience, and aims to take black writing into a new era. Prefers full manuscript submissions rather than proposals, preferably black interest popular fiction from black writers.

Y Lolfa Cyf

Talybont, Ceredigion, SY24 5HE
T 01970 832304
F 01970 832782
E ylolfa@ylolfa.com
W www.ylolfa.com

Contact Managing Director, Garmon Gruffudd;
Chief Editor, Lefi Gruffudd

Established 1967

Imprint(s) Dinas

Insider Info Publishes 50 titles per year. Payment
is via royalties. Catalogue available online.

Publishes Mainstream/Contemporary and
Translation titles.

Recent Title(s) *Welsh Folk Tales in a Flash*, Y Lolfa
(Children's)

Tips Y Lolfa is an independent Welsh publisher
specializing in fiction and non-fiction from, or
about Wales. They print in both Welsh and
English and also offer services as a commercial
print company. The Dinas imprint is a part-
author subsidized press for unusual and non-
mainstream Welsh interest books. Its aim is to
produce interesting and original books, which
enhance the variety of books published in Wales.

AGENCIES & CONSULTANCIES

UK & Irish Literary Agents

A&B Personal Management Ltd

✉ Suite 330 Linen Hall, 162–168 Regent Street, London, W1B 5TD
☎ T 020 7434 4262
F 020 7038 3699
✎ E billellis@aandb.co.uk

Established 1982

Insider Info No unsolicited manuscripts. Please submit query email first. Rejected work will be destroyed with no rejection slip sent. Commission rates of 12.5 per cent for domestic sales, 15 per cent for foreign sales and 12.5 per cent for film sales. Charges a reading fee for full-length book manuscripts.

Tips Enquire about fees before submitting proposal. No unsolicited manuscripts considered.

Aitken Alexander Associates

✉ 18–21 Cavaye Place, London, SW10 9PT
☎ T 020 7373 8672
F 020 7373 6002
✎ E reception@aitkenalexander.co.uk
W www.aitkenalexander.co.uk

Contact Gillon Aitken; Clare Alexander (New Fiction Writers, History, Biography, Memoir and Science); Kate Shaw (Literary and Popular Fiction for Adult's and Children's Authors); Lesley Thorne (Screenplays, Literary Fiction, Crime Thrillers, Memoir, Travelogue/Adventure, Biography and Popular Culture); Matthew Hamilton (Literary Fiction, Thrillers and Popular Culture); Andrew Kidd (Literary and Contemporary Fiction)

Established 1976

Insider Info Actively seeking clients. Aims to respond to queries and proposals within eight weeks. Unsuccessful submissions are returned with SAE. Commission rates are 10 per cent for domestic sales, 20 per cent for foreign sales and 10 per cent for film sales. Does not charge a reading fee. *The agents have mainly come from publishing and editorial backgrounds.

Considers General, Literary and Children's Fiction titles.

Submission Guidelines Send query letter with outline, biography and a 30-page sample of writing. All pages should be single-sided and double-spaced.

Client(s) Josephine Cox, Sebastian Faulks, Helen Fielding, Germaine Greer, JD Salinger, Tom Shakespeare, Andrew Wilson

Tips Formerly known as Gillon Aitken Associates. Aitken Alexander Associates are unable to answer queries by email. Postal queries and submissions only. A list of writing credits (in any genre) would be useful to include with the submission.

Alexandra Nye

✉ 'Craigower', 6 Kinnoull Avenue, Dunblane, Perthshire, FK15 9JG
☎ T 01786 825114

Contact Director, Alexandra Nye

Established 1991

Insider Info Actively seeking clients. Submissions accompanied by SAE will be returned. Clients usually obtained through queries/submissions. Commission rates of 10 per cent for domestic sales, 20 per cent for foreign sales. Reading fee will be charged for a detailed report on manuscripts.

Considers General and Literary Fiction titles.

Submission Guidelines Accepts query with SAE and synopsis. *No telephone enquiries.

Client(s) Dr Tom Gallagher, Harry Mehta

Tips The agency is known for its interest in Scottish history and literary fiction.

AM Heath

6 Warwick Court, Holborn, London, WC1R 5DJ
T 020 7242 2811
F 020 7242 2711
W www.amheath.com

Contact Bill Hamilton (Literary and Commercial Fiction and Non-Fiction); Sara Fisher (Translation Rights, Client Representation); Sarah Molloy (Children's Writers); Victoria Hobbs (Literary and Commercial Fiction and Non-Fiction); Euan Thorneycroft (Literary and Commercial Fiction and Non-Fiction)

Established 1919

Insider Info Actively seeking clients. Aims to respond within four months. Proposals returned if accompanied by SAE. Commission rates of 15 per cent for domestic sales, 20 per cent for foreign sales, 15 per cent for film sales. Does not charge a reading fee.

Considers Literary, Commercial and Children's Fiction titles.

Submission Guidelines Send query letter with SAE, synopsis and three sample chapters. Submission should be double spaced on single-sided A4 paper.

Client(s) Christopher Andrew, Rosemary Ashton, David Conn, Kate Ellis, William Horwood, Helena McEwan

Tips No young children's fiction accepted. Manuscripts or queries will not be accepted via email.

The Ampersand Agency

Ryman's Cottages, Little Tew, Chipping Norton, Oxfordshire, OX7 4JJ
T 01608 683677/683898
F 01608 683449
E info@theampersandagency.co.uk
W www.theampersandagency.co.uk

Contact Peter Buckman (all types of submissions); Anne-Marie Doulton (Literary Fiction, Women's Fiction)

Established 2003

Insider Info Seeking both new and established writers. Represents more than 35 clients, 85 per cent of whom are new or previously unpublished writers. Will consider simultaneous submissions. Aims to respond to queries within two weeks and manuscripts within four weeks. Unsuccessful proposals will be returned with SAE. The Ampersand Agency obtains new clients through recommendations from others and through queries and submissions. Will also sometimes approach writers with ideas. Has seen 17 book projects through publication in the past year. Commission rates of 12.5–15 per cent for domestic sales, 20 per cent for foreign sales and 15 per cent for film sales. Offers a written contract that may be terminated at any time. Does not charge a reading fee or offer a criticism service.

*The agency specializes in good storytelling, whether in fiction or non-fiction, and is made distinct by its candour and rapid responses. Before becoming an agent, Peter Buckman was a publisher and then a full-time writer. Anne-Marie Doulton was an editor and a literary scout.

Considers Children's Fiction, Detective/Police/Crime, Family Saga, Historical, Literary, Mainstream, Mystery, Romance, Thriller/Espionage, Women's/Chick Lit and Young Adult Fiction titles.

Submission Guidelines Send query letter with outline, one or two sample chapters and author biography. Also accepts queries via email. Actively seeking good stories, commercial and literary fiction and non-fiction, for adults and young people. Does not want poetry, science-fiction, fantasy or political satires sent in the future.

Recent Sale(s) *Taking the Medicine*, Druin Burch (Chatto); *Zelah Green: Queen of Clean*, Vanessa Curtis (Egmont); *Dream Machine*, Will Davis (Bloomsbury); *Double Cross*, Tracy Gilpin (Black Star); *Sting of Justice*, Cora Harrison (Macmillan); *Octavia's War*, Beryl Kingston (Allison & Busby); *Smart/Casual*, Niamh Shaw (Headline)

Client(s) Helen Black, SJ Bolton, Martin Conway, Druin Burch, Anna Crosbie, Andrew Cullen, Vanessa Curtis, Will Davis, Catherine Deveney, Tracy Gilpin, Cora Harrison, Georgette Heyer, Michael Hutchinson, Beryl Kingston, Miriam Morrison, Philip Purser, Richard Piers Rayner, Niamh Shaw, P Robert Smith, Georgina Sowerby & Brian Luff, Ivo Stourton, Vikas Swarup, Nick Van Bloss, Michael Walters

Andrew Mann Ltd

1 Old Compton Street, London, W1D 5JA
T 020 7734 4751
F 020 7287 9264
E manuscript@onetel.com

Contact Anne Dewe, Tina Betts, Sacha Elliot

Established 1975

Insider Info Actively seeking clients. Submissions accompanied by SAE will be returned. Clients usually acquired through queries/submissions. Commission rates of 15 per cent for domestic sales, 20 per cent for foreign sales. No reading fees charged.

Submission Guidelines Send submissions with SAE, synopsis and three sample chapters. Queries accepted by email. No poetry considered.

Tips Manuscripts sent by email will not be accepted, send a synopsis only. Unsolicited manuscripts will be accepted only with an accompanying letter.

Andrew Nurnberg Associates Ltd

Clerkenwell House, 45–47 Clerkenwell Green, London, EC1R 0QX
T 020 3327 0400
F 020 7253 4851
E contact@andrewnurnberg.com
W www.andrewnurnberg.com

Contact Director, Andrew Nurnberg

Established 1970s

Insider Info Seeking both new and established writers. Clients usually acquired through queries/submissions. Commission rates of 15 per cent for domestic sales and 20 per cent for foreign sales.

Considers Novels

Submission Guidelines Send short, one-page synopsis and first three chapters (double or 1.5 spaced) with a covering letter and SAE or email submission to: submissions@andrewnurnberg.com.

Tips Represents established authors and agents. Specializes in foreign rights.

Annette Green Authors' Agency

1 East Cliff Road, Tunbridge Wells, Kent, TN4 9AD
T 01892 514275
F 01892 518124
E david@annettegreenagency.co.uk
W www.annettegreenagency.co.uk

Contact Annette Green, David Smith

Established 1998

Insider Info Actively seeking clients. Simultaneous submissions are accepted. Aims to respond to queries/proposals within four weeks. Submissions accompanied by SAE will be returned. Clients usually acquired through queries/submissions. Commission rates of 15 per cent for domestic sales and 20 per cent for foreign sales. Does not charge a reading fee. *Annette Green established her own literary agency in 1998 after working at AM Heath & Co. Ltd for several years. David Smith joined as a partner in 2001.

Submission Guidelines Send query letter with SAE, synopsis and 5,000–10,000 words of the opening chapters. No dramatic scripts, poetry, science-fiction or fantasy considered.

Recent Sale(s) *Mummy Said the F-Word*, Fiona Gibson (Novel)

Client(s) Meg Cabot, Fiona Gibson, Justin Hill, JB Aspinall, Ian Marchant, Anva Khan, Bernadette Strachan

Tips Specializes in discovering new, exciting talent.

Anthony Sheil

18–21 Cavaye Place, London, SW10 9PT
T 020 7373 8672
F 020 7373 6002
E anthony@gillonaitken.co.uk
W www.aitkenalexander.co.uk

Contact Anthony Sheil

Established 1998

Insider Info Actively seeking clients. Aims to respond to queries/proposals within eight weeks. Submissions accompanied by SAE will be returned. Clients usually acquired through queries/submissions. Commission rates of 10 per cent for domestic sales and 20 per cent for foreign sales. Does not charge a reading fee. *Anthony Sheil became an independent agent in association with Gillon Aitken Associates in 1998, after running Anthony Sheil Associates and being Chairman of Sheil Land Associates.

Considers Novels.

Submission Guidelines Send query letter with SAE, synopsis and sample chapters consisting of the first 30 pages of continuous text. Submission should be double spaced, single-sided A4.

Client(s) Caroline Alexander, Paul Arden, Rosalind Belben, Catrine Clay, Piers Dudgeon, John Fowles, Diarmuid Jeffreys, Maurice Keen, Robert Wilson, Benjamin Woolley

Antony Harwood Ltd

103 Walton Street, Oxford, OX2 6EB
T 01865 559615
F 01865 310660
E mail@antonyharwood.com
W www.antonyharwood.com

Contact Antony Harwood, James MacDonald Lockhart

Established 2000

Insider Info Actively seeking clients. Submissions accompanied by SAE will be returned. Clients usually acquired through queries/submissions. Does not charge a reading fee. *Before establishing the agency in 2000, Antony Harwood began publishing at Chatto & Windus in 1978, then became an agent at Gillon Aitken. In 1990 he joined the Curtis Brown Group as a director, before returning for a period at Gillon Aitken. James MacDonald Lockhart was with Hodder Headline before going to Gillon Aitken in 1998. Two years later he joined Antony Harwood to set up their own independent agency.

Submission Guidelines Send query letter with SAE, synopsis and three sample chapters. Queries accepted by email. No material for children under ten.

Recent Sales(s) *The Temporal Void*, Peter F

Hamilton (Tor); *The Woman in the Fifth*, Douglas Kennedy (Arrow Books)

Client(s) Peter F Hamilton, Douglas Kennedy, Malcolm Knox, Deborah Levy, Roger Levy, Mark Lynas

Anubis Literary Agency

6 Birdhaven Close, Lighthorne, Warwick, CV35 0BE
T 01926 642588
F 01926 642588
E writestuff@btinternet.com

Contact Steve Calcutt

Established 1994

Insider Info Specializes in fiction. Submissions accompanied by SAE will be returned. Commission rates of 15 per cent for domestic sales, 20 per cent for foreign sales. Does not charge a reading fee.

Considers Fantasy, Horror and Science-Fiction titles.

Submission Guidelines Send submission with SAE, a one-page synopsis and the first 50 pages only. Queries are not accepted by telephone.

Tips No manuscripts accepted other than fiction from the genres listed above.

AP Watt Ltd

20 John Street, London, WC1N 2DR
T 020 7405 6774
F 020 7831 2154
E apw@apwatt.co.uk
W www.apwatt.co.uk

Contact Caradoc King, Derek Johns, Linda Shaughnessy, Georgia Garrett, Natasha Fairweather, Jon Elek, Juliet Pickering, Elinor Cooper

Established 1875

Insider Info Commission rates of 15 per cent for domestic sales, 20 per cent for foreign sales. No reading fee charged.

Submission Guidelines Send query letter to the relevant agent. Does not accept poetry or any unsolicited manuscripts.

Recent Sales(s) *The Secret Scripture*, Sebastian Barry (Literary Fiction)

Clients(s) Tony Parsons, Rudyard Kipling, John Creed, Michael Innes and Camille Griffin, Robert Heller, Mick Jackson, James Robertson, Elaine Showalter, Zadie Smith

Tips No unsolicited manuscripts accepted. No responsibility accepted for submitted materials.

Artellus Ltd

30 Dorset House, Gloucester Place, London, NW1 5AD
T 020 7935 6972
F 020 8609 0347
E leslie@artellusltd.co.uk
W www.artellusltd.co.uk

Contact Chairperson/Agent/Consultant, Gabriele Pantucci; Director/Agent, Leslie Gardner (Film Rights); Associate Agent/Company Secretary, Darryl Samaraweera (Foreign and Theatrical Rights); Associate Agent/Administrator/Picture Researcher, Liz Mallett

Established 1986

Insider Info Actively seeking clients. Submissions accompanied by SAE will be returned. Clients are usually acquired through recommendation or queries/submissions. Commission rate of ten per cent for domestic sales, 15 per cent for foreign sales. Fee charged for a selective reading service, by invitation.

Considers Crime, Fantasy, Literary Fiction and Science-Fiction titles.

Submission Guidelines Send query letter with SAE, synopsis, three sample chapters and a biography by post only.

Recent Sale(s) *A Visible Darkness*, Michael Gregorio; *The Valley*, JD Landis

Client(s) Anthony Burgess, Lois McMaster Bujold, Sir John Pope-Hennessy, Roger Lewis, Martin van Creveld, Robert Hazen, Robert Gallo, Salma Samar Damluji

Tips The agency has a worldwide client list and is established in the handling of all exploitation of book rights through to periodicals, film, television and radio. Enquire thoroughly about the reading fee before submitting work.

Author Literary Agents

53 Talbot Road, Highgate, London, N6 4QX
T 020 8341 0442
F 020 8341 0442
E agile@authors.co.uk

Contact John Havergal

Established 1997

Insider Info Actively seeking clients. Prefers to receive exclusive submissions. Aims to respond to queries within seven days. Submissions accompanied by SAE will be returned. Clients usually acquired through recommendation or queries/submissions. Does not charge a reading fee.

Considers Action/Adventure, Confessional, Crime, Experimental, Family Saga, Fantasy, Historical, Children's, Literary, Mainstream, Mystery, Religious/Inspirational, Romance, Science-Fiction, Thriller and Young Adult Fiction titles.

Submission Guidelines Send query letter with SAE, synopsis, biography and first chapter. Queries accepted by fax, email and telephone.

Barbara Levy Literary Agency

64 Greenhill, Hampstead High Street, London, NW3 5TZ
T 020 7435 9046
F 020 7431 2063

Contact Director, Barbara Levy; Associate and Solicitor, John Selby

Established 1986

Insider Info Actively seeking clients. Unsuccessful proposals will be returned if accompanied by SAE. Obtains new clients by queries and submissions. Commission rates of 10 per cent for domestic sales, with rates for foreign sales by arrangement. Does not charge a reading fee.

Considers General Fiction titles, mainly full-length Novels.

Submission Guidelines Send query letter with synopsis and SAE.

Tips Do not send entire manuscripts.

Barrie James Literary Agency

Rivendell, Kingsgate Close, Torquay, Devon, TQ2 8QA

T 01803 326617
E mail@newauthors.org.uk
W www.new-writer.co.uk

Contact Barrie James

Established 1997

Insider Info Actively seeking clients. Will consider simultaneous submissions. Unsuccessful proposals will be returned if accompanied by SAE. Obtains new clients through queries and submissions.

Considers Mainstream Fiction titles.

Submission Guidelines Accepts query letter with SAE or queries via email.

Tips Also operates a website for unpublished authors to display their work for a fee: www. newauthors.org.uk. See website for full submission guidelines, costs and new author listings – please research costs and benefits thoroughly before committing.

The Bell Lomax Moreton Agency

James House, 1 Babmaes Street, London, SW1Y 6HF

T 020 7930 4447
F 020 7925 0118
E info@bell-lomax.co.uk
W www.bell-lomax.co.uk

Contact Executives, Eddie Bell, Pat Lomax, Paul Moreton, June Bell

Established 2000

Insider Info Actively seeking clients. Unsuccessful proposals will be returned with SAE. Obtains new clients through queries and submissions. Does not charge a reading fee.

Considers General Fiction titles.

Submission Guidelines Send query letter.

Tips Do not send any manuscripts before first approaching with a query letter.

Binnacle Press

4 The Avenue, Compass Quay, Kinsale, Co. Cork, Republic of Ireland
E info@binnaclepress.com
W www.binnaclepress.com

Contact Agent, Deborah Lysaght

Insider Info Obtains new clients through queries and submissions. Does not accept simultaneous submissions. Commission upon arrangement. Does not charge a reading fee. Also offers a fee-based review service.

Considers Thought-provoking and intelligent Fiction titles.

Submission Guidelines Accepts proposal package (including covering letter, synopsis and author biography) by post or email. Email submissions must use 'Enquiry for Binnacle Press' as the subject line.

Tips Binnacle press is not interested in scripts or Chick Lit.

Blake Friedmann Literary, Film & TV Agency

122 Arlington Road, London, NW1 7HP
T 020 7284 0408
F 020 7284 0442
E info@blakefriedmann.co.uk
W www.blakefriedmann.co.uk

Contact Carole Blake, Oliver Munson (Books)

Established 1977

Insider Info Actively seeking clients. Unsuccessful proposals will be returned if accompanied by SAE. Obtains new clients through queries and submissions. Commission rates of 15 per cent for domestic sales and 20 per cent for foreign sales. Does not charge a reading fee. *Specializes in film and television rights.

Considers General Fiction, Genre Fiction, Literary and Commercial titles.

Submission Guidelines Send query letter with a synopsis and three sample chapters. Do not send any science-fiction.

Client(s) Jane Asher, Elizabeth Chadwick, Maeve

Haran, Ken Hom, Bookey Peek, Craig Russell, Peter James

Tips Caters for a larger overseas market. All ranges of fiction – from genre to literary – are accepted.

The Book Bureau Literary Agency

✉ 7 Duncairn Avenue, Bray, Co. Wicklow, Republic of Ireland
☎ T 00353 1 276 4996
  F 00353 1 276 4834
✎ E thebookbureau@oceanfree.net

Contact Geraldine Nichol

Insider Info Actively seeking clients. Unsuccessful proposals will be returned if accompanied by SAE. Obtains new clients through queries and submissions. Commission rates of ten per cent on domestic sales and 20 per cent on foreign sales. Does not charge a reading fee.

Considers Crime, Literary, Thriller, Women's/ Chick Lit and General Commercial Fiction titles.

Submission Guidelines Send query letter with a synopsis, three to five sample chapters and SAE. Does not accept science-fiction, horror or children's titles.

Tips Writers may usually expect a prompt response to proposals, and may be offered editorial support.

Brie Burkeman & Serafina Clarke Ltd

✉ 14 Neville Court, Abbey Road, London, NW8 9DD
☎ T 0870 199 5002
  F 0870 199 1092
✎ E info@burkemanandclarke.com
  W www.burkemanandclarke.com

Contact Brie Burkeman

Established 2000

Insider Info Both new and established writers considered but taking on few new clients except by recommendation. Prefers to receive

exclusive submissions. Unsuccessful proposals will only be returned SAE. Does not charge a reading fee or offer a criticism service.

Considers Action/Adventure, Crime, Ethnic, Historical, Literary, Mainstream, Mystery and Thriller Fiction titles.

Submission Guidelines Send query letter or email in first instance. Do not send attachments (which will be automatically deleted) or enclosures until invited. See website for detailed guidelines.

Bryan Drew Ltd

✉ Quadrant House, 80–82 Regent Street, London, W1B 5AU
 T 020 7437 2293
  F 020 7437 0561
✎ E bryan@bryandrewltd.com

Contact Literary Manager, Bryan Drew

Established 1962

Insider Info Seeking both new and established writers. Unsuccessful proposals will be returned if accompanied by SAE. Obtains new clients through queries and submissions. Commission rates of 12.5 per cent for domestic sales and 15 per cent for foreign sales. Does not charge a reading fee.

Considers Crime, Thriller and General Fiction titles.

Submission Guidelines Send query letter with synopsis, two to three sample chapters and SAE.

Tips SAE is essential.

Campbell, Thomson & McLaughlin Ltd

✉ 50 Albemarle Street, London, W1S 4BD
☎ T 020 7297 4311
  F 020 7495 8961
✎ E submissions@ctmcl.co.uk
  W www.ctmcl.co.uk

Contact Charlotte Bruton

Established 1931

Insider Info Seeking both new and established writers. Unsuccessful proposals will be returned if accompanied by SAE. Obtains new clients through queries and submissions. Commission rates of 10 per cent for domestic sales and up to 20 per cent for foreign sales. Does not charge a reading fee.

Considers General Fiction titles.

Submission Guidelines Send query letter with SAE, or query via email. Do not send scripts or children's titles.

Tips Do not send entire manuscript before first sending a query letter.

Capel & Land Ltd

29 Wardour Street, London, W1D 6PS
T 020 7734 2414
F 020 7734 8101
E georgina@capelland.co.uk
W www.capelland.com

Contact Directors, Georgina Capel (Literary) and Anita Land (TV & Radio); Agents, Phillipa Brewster, Abi Fellows and Rosie Apponyi (Literary)

Established 2000

Insider Info Actively seeking clients. Obtains new clients through queries and submissions. Commission rates of 15 per cent for domestic and foreign sales. Does not charge a reading fee.

Considers General and Literary Fiction titles.

Submission Guidelines Send query letter with a synopsis, three sample chapters and SAE.

Client(s) Kohn Bew, Matthew Dennison, Julie Burchill, Andrew Greig, Eammon Holmes, Liz Jones, Dr Tristram Hunt, Stella Rimington, Jeremy Paxman, Fay Weldon, Greg Woolf

Tips In some instances revision to proposals or manuscripts may be suggested.

Caroline Davidson Literary Agency

5 Queen Anne's Gardens, London, W4 1TU
T 020 8995 5768
F 020 8994 2770
E caroline@cdla.co.uk
W www.cdla.co.uk

Contact Founder, Caroline Davidson

Established 1988

Insider Info Actively seeking clients. Represents around 30 clients. Aims to respond to queries and proposals within four weeks. Obtains new clients through queries and submissions. Commission rates of 12.5 per cent for domestic sales and foreign sales (20 per cent for foreign sales if sub-agents are involved). Does not charge a reading fee. *Caroline Davidson has been a journalist for Reuters in London and BBC television in the USA, and has wide experience of the international market. She has been the author of five books including A Woman's Work is Never Done.

Considers Literary Fiction titles.

Submission Guidelines Send query letter with a synopsis, the first 50 pages, author biography and SAE. Do not send fantasy, thrillers, crime, occult or children's titles.

Client(s) Perter Barham, Nigel Barlow, Emma Donoghue, Paul Luff, Malachi McIntosh, Simon Unwin, Helena Whitbread

Tips A CV must accompany the preliminary letter and submission. The agency will endeavour to respond to submissions as quickly as possible. No response will be given to submissions by fax or email.

Caroline Sheldon Literary Agency

71 Hillgate Place, London, W8 7SS
T 020 7727 9102
E carolinesheldon@carolinesheldon.co.uk
W www.carolinesheldon.co.uk

Contact Caroline Sheldon, Penny Holroyde

Established 1985

Insider Info Actively seeking clients. Aims to respond to proposals within four weeks. Unsuccessful proposals will be returned with SAE. Obtains new clients through queries and submissions. Commission rates of 10–15 per cent for domestic sales and 20 per cent for foreign sales. Does not charge a reading fee. *Before establishing her agency, Caroline Sheldon was a publisher at Hutchinson Arrow, specializing in women's and children's books. Penny Holroyde has worked at Walker Books and as a rights director for Candlewick Press in the USA. She joined Caroline Sheldon in 2004.

Considers Adult's and Children's Fiction titles.

Submission Guidelines Send query letter with a synopsis, three sample chapters and SAE. Pages should be double-spaced and single-sided A4. No staples or bound manuscripts. Do not send scripts.

Tips The Caroline Sheldon Literary Agency is always looking out for exciting projects by debut authors in both adult and children's books, but out of the enormous amount they see, only a few are selected. There are occasions when they make detailed editorial suggestions and comments but only when they see real promise in the work. Caroline Sheldon does not charge a reading fee.

Cat Ledger Literary Agency

✉ 20–21 Newman Street, London, W1T 1PG
☎ T 020 7861 8226
F 020 7861 8001

Contact Cat Ledger

Insider Info Seeking both new and established writers. Unsuccessful proposals will be returned with SAE.

Considers General Adult Fiction titles.

Submission Guidelines Send query letter with SAE. Do not send science-fiction, fantasy, romance or children's titles.

Tips Mostly deals with non-fiction titles.

Chapman & Vincent

✉ The Mount, Sun Hill, Royston, Hertfordshire, SG8 9AT
☎ T 01763 245005
F 01763 243033
✎ E info@chapmanvincent.co.uk

Contact Directors, Jennifer Chapman and Gilly Vincent

Established 1992

Insider Info Seeking mostly established writers through referrals. Simultaneous submissions are accepted. Unsuccessful proposals will be returned with SAE. Obtains new clients through recommendations from others as well as queries and submissions. Commission rates of 15 per cent for domestic sales and 20 per cent for foreign sales. Does not charge a reading fee.

Considers Up-market Adult Fiction titles.

Submission Guidelines Send query letter with two sample chapters and SAE. No thrillers, adventure or children's books.

Client(s) George Carter, Leslie Geddes-Brown, Rowley Leigh, Eve Pollard

Tips The agency does not accept telephone calls, or any proposals by fax or email.

Christine Green Authors' Agent

✉ 6 Whitehorse Mews, Westminster Bridge Road, London, SE1 7QD
☎ T 020 7401 8844
F 020 7401 8860
✎ E info@christinegreen.co.uk
W www.christinegreen.co.uk

Contact Christine Green

Established 1984

Insider Info Actively seeking clients. Prefers to receive exclusive submissions. Aims to respond to queries and proposals within four weeks. Unsuccessful proposals will be returned with SAE. Obtains new clients through queries and submissions. Commission rates of 10 per cent for domestic sales and 20 per cent for foreign sales. Does not charge a reading fee.

Considers General Fiction titles.

Submission Guidelines Send a query letter with the first three chapters, a synopsis and SAE. Pages should be double-spaced, single-sided, numbered and A4 sized. Do not send science-fiction, fantasy or children's titles.

Recent Sale(s) *Heart and Soul*, Maeve Binchy; *Bitter Chocolate*, Lesley Lokko

Client(s) Mary Beckett, Maeve Binchy, Allie Cresswell, Ita Daly, Winston Fletcher, Carl

Gibeily, Sylvian Hamilton, Marilyn Heward Mills, Mary Joyce, Leslie Lokko, Gaile Parkin

The Christopher Little Literary Agency

Eel Brook Studios, 125 Moore Park Road, London, SW6 4PS
T 020 7736 4455
F 020 7736 4490
E info@christopherlittle.net
W www.christopherlittle.net

Contact Christopher Little

Established 1979

Insider Info Actively seeking clients. Aims to respond to queries and manuscripts within six weeks. Unsuccessful proposals will be returned with SAE. Obtains new clients through queries and submissions. Commission rates of 15 per cent for domestic sales, and 20 per cent for foreign sales and film rights. Does not charge a reading fee.

Considers Mainstream and Literary full-length Fiction titles.

Submission Guidelines Check the website for submission status. No science-fiction, fantasy or illustrated material.

Client(s) Paul Bajoria, AJ Butcher, Janet Gleeson, Gorillaz, Christopher Hale, Pete Howells, Carol Hughes, General Sir Mike Jackson, Lauren Liebenberg, Alistair McNeill, Christopher Matthew, Robert Mawson, Haydn Middleton, Shiromi Pinto, Robert Radcliffe, Dr Nicholas Reeves, JK Rowling, Darren Shan, Wladyslaw Szpilman, Shayne Ward, Pip Vaughn-Huges, John Watson, Anne Zouroudi

Tips The agency also handles merchandising, in-house legal matters, contract affairs, royalties and accounting for their clients, as well as offering a high level of personal, hands-on representation.

Conville & Walsh Ltd

2 Ganton Street, Westminster, London, W1F 7QL
T 020 7287 3030
F 020 7287 4545

E info@convilleandwalsh.com
W www.convilleandwalsh.com

Contact Directors, Clare Conville and Patrick Walsh; Agents, Jake Smith-Bosanquet (Foreign Rights), Susan Armstrong (Debut Fiction), Ben Mason, Jo Unwin

Established 2000

Insider Info Seeking both new and established writers. Unsuccessful proposals will be returned if accompanied by SAE. Obtains new clients through queries and submissions. Commission rates of 15 per cent for domestic sales and 20 per cent for foreign sales. Aims to respond to submissions within two months. Does not charge a reading fee. Does not accept unsolicited submissions by email or fax.

Considers Children's, Literary and Commercial Fiction titles.

Submission Guidelines Accepts query letter with a synopsis, three sample chapters and SAE.

Client(s) John Burningham, Helen Castor, Mike Dash, Professor John Emsley, Dermot Healy, Manjit Kumar, Patrick Redmon

Tips Has an interest in first-time novelists.

Coombs Moylett Literary Agency

3 Askew Road, London, W12 9AA
T 020 8740 0454
F 020 8354 3065
E lisamoylett@dial.pipex.com

Contact Lisa Moylett, Nathalie Sfakianos

Insider Info Seeking both new and established writers. Aims to respond to queries and proposals within one week. Unsuccessful proposals will be returned if accompanied by SAE. Obtains new clients through queries and submissions. Commission rates of 15 per cent for domestic sales, foreign sales and film rights. Does not charge a reading fee.

Considers Crime, Literary, Thriller, Women's/Chick Lit and Contemporary Fiction titles.

Submission Guidelines Send query letter with SAE, synopsis and three sample chapters.

Tips The agency is known for its speed in responding to submissions. No electronic submissions.

Crawford & Pearlstine Associates Ltd

31 Ashley Gardens, Ambrosden Avenue, London, SW1P 1QE
T 0845 262 4212
F 0845 262 5546

Contact Jamie Crawford, Maggie Pearlstine

Established 1989

Insider Info Seeking both new and established writers. Commission rates are variable for domestic sales and 20 per cent for foreign sales and film rights. Does not charge a reading fee.

Considers General Fiction titles.

Submission Guidelines Send query letter with SAE and sample chapters. No science-fiction, horror or children's titles.

Tips No fax or email submissions, and no submissions from outside the UK.

Curtis Brown Group Ltd

Haymarket House, 28–29 Haymarket, London, SW1Y 4SP
T 020 7393 4400
F 020 7393 4401
E cb@curtisbrown.co.uk
W www.curtisbrown.co.uk

Contact CEO, Jonathan Lloyd (Fiction, Autobiographies); Managing Director, Jonny Geller (Book Division); Gordon Wise (History, Lifestyle, Literary Estate of Winston Churchill); Camilla Hornby, Vivienne Schuster, Jonathan Pegg (Non-Fiction, Literary Estates, Literary Commercial Fiction, Biographies, Memoirs, History and Travel); Elizabeth Sheinkman, Janice Swanson, Stephanie Thwaite (Debut Novelists, Journalism, Memoirs, Culture and History, Children's Authors, Author Illustrators, Literary Estates); Kate Cooper, Carol Jackson, Betsy Robbins (Foreign Rights)

Established 1899

Insider Info Aims to respond to queries and proposals within eight weeks. Unsuccessful proposals are returned if accompanied by SAE. Obtains new clients by queries and submissions. Does not charge a reading fee. *Jonathan Lloyd was with HarperCollins before joining the Curtis Brown Group Ltd in 1994. He was also President of the Association of Author's Agents (AAA) from 1999 to 2002. Jonny Geller originally trained as an actor, but joined the group in 1993 as a book agent.

Considers Humour, Literary, Women's/Chick Lit Fiction titles.

Submission Guidelines Send query letter with SAE, a synopsis, and three sample chapters. Pages should be double-spaced, single-sided and A4 sized.

Recent Sale(s) *Child 44*, Tom Rob Smith (Simon & Schuster); *The Painter of Shanghai*, Jennifer Cody (Penguin)

Client(s) Jake Arnott, Barbara Davies, Jane Fallon, Jane Harris, David Hewson, FE Higgins, Cathy Kelly, Marion Keyes, Josie Lloyd, Emlyn Rees, David Mitchell, Christopher Skidmore

Tips When submitting sample chapters make sure your name, contact number and email address are clearly written on the cover. No stapled, bound or emailed manuscripts.

Darley Anderson Literary, TV & Film Agency

Estelle House, 11 Eustace Road, London, SW6 1JB
T 020 7385 6652
F 020 7386 5571
E enquiries@darleyanderson.com
W www.darleyanderson.com

Contact Darley Anderson (Crime and Thrillers); Becky Stradwick (Children's); Ella Andrews (Women's Fiction); Camilla Bolton (Crime and Thrillers)

Established 1988

Insider Info Actively seeking clients. 95 per cent of clients are new or previously unpublished writers. Simultaneous submissions are accepted. Aims to respond to queries, proposals and manuscripts within one month. Unsuccessful proposals will be returned if accompanied by SAE. Obtains new clients through recommendations from others, queries and submissions.

Considers Action/Adventure, Confessional, Crime, Erotica, Ethnic, Family Saga, Fantasy, Gay/Lesbian, Glitz, Historical, Horror, Children's, Mainstream, Mystery, Psychic/Supernatural, Regional, Religious, Romance, Science-Fiction, Sports, Thriller, Women's/Chick Lit and Young Adult titles.

Submission Guidelines Send query letter with SAE, synopsis and the first three chapters. Also accepts queries by email or phone.

David Grossman Literary Agency Ltd

✉ 118b Holland Park Avenue, London, W11 4UA
☎ T 020 7221 2770
F 020 7221 1445

Established 1976

Insider Info Actively seeking clients. Simultaneous submissions are accepted. Unsuccessful manuscripts are returned if accompanied by SAE. Obtains new clients through queries and submissions. Commission rates are variable for domestic sales and 20 per cent for foreign sales. Does not charge a reading fee.

Considers Literary and General Fiction titles.

Submission Guidelines Send query letter with SAE, synopsis and the first 50 pages.

Tips No faxed or emailed submissions will be accepted. Debut novelists' well-written, original works will be considered.

David Higham Associates Ltd

✉ 5–8 Lower John Street, Golden Square, London, W1F 9HA
☎ T 020 7434 5900
F 020 7437 1072
✎ E dha@davidhigham.co.uk
W www.davidhigham.co.uk

Contact Veronique Baxter, Georgia Glover, Anthony Goff, Andrew Gordon, Bruce Hunter, Lizzy Kremer, Caroline Walsh, Alice Williams

Established 1935

Insider Info Seeking both new and established writers. Simultaneous submissions are accepted. Unsuccessful proposals will be returned with SAE. Obtains new clients through recommendations from others, queries and submissions. Commission rates of 15 per cent for domestic sales, 20 per cent for foreign sales and 15 per cent for film rights (scripts 10 per cent). Offers a written contract until it is terminated by either party. Does not charge a reading fee or offer a criticism service.

Submission Guidelines Send query letter with SAE, outline, synopsis, three sample chapters and an author biography. The agency is actively seeking good commercial and literary fiction.

Client(s) Lauren Child, JM Coetzee, Roald Dahl, Anne Fine, Jane Green, James Herbert, Penelope Lively, Michael Morpurgo, Alexander McCall Smith, Alice Sebold, Lynne Truss, Jacqueline Wilson

Tips Postal submissions only.

David O'Leary Literary Agency

✉ 10 Lansdowne Court, Lansdowne Rise, London, W11 2NR

☎ T 020 7229 1623
F 020 7229 1623
✎ E d.o'leary@virgin.net

Contact David O'Leary

Established 1988

Insider Info Seeking both new and established writers. Simultaneous submissions are accepted. Unsuccessful proposals will be returned if accompanied by SAE. Obtains new clients through queries and submissions. Commission rates of 10 per cent for domestic and foreign sales. Does not charge a reading fee.

Considers Literary and Thriller/Espionage Fiction titles.

Submission Guidelines Send query letter with SAE and outline proposal. Also accepts queries by email and phone. No science-fiction.

Client(s) Nick Kochan, Jim Lusby, Derek Malcolm, Ken Russell

Tips The agency is happy to discuss proposals, but does not accept unsolicited manuscripts.

The Dench Arnold Agency

✉ 10 Newburgh Street, London, W1F 7RN
☎ T 020 7437 4551
  F 020 7439 1355
✎ E contact@dencharnold.co.uk
  W www.dencharnold.co.uk

Contact Elizabeth Dench, Michelle Arnold, Matthew Dench, Fiona Grant, Davinia Andrew-Lynch

Established 1972

Insider Info Seeking both new and established writers. Unsuccessful proposals will be returned if accompanied by SAE. Obtains new clients through queries and submissions. Commission rates of 10–15 per cent on domestic sales.

Considers General Fiction titles.

Submission Guidelines Send query letter with SAE, author biography and a sample of work for scripts.

Client(s) Karen Brown, Lucy Flannery, Jeff Gross, Michael Hines, Phil O'Shea, Julian Kemp

DGA Ltd

✉ 55 Monmouth Street, London, WC2H 9DG
☎ T 020 7240 9992
  F 020 7395 6110
✎ E assistant@davidgodwinassociates.co.uk
  W www.davidgodwinassociates.co.uk

Contact Directors, David Godwin and Heather Godwin; Sophie Hoult, Charlotte Knight (Publicity & Client Enquiries); Kerry Glencorse (Foreign Rights); Kirsty McLachan (Film/TV rights)

Established 1995

Insider Info Aims to respond to queries within three weeks. Unsuccessful proposals will be returned if accompanied by SAE. *Specializes in

film and television rights worldwide.

Considers Literary Fiction titles.

Submission Guidelines Send query letter with SAE, synopsis, three sample chapters and an author biography. No children's books, science-fiction, graphic or illustrated novels.

Client(s) Diane Atkinson, Arundhati Roy, Aiden Hartley, Jim Crace, Brian Lara, Michael Pye, Simon Armitage, Ronan Bennett, William Dalrymple, Joe Lovejoy, Clare Tomalin, Donald Sassoon, Ben Rice, Alan Warner

Tips Does not accept submissions by email.

Diane Banks Associates

✎ E submissions@dianebanks.co.uk

Contact Diane Banks

Established 2006

Insider Info Seeking both new and established writers. Simultaneous submissions will be accepted. Aims to respond to queries within two weeks. Obtains new clients through queries and submissions. Commission rates of 15 per cent for domestic sales and 20 per cent for foreign sales. Does not charge a reading fee.

Considers Crime, Literary Fiction, Thriller/Espionage and Women's/Chick Lit titles.

Submission Guidelines Send a synopsis, two to three sample chapters, and an author biography. Also accepts queries by email. No science-fiction or children's titles.

Tips Will only accept submissions via email.

Dinah Wiener Ltd

✉ 12 Cornwall Grove, London, W4 2LB
☎ T 020 8994 6011
  F 020 8994 6044
✎ E dinahwiener@enterprise.net

Contact Dinah Wiener

Established 1985

Insider Info Actively seeking clients. Simultaneous submissions are accepted. Unsuccessful submissions will be returned with

SAE. Obtains new clients through queries and submissions. Commission rates of 15 per cent for domestic sales and 20 per cent for foreign sales.

Considers General Fiction titles.

Submission Guidelines Send query letter, SAE, two sample chapters and a CV giving information on past work and future plans. No children's books.

Tips All submitted manuscripts must be double-spaced, single-sided and A4 sized.

Dorian Literary Agency (DLA)

 Upper Thornehill, 27 Church Road, St Marychurch, Torquay, Devon, TQ1 4QY
T 01803 312095
F 01803 312095

Contact Proprietor, Dorothy Lumley

Established 1986

Insider Info Actively seeking clients. Simultaneous submissions are accepted. Unsuccessful proposals will be returned if accompanied by SAE. Obtains new clients through queries and submissions. Commission rates are variable for domestic sales and 15 per cent for foreign sales. Does not charge a reading fee.

Considers Crime, Family Saga, Fantasy, Historical, Horror, Romance, Science-Fiction, Thriller/Espionage and Women's/Chick Lit titles.

Submission Guidelines Send query letter with SAE, synopsis and three sample chapters. No children's books for children aged under ten.

Client(s) Gillian Bradshaw, Brian Lumley, Rosemary Rowe, Lyndon Stacey

Tips No enquiries via telephone, or manuscripts via email or fax.

Dorie Simmonds Agency

 Riverbank House, 1 Putney Bridge Approach, London, SW6 3JD
T 020 7736 0002
E dhsimmonds@aol.com

Contact Dorie Simmonds

Insider Info Seeking both new and established writers. Unsuccessful proposals will be returned if accompanied by SAE. Obtains new clients through queries and submissions. Commission rates of 15 per cent for domestic and North American sales; commission rate of 20 per cent for foreign translations. Does not charge a reading fee.

Considers Commercial, Crime/Thriller, General, Historical and Women's Fiction titles, as well as Children's Novels.

Submission Guidelines Send a query letter with SAE, synopsis, and two to three sample chapters. Include any publishing history in the letter.

Duncan McAra

28 Beresford Gardens, Edinburgh, EH5 3ES
T 0131 552 1558
F 0131 552 1558
E duncanmcara@hotmail.com

Contact Duncan McAra

Established 1988

Insider Info Actively seeking clients. Commission rates of 10 per cent on domestic sales and 20 per cent on foreign sales. Does not charge a reading fee.

Considers Literary Fiction titles.

Submission Guidelines Send query letter with SAE, synopsis and sample chapters.

Eddison Pearson Ltd

West Hill House, 6 Swains Lane, London, N6 6QS
T 020 7700 7763
F 020 7700 7866
E enquiries@eddisonpearson.com
W www.eddisonpearson.com

Contact Clare Pearson

Established 1996

Insider Info Simultaneous submissions are accepted. Aims to respond to queries and proposals within four weeks. Obtains new clients through queries and submissions. Commission rates of 10 per cent for domestic sales and 15–20 per cent for foreign sales. Does not charge a reading fee.

Considers Literary and Children's Fiction titles.

Submission Guidelines Send query letter and outline by email only.

Client(s) Valerie Bloom, Sue Heap, Robert Muchamore

Tips Query by email for up-to-date submission guidelines. The agency endeavours to reply promptly to all submissions.

Ed Victor Ltd

6 Bayley Street, Bedford Square, London, WC1B 3HE
T 020 7304 4100
F 020 7304 4111

Contact Executive Chairman, Ed Victor; Directors, Sophie Hicks and Margaret Phillips

Established 1976

Insider Info Obtains new clients through queries and submissions. Commission rates of 15 per cent on domestic and foreign sales. Does not charge a reading fee.

Considers Action/Adventure, Children's, Mystery, Romance, Thriller/Espionage, and Women's/Chick Lit titles.

Submission Guidelines Send query letter with SAE and synopsis.

Client(s) John Banville, Herbie Brennan, Eoin Colfer, Frederick Forsyth, AA Gill, Josephine Hart, Jack Higgins, Nigella Lawson, Kathy Lette, Allan Mallinson, Andrew Marr, Janet Street-Porter

Tips Ed Victor does not accept unsolicited manuscripts. The agency also represents the estates of Douglas Adams, Raymond Chandler, Dame Iris Murdoch, Sir Stephen Spender and Irving Wallace.

Edwards Fuglewicz

49 Great Ormond Street, London, WC1N 3HZ
T 020 7405 6725
F 020 7405 6726

Contact Partners, Ros Edwards and Helenca Fuglewicz

Established 1996

Insider Info Actively seeking clients. Simultaneous submissions are accepted. Unsuccessful submissions will be returned if accompanied by SAE. Obtains new clients through queries and submissions. Commission rates of 15 per cent on domestic sales and 20 per cent on foreign sales. Does not charge a reading fee.

Considers Literary and Commercial Fiction titles.

Submission Guidelines Send query letter with SAE, three sample chapters and a brief CV. No science-fiction, fantasy, horror or scripts.

Tips No unsolicited submissions or electronic manuscripts.

Elaine Steel

110 Gloucester Avenue, London, NW1 8HX
T 01273 739022
E info@elainesteel.com
W www.elainesteel.com

Contact Elaine Steel

Established 1986

Insider Info Seeking both new and established writers. Unsuccessful proposals will be returned if accompanied by SAE. Obtains new clients through queries and submissions. Commission rates of 10 per cent for domestic sales, and 20 per cent for foreign sales.

Considers General Fiction titles.

Submission Guidelines Send query letter with SAE.

Tips First contact by telephone is preferred.

Elspeth Cochrane Personal Management

16 Trinity Close, The Pavement, London, SW4 0JD
T 020 7622 3566
E elspethcochrane@talktalk.net
W www.elspethcochrane.com

Contact Elspeth Cochrane

Established 1960

Insider Info Actively seeking clients. Obtains new clients through queries and submissions. Commission rates are variable on domestic sales. Does not charge a reading fee.

Considers General Adult's Fiction titles.

Submission Guidelines Send query letter with SAE and synopsis. Telephone in the first instance before submitting any proposal. No children's fiction.

Client(s) Alex Jones, Dominic Leyton, Royce Ryton, FE Smith, Robert Tannitch

Eric Glass Ltd

25 Ladbroke Crescent, London, W11 1PS
T 020 7229 9500
F 020 7229 6220
E eglassltd@aol.com

Contact Janet Glass

Established 1932

Insider Info Actively seeking clients. Simultaneous submissions are accepted. Unsuccessful proposals will be returned if accompanied by SAE. Obtains new clients through queries and submissions. Commission rates of 15 per cent for domestic sales and 20 per cent for foreign sales. Does not charge a reading fee.

Considers General Fiction titles.

Submission Guidelines Send query letter with SAE and the entire manuscript if requested. No children's titles.

Client(s) Herbert Appleman, Henry Fleet, Alan Melville

Tips No unsolicited manuscripts.

Eve White

54 Gloucester Street, London, SW1V 4EG
T 020 7630 1155
E eve@evewhite.co.uk
W www.evewhite.co.uk

Contact Eve White

Established 2003

Insider Info Seeking both new and established writers. Receives 150 manuscripts per month. Represents 40 clients, 25 of whom are new or previously unpublished writers. Prospective clients must see the website for submission requirements. Aims to respond to manuscripts within two months. Unsuccessful proposals will be returned if accompanied by SAE. Obtains new clients through recommendations from others, queries and submissions. Commission rates of 15 per cent on domestic sales and 20 per cent on foreign sales and film rights. Does not charge a reading fee or offer a criticism service. They will sometimes suggest a literary consultancy or a specific editor where work looks promising but not right for them at the time. Eve White Literary Agency is a member of The Association of Authors' Agents. *Eve White has a degree in Education (with English and Drama). She worked as a teacher and then as a writer, director and actress in theatre and television. The agency will frequently get involved in the PR side of an author's career.

Considers Literary and Commercial Fiction titles, but always check the website as requirements may change.

Submission Guidelines See www.evewhite.co.uk for up-to-date requirements.

Faith Evans Associates

27 Park Avenue North, London, N8 7RU
T 020 8340 9920
F 020 8340 9410
E faith@faith-evans.co.uk

Contact Faith Evans

Established 1987

Insider Info Actively seeking clients. Obtains commissions through recommendations from others. Commission rates of 15 per cent for domestic sales and 20 per cent for foreign sales.

Considers General Fiction titles.

Submission Guidelines Does not accept scripts.

Client(s) Melissa Benn, Shyam Bhatia, Cherie Booth, Carolyn Cassady, Caroline Conran, Alicia Foster, Helena Kennedy, Seumas Milne, Jim Kelly

Tips Does not accept telephone queries. Manuscripts are only accepted by recommendations.

Felicity Bryan Literary Agency

2a North Parade Avenue, Oxford, OX2 6LX
T 01865 513816
F 01865 310055
E agency@felicitybryan.com
W www.felicitybryan.com

Established 1988

Insider Info Seeking both new and established writers. Simultaneous submissions are accepted. Aims to respond to queries and manuscripts within eight weeks. Unsuccessful proposals are returned if accompanied by SAE. Obtains new clients through recommendations from others and queries/submissions. Written contract offered. Does not charge a reading fee, or offer a criticism service.

Considers Crime, Literary Fiction, Thriller/Espionage and Young Adult titles.

Submission Guidelines Send query letter with SAE, outline, synopsis, sample chapters, biography and a proposal. Does not accept science-fiction, horror, fantasy, light romance or illustrated children's books .

Client(s) Roy Strong, John Julius Norwich, AC Grayling, Meg Rosoff, Iain Pears, Miriam Stoppard, Karen Armstrong, John Dickie, Simon Blackburn, Katherine Langrish, Eleanor Updale, Matthew Skelton, Jenny Downham, Sadie Jones, Tim Harford, James Naughtie

Tips Does not accept authors from North America for practical reasons.

Felix De Wolfe

Kingsway House, 103 Kingsway, London, WC2B 6QX

T 020 7242 5066
F 020 7242 8119
E info@felixdewolfe.com
W www.felixdewolfe.com

Insider Info Seeking both new and established writers. Obtains new clients by queries/submissions. Commission rates of 10–15 per cent for domestic sales and 20 per cent for foreign sales. Does not charge a reading fee.

Considers General Fiction titles.

Tips Approach first by telephone.

Font Literary Agency

Hollyville House, Hollybrook House, Clontarf, Dublin 3, Republic of Ireland
T 00353 1 853 2365
E info@fontlitagency.com
W www.fontlitagency.com

Contact Director/Agent, Ita O'Driscoll; Founder/Agent, Orna Ross

Established 2003

Insider Info Currently handles fiction and non-fiction internationally. Obtains new clients through queries and submissions. Does not accept simultaneous submissions. Commission rate of 15 per cent for domestic sales. Does not charge a reading fee.

Considers Commercial Fiction titles, but does not handle Science-Fiction or Children's writing.

Submission Guidelines As an initial contact send a query by email outlining the subject matter of the book, its title and purpose, as well as proposed length and target readership.

Recent Sale(s) *Champagne Kisses*, Amanda Brunker (Novel)

Client(s) Amanda Brunker, Evelyn Cosgrave, Cornucopia Creative Team, Garbhan Downey, Paul Kilduff, Karen Lotter, Paul Lynch, Susanne O'Leary, Dearbhail McDonald, Donal Maguire, Orna Ross, Audrey Talbot

Tips Authors are asked to submit an email query in the first instance, but only if they have completed their manuscript. Font will then request a full submission if they are interested. See the website for further details.

Fraser Ross Associates

6 Wellington Place, Edinburgh, EH6 7EQ
T 0131 657 4412/0131 553 2759
E kjross@tiscali.co.uk
E lindsey.fraser@tiscali.co.uk
W www.fraserross.co.uk

Contact Lindsey Fraser, Kathryn Ross

Established 2002

Insider Info Actively seeking clients. Unsuccessful proposals are returned if accompanied by SAE. Obtains new clients by queries/submissions. Commission rates of 12.5 per cent for domestic sales and 20 per cent for foreign sales. Does not charge a reading fee. *Both partners had careers in readership development, bookselling and teaching before establishing their own agency, and they also ran the Scottish Book Trust from 1991 to 2002. They have been judges on panels for such prizes as the Whitbread, Blue Peter, Smarties and Fidler, and have addressed conferences on readership development worldwide. Presently they run the Pushkin Prizes (www.pushkinprizes.net) and offer readership development workshops and training to teachers and librarians.

Considers Commercial and Literary Fiction titles.

Submission Guidelines Send query letter with SAE for return of material, synopsis, three sample chapters and a short biography. Pages should be one-sided, double-spaced, numbered and A4 sized. Please do not send any unfinished work. General information and full submission guidelines are on the website.

Client(s) Gill Arbuthnott, Erica Blaney, Tom Bloor, John Cresswell, Samantha David, Robert Dodds, Lari Don, Jane Eagland, Richard Edwards, Anne Forbes, Vivian French, Edward Hardy, Chris Higgins, Barry Hutchinson, Janey Louise Jones, Ann Kelley, Joan Lennon, Joan Lingard, Tanya Landman, Jack McLean, Helena Pielichaty, Sue Purkiss, Lynne Rickards, Jamie Rix, Dugald Steer, Linda Strachan, Chae Strathie and Matilda Webb. Illustrators: Ella Burfoot, Sally Collins, Teresa Flavin, Shona Grant, Iain McIntosh, Moira Munro, Katie Pamment

Tips If acknowledgement of submitted material is required, a paid reply postcard must be included with manuscript. Material will only be returned if an SAE is enclosed.

Futerman, Rose & Associates (FRA)

91 St Leonards Road, London, SW14 7BL
T 020 8255 7755
F 020 8286 4860
E enquiries@futermanrose.co.uk
W www.futermanrose.co.uk

Contact Betty Schwartz (Commercial and Literary Fiction)

Established 1984

Insider Info Actively seeking clients. Unsuccessful proposals are returned with SAE. Obtains new clients by queries and submissions. Commission rates of 10 per cent for domestic sales and 20 per cent for foreign sales. Does not charge a reading fee. Affiliated to the Authors' Agents Association and the Personal Managers Association.

Considers Commercial, Literary and Young Adult Fiction titles.

Submission Guidelines Send query letter with SAE, synopsis, three sample chapters and a biography. Does not accept science-fiction or young children's titles.

Recent Sale(s) *Jumping to Confusions*, Liz Rettig (Young Adult)

Client(s) Paul Hendy, Ciaran O'Keeffe, Sue Lenier, David Brett, Kenneth Branagh, Susan George, Stephen Griffin, Yvette Fielding, Iain Duncan Smith, Peter Sallis, Elizabeth Taylor, Tom Conti, Toyah Wilcox, Paul Marx, Philip Dart

Greene & Heaton Ltd

37 Goldhawk Road, London, W12 8QQ
T 020 8749 0315
F 020 8749 0318
E info@greeneheaton.co.uk
W www.greeneheaton.co.uk

Contact Director, Carol Heaton (Authors); Judith Murray (Authors); Antony Topping

(Authors); Nick Harrop (Authors); Linda Davis (Children's Authors); Ellie Glason (Translations and Subsidiary Rights); Belou Charlaff (Authors)

Established 1963

Insider Info Actively seeking clients. Simultaneous submissions are accepted. Aims to respond to queries and proposals within six weeks. Unsuccessful submissions returned with SAE. Obtains new clients by queries and submissions. Commission rates of 10–15 per cent for domestic sales and 20 per cent for foreign sales. Does not charge a reading fee.

Considers Children's, Literary, Mainstream, Science-Fiction, Fantasy, Crime and Graphic Novel titles.

Submission Guidelines Send query letter with SAE, synopsis and three sample chapters. Does not accept scripts.

Recent Sale(s) *Urban Sanctuaries*, Stephen Anderton; *How to be Cool*, Will Smith; *Unknown Soldiers*, Matthew Carr; *Voyaging the Pacific*, Miles Hordern

Client(s) Michael Frayn, PD James, William Shawcross, Mark Barrowcliffe, Bill Bryson, Hugh Fearnley-Whittingstall, CJ Sansom, Marcus du Sautoy, Sarah Waters, Kathryn Hymen, Tom Ryan, Russell Davis, Tabitha Suzuma

Tips The agency has a very diverse list of clients, handling all types of fiction and non-fiction. Greene & Heaton is also the first literary agency to open an office in 'Second Life', the online virtual world.

Gregory & Company Authors' Agents

3 Barb Mews, Hammersmith, London W6 7PA
T 020 7610 4676
F 020 7610 4686
E info@gregoryandcompany.co.uk
W www.gregoryandcompany.co.uk

Contact Director, Jane Gregory; Agent, Emma Dunford (Editorial); Rights Manager, Claire Morris (Foreign & Audio Rights); Rights Executive, Jemma McDonagh (Publicity)

Established 1987

Insider Info Actively seeking clients. Accepts simultaneous submissions. Unsuccessful manuscripts will be returned if accompanied by SAE. Clients usually obtained through queries and submissions. Commission of 15 per cent for domestic sales, 20 per cent for foreign sales. Does not charge a reading fee.

Considers Crime, Family Saga, Historical, Literary, and Thriller/Espionage titles.

Submission Guidelines Authors should include query letter, SAE, synopsis and three sample chapters as double-spaced, one-sided A4. Accepts queries by email. Children's, chick lit, science-fiction and fantasy not considered.

Recent Sale(s) *Singing to the Dead*, Carol Ramsay (WF Howes); *Mad Dogs and an Englishwoman*, Polly Evans (Oakhill)

Client(s) Julian Thompson, John Ryan, Eileen Dewhurst, Betty Boothroyd, Jo Bannister, Minette Walters, Robert Barnard, Gladys Mitchell, Sarah Diamond, Val McDermid

Tips If submission is by email, send a brief letter with a synopsis, but no more than ten pages. When entering the book title also write 'Submission' in subject line. Do not send an entire manuscript without prior authorization.

Gunn Media Associates

50 Albemarle Street, London, W1S 4BD
T 020 7529 3745
E ali@gunnmedia.co.uk

Contact Ali Gunn

Established 2005

Insider Info Seeking both new and established writers. Does not accept simultaneous submissions. Unsuccessful proposals will be returned with SAE. Obtains new clients through queries and submissions. Commission rate of 15 per cent on domestic sales and 20 per cent on foreign sales. Does not charge a reading fee.

Considers Commercial Fiction titles.

Submission Guidelines Send query letter with SAE, synopsis and two to three sample chapters. No scripts.

Tips Unsolicited proposals are welcome by post only.

The Hanbury Agency

28 Moreton Street, London, SW1V 2PE
T 020 7630 6768
E enquiries@hanburyagency.com
W www.hanburyagency.com

Contact Margaret Hanbury

Established 1983

Insider Info Actively seeking clients. Currently handles novels. Proposals returned if accompanied by SAE. Commission rates of 15 per cent for domestic sales and 20 per cent for foreign sales.

Considers Literary Fiction titles.

Submission Guidelines Send query, including SAE, before sending submission. Will not accept children's fiction, fantasy or horror.

Client(s) George Alagiah, JG Ballard, Simon Callow, Judith Lennox

Tips No unsolicited manuscripts.

Henser Literary Agency

174 Pennant Road, Llanelli, Wales, SA14 8HN
T 01554 753520
E henserliteraryagency@btopenworld.com

Contact Steve Henser

Established 2002

Insider Info Seeking both new and established writers. Simultaneous submissions are accepted. Obtains new clients through queries and submissions. Commission rates of 15 per cent on domestic sales and 20 per cent on foreign sales.

Considers Fantasy, Literary, Mainstream, Mystery and Science-Fiction titles.

Submission Guidelines Send query letter with SAE and synopsis. No horror.

Tips Does not accept unsolicited manuscripts.

ICM

66 Charlotte Street, London, W1T 4QE
T 020 7631 4232
W www.icmtalent.com

Contact Margaret Halton

Insider Info Obtains new clients through queries. Does not charge a reading fee.

Considers General Commercial Fiction titles.

Submission Guidelines No unsolicited submissions.

Tips ICM has a very strict policy of not accepting unsolicited materials of any kind.

International Scripts

1a Kidbrooke Park Road, London, SE3 0LR
T 020 8319 8666
F 020 8319 0801
E internationalscripts@btinternet.com

Contact HP Tanner, J Lawson

Established 1979

Insider Info Actively seeking clients. Simultaneous submissions are accepted. Unsuccessful proposals will be returned with SAE. Obtains new clients through queries and submissions. Commission rates of 15 per cent on domestic sales and 20 per cent on foreign sales. May charge reading fees.

Considers Detective/Police/Crime, Women's/Chick Lit and General Contemporary Fiction titles.

Submission Guidelines Send query letter with SAE.

Client(s) Jane Adams, Ashleigh Bingham, Dr James Fleming, Trevor Lummis, Chris Pascoe, Anne Spencer

Tips If a full manuscript is requested, an editorial financial contribution may be required along with SAE.

Jane Conway-Gordon Ltd

1 Old Compton Street, London, W1D 5JA
T 020 7494 0148
F 020 7287 9264
E jconway_gordon@dsl.pipex.com

Contact Jane Conway-Gordon

Established 1982

Insider Info Actively seeking clients. Accepts simultaneous submissions. Manuscripts returned with SAE. Clients usually obtained through queries/submissions. Commission rate of 15 per cent for domestic sales, 20 per cent for foreign sales. Does not charge a reading fee.

Submission Guidelines Authors should include query letter and SAE with submissions. No science-fiction or children's books considered.

Tips The agency is represented worldwide.

Jane Judd Literary Agency

✉ 18 Belitha Villas, London, N1 1PD
☎ T 020 7607 0273
✐ E Online form
🖱 W www.janejudd.com

Contact Jane Judd

Established 1986

Insider Info Actively seeking clients. Accepts simultaneous submissions. Manuscripts returned with SAE. Clients usually obtained through queries/submissions. Commission rates of 10 per cent for domestic sales, 20 per cent for foreign sales. Does not charge a reading fee.

Considers Detective/Police/Crime, Thriller/Espionage, Women's/Chick Lit and Literary Fiction titles.

Submission Guidelines Authors should include query letter, SAE, synopsis, one sample chapter, complete contact details and an email address with their submission.

Jane Turnbull

✉ Barn Cottage, Veryan, Truro, TR2 5QA
☎ T 01872 501317/020 7727 9409
✐ E jane@janeturnbull.co.uk
🖱 W www.janeturnbull.co.uk

Contact Jane Turnbull

Insider Info Actively seeking clients. Manuscripts returned with SAE. Clients usually obtained through personal recommendations or queries/submissions. Commission rates of 15 per cent for domestic sales, 20 per cent for foreign sales. Works with specialized sub-agents

for sale of film/TV, and translation rights. Does not charge a reading fee.

Considers General Fiction titles.

Submission Guidelines Authors should include query letter and SAE with submissions. Science-fiction for young children will not be considered.

Tips Jane Turnbull does not accept unsolicited submissions of full manuscripts – always send a query letter first.

Janklow & Nesbit (UK) Ltd

✉ 33 Drayson Mews, London, W8 4LY
☎ T 020 7376 2733
   F 020 7376 2915
✐ E queries@janklow.co.uk
🖱 W www.janklowandnesbit.co.uk

Contact Tif Loehnis, Claire Paterson, Jenny McVeigh

Established 2000

Insider Info Seeking both new and established writers. Accepts simultaneous submissions. Manuscripts returned with SAE. Does not charge reading or office fees, and does not offer a criticism service. Does not refer to an editing service.

Considers General Fiction titles.

Submission Guidelines Authors should include query letter, SAE, outline, synopsis, three sample chapters, author biography and proposal with submissions. Actively seeking commercial and literary fiction. Email submissions are not accepted.

Jeffrey Simmons

✉ 15 Penn House, Mallory Street, London, NW8 8SX
☎ T 020 7224 8917
   F 020 7224 8918
✐ E jasimmons@unicombox.com

Contact Jeffrey Simmons

Insider Info Manuscripts returned with SAE. Clients usually obtained through recommendations and direct submissions.

Commission rate for new clients, 15 per cent. Does not charge a reading fee.

Considers Quality Commercial Fiction titles.

Submission Guidelines Authors should include query letter, SAE, synopsis, two or three sample chapters (not with email submissions), author biography, brief publishing history – including list of manuscripts with submission. No science-fiction, fantasy, horror or children's titles considered.

Tips Genuinely interested in new, exciting young writers. Will suggest revisions, include any publishing history and a list of agents/publishers that the manuscript has been submitted to.

Jenny Brown Associates

✉ 33 Argyle Place, Edinburgh, EH9 1JT
☎ T 0131 229 5334
✎ E info@jennybrownassociates.com
W www.jennybrownassociates.com

Contact Jenny Brown (Literary Fiction & Non-fiction); Allan Guthrie (Novels); Lucy Juckes (Children's Books); Kevin Pocklington (Rights)

Established 2002

Insider Info Actively seeking clients. Accepts simultaneous submissions. Aims to respond to queries/proposals within six weeks. Manuscripts returned with SAE. Clients usually obtained through queries/submissions. Commission rate of 12.5 per cent for domestic sales, 20 per cent for foreign sales. Does not charge a reading fee. *Before establishing the agency, Jenny Brown was formerly Director of the Edinburgh International Book Festival and Head of Literature at the Scottish Arts Council.

Considers Detective/Police/Crime, Children's and Literary Fiction titles.

Submission Guidelines Authors should include SAE, synopsis, sample chapters (30 pages), author biography, one-page synopsis and brief CV with submission. No poetry, science-fiction, fantasy, sagas or academia considered.

Recent Sale(s) *Enchanted Forests*, Sara Maitland (Granta); *Easy Kill*, Lin Anderson (Hodder)

Client(s) Lin Anderson, Richard Blandford, Linda Cracknell, David White, Patrick Lambe, Esther Woolfson, Dennis O'Donnell, Erica Munro, Alex Gray, Diana Hendry, David Barnes, Catherine De Courcy, Neil Drysdale, Guy Kennaway, Richard Moore, Aidan Smith

JM Thurley Management

✉ Archery House, 33 Archery Square, Walmer, Deal, Kent, CT14 7JA
☎ T 01304 371721
F 01304 371416
✎ E jmthurley@aol.com
W www.thecuttingedge.biz

Contact Jon Thurley, Patricia Preece

Established 1976

Insider Info Seeking both new and established writers. Accepts simultaneous submissions. Manuscripts returned with SAE. Clients usually obtained through queries/submissions. Commission of 15 per cent for domestic sales, 20 per cent for trade sales. Does not charge a reading fee.

Considers Literary and Commercial Fiction titles.

Submission Guidelines Authors should include query letter and SAE with submissions. No fantasy titles considered.

Tips The agency provides editorial and creative assistance to new, exciting writers and constructive revision advice to authorized manuscripts that are rejected.

John Pawsey

✉ 60 High Street, Tarring, Worthing, Essex, BN14 7NR
☎ T 01903 205167
F 01903 205167
Contact John Pawsey

Established 1981

Insider Info Actively seeking clients. Accepts simultaneous submissions. Manuscript returned with SAE. Clients usually obtained through queries/submissions. Commission for domestic and foreign sales variable. Does not charge a reading fee.

Considers Detective/Police/Crime, Mystery and Thriller/Espionage titles.

Submission Guidelines Authors should submit query letter, SAE, synopsis and three sample chapters with submission. No science-fiction, fantasy, horror or children's titles considered.

Client(s) Jennie Bond, David Ashforth, William Fotheringham, Don Hale, Patricia Hall, Dr David Lewis, Anne Mustoe

Tips Has a strong list of established clients, but is always looking to meet bright new talent.

Johnson & Alcock Ltd

✉ Clerkenwell House, 45–47 Clerkenwell Green, London, EC1R 0HT
☎ T 020 7251 0125
F 020 7251 2172
✎ E Online form
W www.johnsonandalcock.co.uk

Contact Michael Alcock, Anna Power, Andrew Hewson, Ed Wilson

Established 1956

Insider Info Actively seeking clients. Accepts simultaneous submissions. Manuscripts returned with SAE. Clients usually obtained through queries/submissions. Commission of 15 per cent on domestic sales, 20 per cent on foreign sales. Does not charge a reading fee.

Considers Children's, Literary and Commercial Fiction titles.

Submission Guidelines Authors should include query letter, SAE, synopsis, and author biography with submissions. Include details of media/writing experience. No science-fiction titles considered.

Tips No unsolicited manuscripts, but fiction writers may submit the first three chapters with first contact. No email submissions.

Jonathan Clowes Ltd

✉ 10 Iron Bridge Road, Bridge Approach, London, NW1 8BD
☎ T 020 7722 7674
F 020 7722 7677

✎ E admin@jonathanclowes.co.uk
W www.jonathanclowes.co.uk

Contact Jonathan Clowes

Established 1960

Insider Info Actively seeking clients. Manuscripts returned with SAE. Clients usually obtained through recommendations from others and queries/submissions. Commission rate of 15 per cent for domestic sales, variable for foreign sales. Does not charge a reading fee.

Considers Literary Fiction titles.

Submission Guidelines Authors should include a query letter, CV and SAE with submissions. No children's titles considered.

Tips No unsolicited manuscripts. Always contact with a query letter in the first instance.

Jonathan Williams Literary Agency

✉ Rosney Mews, Upper Glenageary Road, Glenageary, Co. Dublin, Republic of Ireland
☎ T 00353 1 280 3482
F 00353 1 280 3482

Contact Director, Jonathan Williams

Established 1981

Insider Info Seeking both new and established writers. Manuscripts returned with SAE. Clients usually obtained through queries/submissions. Commission rate of 10 per cent on domestic sales. Does not charge reading fee (see **Tips**).

Considers General Fiction titles.

Submission Guidelines Authors should include query letter, SAE, synopsis, and two to three sample chapters.

Tips Reading fees will be charged if a quick response is required. Include IRCs with submissions instead of UK stamps.

Judith Chilcote Agency

✉ 8 Wentworth Mansions, Keats Grove, London, NW3 2RL
☎ T 020 7794 3717

E judybks@aol.com

Contact Judith Chilcote

Established 1990

Insider Info Actively seeking clients. Accepts simultaneous submissions. Manuscripts returned with SAE. Clients usually obtained through queries/submissions. Does not charge a reading fee.

Considers Commercial Fiction titles.

Submission Guidelines Authors should include query letter, SAE, three sample chapters and biography with submission. No children's titles considered.

Tips A CV is essential with submissions. The agency is primarily interested in cinema/television tie-ins for its clients.

Judith Murdoch Literary Agency

19 Chalcot Square, London, NW1 8YA
T 020 7722 4197

Contact Judith Murdoch

Established 1993

Insider Info Commission rate of 15 per cent for domestic sales, 20 per cent for foreign sales. Editorial advice is given and the agency does not charge a reading fee. Translation rights are handled by the Marsh Agency Ltd.

Considers Full-length Fiction only, particularly accessible Literary and Commercial Women's Fiction titles.

Submission Guidelines Author should include synopsis and two sample chapters with submission, including an SAE for return. No science-fiction/fantasy or children's titles considered. Does not accept queries by telephone or email.

Client(s) Alison Bond, Anne Bennett, Meg Hutchinson, Lisa Jewell, Pamela Jooste, Eve Makis

Juliet Burton Literary Agency

2 Clifton Avenue, London, W12 9DR
T 020 8762 0148
F 020 8743 8765
E juliet.burton@btinternet.com

Contact Juliet Burton

Established 1999

Insider Info Seeking both new and established writers. Manuscripts returned with SAE. Clients usually obtained through queries/submissions. Commission rate of 15 per cent for domestic sales, 20 per cent for foreign sales. Does not charge a reading fee.

Considers Crime, Detective and Women's Fiction titles.

Submission Guidelines Authors should include query letter, SAE, synopsis, and two or three sample chapters with submission.

Tips No unsolicited or emailed manuscripts.

Juri Gabriel

35 Camberwell Grove, London, SE5 8JA
T 020 7703 6186
F 020 7703 6186

Contact Juri Gabriel

Insider Info Actively seeking clients. Currently handles novels. Simultaneous submissions accepted. Manuscripts returned with SAE. Clients usually obtained through queries/submissions. Commission rate of 10 per cent for domestic sales, 20 per cent for foreign sales. Does not charge a reading fee. *Juri Gabriel worked in television for many years and is the author of several books. He is also chairman of Dedalus Publishers.

Considers Literary Fiction titles.

Submission Guidelines Authors should include query letter, SAE, three sample chapters, biography and written query with submissions. No children's titles considered.

Client(s) Maurice Caldera, Diana Constance, Miriam Dunne, Richard Mankiewicz, Karina Mellinger, Dr Terence White

Tips Juri Gabriel handles mainly established clients and insists on a high quality of manuscript. Mainly focuses on television, film and radio rights.

Kate Hordern Literary Agency

✉ 18 Mortimer Road, Clifton, Bristol, BS8 4EY
☎ T 0117 923 9368
F 0117 973 1941
✎ E katehordern@blueyonder.co.uk

Contact Kate Hordern

Established 1999

Insider Info Actively seeking clients. Will consider simultaneous submissions and unsuccessful proposals will be returned with SAE. Obtains new clients via queries/submissions. Commission rates of 15 per cent for domestic sales and 20 per cent for foreign sales. Does not charge a reading fee.

Considers Quality General Fiction titles.

Submission Guidelines Send proposal package with query letter, SAE and synopsis.

Tips Sample chapters for fiction upon request only. No unsolicited manuscripts will be accepted.

Laura Morris Literary Agency

✉ 21 Highshore Road, London, SE15 5AA
☎ T 020 7732 0153
F 020 7732 9022
✎ E laura.morris@btconnect.com

Contact Laura Morris

Established 1998

Insider Info Actively seeking clients. Will consider simultaneous submissions, and unsuccessful proposals will be returned with SAE. Obtains new clients via queries/submissions. Commission rates of 10 per cent for domestic sales and 20 per cent for foreign sales. Does not charge a reading fee.

Considers Literary Fiction titles.

Submission Guidelines Send proposal package with query letter and SAE. No children's books will be considered.

Tips No unsolicited manuscripts will be accepted.

Lavinia Trevor

✉ The Glasshouse, 49a Goldhawk Road, London, W12 8QP
☎ T 020 8749 8481
F 020 8749 7377

Contact Lavinia Trevor

Established 1993

Insider Info Actively seeking clients. Will consider simultaneous submissions. Unsuccessful proposals will be returned with SAE. Obtains clients via queries/submissions. Commission paid for domestic and foreign sales by agreement. Does not charge a reading fee.

Considers Literary and Commercial titles.

Submission Guidelines Send proposal package with query letter, SAE, synopsis, sample chapters, brief biography and the first 50–60 pages only. No science-fiction, fantasy or children's titles will be considered.

Tips Concentrates mainly on literary and commercial fiction/non-fiction.

LAW Ltd

✉ 14 Vernon Street, London, W14 0RJ
☎ T 020 7471 7900
F 020 7471 7910
✎ E admin@lawagency.co.uk
W www.lawagency.co.uk

Contact Mark Lucas, Julian Alexander, Araminta Whiteley (Fiction & Non-Fiction); Lucinda Cook (Translation Rights & Literary Estates); Philipaa Milnes-Smith (Children's & Young Adults); Alice Saunders (Audio Rights & Speaker Engagements)

Established 1996

Insider Info Actively seeking clients. Will consider simultaneous submissions. Aims to respond to queries/proposals within eight weeks. Unsuccessful proposals will be returned with SAE. Obtains new clients via queries/ submissions. Commission rates are 15 per cent for domestic sales and 20 per cent for foreign sales. Does not charge a reading fee.

Considers Children's, Literary and Young Adult Fiction titles.

Submission Guidelines Send proposal package with query letter, SAE, synopsis, and two sample chapters, or up to 30 pages in single-sided, double-spaced A4 format.

Recent Sale(s) *The Accident Man*, Tom Cain; *The Ultimate Teen Book Guide*, Daniel Hahn

Client(s) Tracy Edwards, Gene Kemp, Felicity Kendall, Sophie Kinsella, Andy McNab, Livi Michael, Philip Reeve, John Sergeant, Nigel Slater

Tips LAW are happy to consider material from potential new clients although it should be noted that they take on very few of those projects submitted to them. Submissions by email, fax or disk will not be accepted.

Lisa Eveleigh Literary Agency

3rd Floor, 11/12 Dover Street, London, W1S 4LJ
T 020 7399 2803
F 020 7399 2801
E eveleigh@dial.pipex.com

Contact Lisa Eveleigh

Established 1996

Insider Info Actively seeking clients. Unsuccessful submissions will be returned with SAE. Obtains new clients via queries/ submissions. Commission rate is 15 per cent for domestic sales and 20 per cent for foreign sales. Does not charge a reading fee.

Considers Children's, Literary, Young Adult and Commercial Fiction titles.

Submission Guidelines Send proposal package with query letter, SAE, synopsis, two to three sample chapters, and author biography. Accepts queries by email. No scripts, children's picture books, horror or science-fiction titles will be accepted.

Tips Send preliminary letter only, via email (no manuscripts).

The Lisa Richards Agency

108 Upper Leeson Street, Dublin 4, Republic of Ireland
T 00353 1 637 5000
F 00353 1 667 1256
E info@lisarichards.ie
W www.lisarichards.ie

Contact Literary Agent, Faith O'Grady

Established 1998

Insider Info Seeking both new and established writers. Unsuccessful proposals will be returned with SAE. Obtains new clients via queries/ submissions. Commission rates are 10–15 per cent for domestic sales, 20 per cent for foreign sales and 15 per cent for film sales. Does not charge a reading fee.

Considers General Fiction titles for both adults and children.

Submission Guidelines Send proposals package with query letter, SAE, synopsis and two to three sample chapters.

Client(s) Helena Close, Susan Connolly, Matt Cooper, Denise Deegan, Christine Dwyer Hickey, Robert Fannin, Karen Gillece, Paul Howard aka Ross O'Carroll-Kelly, Arlene Hunt, Roisin Ingle, Alison Jameson, George Lee, Declan Lynch, Anna McPartlin, Pauline McLynn, Roisin Meaney, David O'Doherty, Jarlath Regan

London Independent Books

26 Chalcot Crescent, London, NW1 8YD
T 020 7706 0486
F 020 7724 3122

Contact Carolyn Whitaker

Established 1971

Insider Info Actively seeking clients. Simultaneous submissions will be accepted. Unsuccessful proposals will be returned with SAE. Obtains new clients via queries/ submissions. No reading fee.

Considers Fantasy, Young Adult and Commercial Fiction titles.

Submission Guidelines Send proposal package with query letter, SAE, synopsis, two sample chapters or up to 30 pages. No young children's books.

Tips The agent will suggest revision and offer constructive criticism.

Lorella Belli Literary Agency (LBLA)

✉ 54 Hartford House, 35 Tavistock Crescent, Notting Hill, London, W11 1AY

☎ T 020 7727 8547
F 0870 787 4194

✎ E info@lorellabelliagency.com
W www.lorellabelliagency.com

Contact Lorella Belli

Established 2002

Insider Info A small agency seeking both new and established writers. Aims to respond to queries/proposals within one week and manuscripts within one month. Manuscripts will be returned with SAE. Clients are usually obtained through recommendations from others, queries/submissions and conferences. Commission rate of 15 per cent for domestic sales, 20 per cent for foreign sales and 20 per cent for film sales. Offers a written contract that is binding until terminated by either party, 60 days notice must be given to terminate. Does not charge a reading fee, or offer a criticism service.

Considers Adventure, Confessional, Crime, Erotica, Ethnic, Experimental, Family saga, Feminist, Gay/Lesbian, Glitz, Historical, Humour/Satire, Literary, Mainstream, Mystery, Supernatural, Romance, Sports, Thriller and Women's Fiction titles.

Submission Guidelines Authors should include query letter, SAE, outline, synopsis, sample chapters (initial three for fiction), biography and proposal with submission. Accepts queries by fax, email and phone. Actively seeking first novelists, journalists, international and multicultural writing and books on Italy/with an Italian connection. Does not accept children's books, fantasy or science-fiction.

Client(s) Michael Bess, Zoe Bran, Sean Bidder, Annalisa Coppolaro-Nowell, Dario Fo, Emily Giffin, Rick Mofina, Paul Marting, Nisha Minhas, Alanna Mitchell, Angela Murrills, Jennifer

Quellette, Robert Ray, Grace Saunders, Dave Singleton, Rupert Steiner, Diana Winston

Tips Lorella Belli also represents a number of US, Canadian, Australian and European agencies in the UK.

Louise Greenberg Books Ltd

✉ The End House, Church Crescent, London, N3 1BG

☎ T 020 8349 1179
F 020 8343 4559

✎ E louisegreenberg@msn.com

Contact Louise Greenberg

Established 1997

Insider Info Actively seeking clients. Manuscripts returned with SAE. Clients usually obtained through queries/submissions. Commission rate of 15 per cent for domestic sales, 20 per cent for foreign sales. Does not charge a reading fee.

Considers Literary Fiction titles.

Submission Guidelines Author should submit query letter, SAE and three sample chapters with submissions.

Tips No telephone enquiries.

Lucy Luck Associates

✉ 18–21 Cavaye Place, London, SW10 9PT
✎ E lucy@lucyluck.com
W www.lucyluck.com

Contact Lucy Luck

Established 2006

Insider Info Seeking both new and established writers. Currently represents 20 clients, 50 per cent of which are new/previously unpublished writers. Accepts simultaneous submissions. Aims to respond to queries/proposals and manuscripts within three months. Manuscripts returned with SAE. Clients usually obtained through recommendations from others. 60 days notice required to terminate contract. Does not charge reading or office fees, and also offers a criticism service. *Lucy Luck has worked as an agent since 1997 and specializes in edgy, thoughtful literary fiction and quirky, narrative non-fiction.

The agency works with young writers to establish a writing career, in the first instance forming a relationship with a publisher, but then working on related areas such as journalism. Their experience ranges from working with first-time novelists to established writers, and their stated strength is their commitment to personal relationships and a belief that books matter.

Considers Action/Adventure, Crime, Historical, Literary, Mystery, Thriller and Young Adult Fiction titles.

Submission Guidelines Authors should include query letter, SAE, sample chapters and biography with submission. Accepts queries by email. Actively seeking writers of ability, who are looking to build a career through their writing. Illustrated books or one-off books, anything too technical or academic, or anything too derivative will not be considered.

Recent Sale(s) *Hodd*, Adam Thorpe (Cape); *Menage*, Ewan Morrison (Cape); *What Was Lost*, Catherin O'Flynn (Tindal Street Press); *Black Rock*, Amanda Smyth (Serpent's Tail); *The Years of the Locust*, Jon Hotten (Yellow Jersey); *Take Me To The Source*, Rupert Wright (Harvill Secker)

Client(s) Ewan Morrison, Doug Johnstone, Philip O Ceallaigh, Jon Hotten, Lorelei Matthias, Tom Chesshyre, JA Henderson, Catherine O'Flynn

Tips The website has a secure online form for submissions.

Luigi Bonomi Associates Ltd

91 Great Russell Street, London, WC1B 3PS
T 020 7637 1234
F 020 7637 2111
E info@bonomiassociates.co.uk
W www.bonomiassociates.co.uk

Contact Luigi Bonomi, Amanda Preston

Established 2005

Insider Info Actively seeking clients. Manuscripts are returned with SAE. Clients usually obtained through queries/submissions. Commission rate of 15 per cent for domestic sales, 20 per cent for foreign sales and 15 per cent for film sales. Does not charge a reading fee.

Considers Crime, Literary, Thriller, Women's and

Young Adult Fiction titles.

Submission Guidelines Authors should submit query letter, SAE, synopsis and three sample chapters with submission. No science-fiction, fantasy or children's titles considered.

Client(s) James Barrington, John Humphreys, Nick Foulkes, Eamonn Holmes, James May, Richard Madeley and Judy Finnigan, Esther Rantzen, Professor Bryan Sykes, Alan Titchmarsh, Kim Woodburn and Aggie MacKenzie, Sir Terry Wogan

Tips Interested in new authors and television tie-ins.

Lutyens & Rubinstein

21 Kensington Park Road, London, W11 2EU
T 020 7792 4855
E submissions@lutyensrubinstein.co.uk
W www.lutyensrubinstein.co.uk

Contact Susannah Godman

Established 1991

Insider Info Accepts simultaneous submissions. Aims to respond to queries/proposals within six weeks. Manuscripts returned with SAE.

Considers Children's and Adult's Fiction titles.

Submission Guidelines Authors should include query letter, SAE, synopsis and two sample chapters with submissions. Queries accepted by email.

Marianne Gunn O'Connor Literary Agency

Morrison Chambers, Suite 17, 32 Nassau Street, Dublin 2, Republic of Ireland
E magoclitagency@eircom.net

Contact Marianne Gunn O'Connor

Established 1996

Insider Info Seeking both new and established writers. Proposals accompanied by SAE will be returned. Commission rates are 15 per cent for domestic sales, 20 per cent for foreign sales and 20 per cent for films.

Considers Children's, Literary and Commercial Fiction titles.

Submission Guidelines Send proposal package including a brief synopsis and two or three sample chapters.

Tips No unsolicited manuscripts.

Marjacq Scripts Ltd

✉ 34 Devonshire Place, London, W1G 6JW
☎ T 020 7935 9499
🖷 F 020 7935 9115
✎ E enquiries@marjacq.com
W www.marjacq.com

Contact CEO, Jacqui Lyons; Literary Agent, Philip Patterson; Film and TV Agent, Luke Speed

Established 1974

Insider Info Actively seeking clients. Will consider simultaneous submissions. Aims to respond to queries/proposals within six weeks. Commission rates are 10 per cent for domestic sales and 20 per cent for foreign sales. Does not charge a reading fee.

Considers Commercial and Literary Fiction titles.

Submission Guidelines Send proposal package with synopsis and three sample chapters (typed, single-side and double-spaced on A4 paper).

Recent Sale(s) *Magda's Daughter*, Catrin Collier; *The Church Mouse*, Graham Oakley (Templar)

Client(s) Anita Anderson, Bill Brown, David Evans and Scott Michaels, James Follett, Ian Pryor, Richard Templar, Stuart Macbride, Jeannie Johnson

Tips Will not accept handwritten/illegible material or queries without submission. Submissions are usually shredded. The agency does not discuss manuscripts unless the author becomes a client.

The Marsh Agency Ltd

✉ 50 Albermarle Street, London, W1S 4BD
☎ T 020 7297 4311
🖷 F 020 7495 8961
✎ E Online form
W www.marsh-agency.co.uk

Contact Managing Director, Paul Marsh (Serious Non-Fiction, Literary Fiction, Client Development, Business Development & Client Account Management); Rights Director, Camilla Ferrier; Agents, Charlotte Bruton, Geraldine Cooke, Hannah Ferguson, Piers Russell-Cobb, Jessica Woollard, Stephanie Ebdon (Translation), Caroline Hardman (Translation)

Established 1994

Insider Info Seeking both new and established writers. Proposals accompanied by SAE will be returned. Commission rates are 15 per cent for domestic sales and 20 per cent for foreign sales. *Paul Marsh worked for Anthony Sheil Associates Ltd, from 1977 and became their Foreign Rights Director in 1979. He left in 1993 and went on to establish The Marsh Agency in 1994 with his wife. Camilla Ferrier worked for HarperCollins prior to joining the agency in 2002, and Geraldine Cooke was an editor for many years at Penguin before joining in 2004. She also founded the Headline Review List. Jessica Woollard was a Director for Toby Eady Associates before joning the agency in 2006, and Leyla Moghadam worked for some time at the European Commission. Leyla is multi-lingual, speaking English, German, French and Farsi.

Considers Action/Adventure, Children's Fiction, Crime, Fantasy, Historical, Literary, Mystery, Romance, Science-Fiction, Thriller and Young Adult titles.

Submission Guidelines Send proposal package with SAE, synopsis, three sample chapters and author biography (double-spaced, numbered A4 pages). Can also submit via an online form. Will not accept children's picture books.

Recent Sale(s) *The Drop Edge of Yonder*, Rudolph Wurlitzer (Novel); *The Good Thief*, Hannah Tinti (First Novel)

Client(s) Monica Ali, Kate Atkinson, Jonathan Safran Foer, Meg Cabot, Toby Litt, Vikram Seth, Bill Bryson

Tips When submitting manuscripts, print your name, address and contact number on the front, and your name and the title on all pages.

Mary Clemmey Literary Agency

6 Dunollie Road, London, NW5 2XP
T 020 7267 1290
F 020 7482 7360

Contact Mary Clemmey

Established 1992

Insider Info Actively seeking both new and established clients. Proposals returned with SAE. Commission rates of 10 per cent for domestic sales and 20 per cent for foreign sales. Usually obtains new clients through queries and submissions. Does not charge a reading fee.

Considers General Fiction titles.

Submission Guidelines Accepts proposal package with query letter, SAE and outline.

Tips Accepts scripts from existing clients only. Does not deal with science-fiction, fantasy or children's titles.

MBA Literary Agents Ltd

62 Grafton Way, London, W1T 5DW
T 020 7387 2076
F 020 7387 2042
E diana@mbalit.co.uk
W www.mbalit.co.uk

Contact Managing Director and Literary Agent, Diana Tyler; Director, Meg Davis (Scriptwriters/ Authors all genres); Director, Laura Longrigg (Fiction/Non-Fiction); Agents, Sophie Gorell Barnes, Susan Smith, Stella Kane, David Riding, Jean Kitson

Established 1971

Insider Info Actively seeking clients. Will consider simultaneous submissions. Unwanted material will be returned with SAE. New clients are usually obtained through queries and submissions. Commission rates of 15 per cent for domestic sales, 20 per cent for foreign sales and 10–20 per cent for film sales.

Considers Fantasy, Literary, Commercial and Science-Fiction titles.

Submission Guidelines See submission details for each individual agent on the website.

Recent Sale(s) *A Mile of River*, Judith Allnatt (Fiction); *We're British, Innit*, Iain Aitch (Humour); *Flight Into Darkness*, Sarah Ash (Fantasy)

Client(s) Robert Jones, Nick Angel, Dr Mark Atkinson, Anila Baig, Rob Bailey, Ed Hurst, Christopher Bird, Vivienne Bolton, Audrey and Sophie Boss, Martin Buckley, Debbie Cash, Vic Darkwood, Sarah Ash, Michael Cobley, Murray Davis, Alan Dunn, Stef Penney

Tips Authors are advised to check the submission details and email address of the relevant agent before sending a submission.

McKernan Agency

5 Gayfield Square, Edinburgh, EH1 3NW
T 0131 557 1771
E info@mckernanagency.co.uk
W www.mckernanagency.co.uk

Contact Maggie McKernan

Established 2005

Insider Info Actively seeking both new and established clients. Currently working with 20 clients, around 50 per cent of whom are previously unpublished writers. Accepts queries by email. Will accept simultaneous submissions. Will return unwanted material with SAE. Usually obtains new clients through recommendations from others, queries and submissions. *A small agency, therefore clients receive very individual attention. During Maggie McKernan's career she edited many prize-winning authors, including Jim Crace, Ben Okri and Vikram Seth.

Considers Crime, Ethnic, Experimental, Family Saga, Fantasy, Feminist, Gay/Lesbian, Glitz, Historical, Horror, Humour/Satire, Literary, Mainstream, Mystery, Supernatural, Thriller, Women's and Young Adult titles.

Submission Guidelines Accepts queries by email, no attachments. Prefers initial contact by letter without attachments.

Tips Seeks novels of all kinds, both commercial and literary.

Mic Cheetham
Literary Agency

✉ 50 Albermarle Street, London, W15 4BD
☎ T 020 7495 2002
  F 020 7399 2801
✎ E info@miccheetham.com
  W www.miccheetham.com

Contact Director, Mic Cheetham

Established 1994

Insider Info Actively seeking both new and established clients. Deals with fiction titles. Unwanted material will be returned with SAE. Obtains new clients mostly through queries and submissions. Commission rates of 10–15 per cent for domestic sales, 10–15 per cent for foreign sales and 10–20 per cent for film sales. Does not charge a reading fee.

Considers Fantasy, Genre, Mainstream, Literary, Science-Fiction, Crime and Historical Fiction titles.

Submission Guidelines Accepts proposals with SAE, one-page synopsis and three sample chapters by post only.

Recent Sale(s) *The Temporal Void*, Iain M Banks (Science-Fiction)

Client(s) Iain M Banks, Simon Beckett, Mark Behr, John Binias, Carol Birch, NM Browne, Stuart Browne, Anita Burgh, Alan Campbell, Paul Cornell, Barbara Ewing, Laurie Graham, David Gunn, Jon Courtenay Grimwood, M John Harrison, Toby Litt, Ken MacLeod, Graham McCann, China Mieville, Sharon Penman, Anthony Sher, Harry Shapiro, Peter Smalley, Veronica Stallwood, Tricia Sullivan, Steph Swainston

Tips Will not accept entire manuscripts, except from existing clients.

Mulcahy Conway Associates

✉ 15 Canning Passage, Kensington, London, W8 5AA
✎ E Online form
  W www.mca-agency.com

Contact Ivan Mulcahy, Jonathan Conway, Laetitia Rutherford, Stephanie Cohen

Established 2008

Insider Info Seeking both new and established writers. The agents' backgrounds include periods in journalism, publishing, printing, business and research. Does not charge a reading fee.

Considers Children's and Adult Fiction titles.

Submission Guidelines Accepts proposals package (including query letter, outline, synopsis, 50–100 sample pages, biography and a summary of competitor books in the market).

Recent Sale(s) *War Child*, Emmanuel Jal (Film)

Client(s) Catherine Arnold, Tony Allan, Michelle Dewberry, David Hencke, Shrabani Basu, Ian Kelly, Leslie Ash, Emmanuel Jal, Nigel Smith

Tips Formerly part of the Mulcahy & Viney agency.

PFD (Peters, Fraser & Dunlop)

✉ Drury House, 34–43 Russell Street, London, WC2B 5HA

☎ T 020 7344 1000
  F 020 7836 9543
✎ E info@pfd.co.uk
  W www.pfd.co.uk

Contact CEO, Caroline Michel; Managing Director, Lesley Davey; Book Agents, Marcella Edwards, Annabel Merullo, Caroline Michel; Michael Sissons, Suzy Jenvey (Children's), Zoe Pagnamenta (US Authors/US Rights), Louisa Pritchard (Foreign Rights); Theatre, Film & Television Agents, Michelle Archer (Film & Television only), Jessica Cooper, Kenneth Ewing, Gemma Hirst, Nicki Stoddart

Insider Info Will consider all genres of work. Prefers to receive exclusive submissions. Commission rates of 10 per cent for domestic sales, and 20 per cent for foreign sales.

Considers Titles in all genres.

Submission Guidelines Send query letter, SAE, synopsis, two to three sample chapters and author biography. Submission should be double-spaced, on single-sided A4. Do not bind or staple. Include a brief CV.

Recent Sale(s) *Archibald Wavell: The Life and Times of An Imperial Servant*, Adrian Fort (Jonathan Cape); *Passion*, Lousie Bagshawe (Headline)

Client(s) Sandy Gall CBE, Mary Alexander, Paul Arnott, Hilaire Belloc (Estate), Michael Collins, Lucy Diamond, Rick Parfitt, Richard Pitman, Robery Uhlig, Ann Widdecombe, Barbara Vine, Clive James, Rt. Hon. William Hague MP

Tips PFD has a vast worldwide client list. Visit the website before submitting material, as submission details may vary.

Pollinger Ltd

9 Staple Inn, Holborn, London, WC1V 7QH
T 020 7404 0342
F 020 7242 5737
E info@pollingerltd.com
W www.pollingerltd.com

Contact Managing Director/Agent, Lesley Pollinger; Agents, Joanna Devereux, Tim Bates, Ruth Needham (Film & TV); Consultants, Leigh Pollinger, Joan Deitch

Established 1935

Insider Info Manuscripts will be returned with SAE. Clients usually obtained through queries/submissions. Commission rate of 15 per cent for domestic sales, 20 per cent for foreign sales. *The agency has always been a family business.

Considers Titles in all genres.

Submission Guidelines Authors should include query letter, SAE, synopsis, three sample chapters and biography with submissions, which should be in black type, double-spaced, on one-sided A4.

Recent Sale(s) *Billie Jo*, Kimberley Chambers (Random House)

Client(s) Max Allen, Peter Clover, Michael Coleman, Laura Denham, Teresa Driscoll, Jacqui Farley, Catherine Fisher, Helen Macgee, Anne Miller, Gareth Owen, Roger Forsdyke, Philip Cross, Bruce Hobson, Alan Wilkinson, Peter Walker, Mark Stay, Robert Sellers

Tips Manuscripts will not be accepted by email or fax.

Real Creatives Worldwide

14 Dean Street, London, W1D 3RS
T 020 7437 4188
E Malcolm.rasala@realcreatives.com

Contact Malcolm Rasala, Mark Maco

Established 1984

Insider Info Seeking established writers. Obtains new clients by queries or submissions. Does not charge a reading fee.

Considers General and Commercial Fiction titles.

Submission Guidelines Send query letter by post with SAE.

Tips Real Creatives Worldwide specializes in literature, film and television scripts. The initial contact should be to request a writer's submission agreement. The agency also has a production interest; see their website at: www.tvmyworld.com.

Redhammer Management Ltd

186 Bickenhall Mansions, London, W1U 6BX
T 020 7224 1748
F 020 7224 1802
E info@redhammer.info
W www.redhammer.info

Contact Managing Director, Peter Cox

Insider Info Seeking both new and established writers. Accept simultaneous submissions. Aims to respond to queries, proposals and manuscripts within six weeks. Proposals will be returned if accompanied by SAE. Obtains new clients by queries or submissions. Commission rates of 17.5 per cent for domestic sales and 20 per cent for foreign sales. Does not charge a reading fee.

Considers Action/Adventure, Children's Fiction, Erotica, Family Saga, Feminist, Gay/Lesbian, Historical, Horror, Humour/Satire, Literary, Mainstream, Mystery, Romance, Science-Fiction, Sports, Thriller, Women's and Young Adult Fiction titles.

Recent Sale(s) *The Joshua Files*, MG Harris (Scholastic Children's Books)

Client(s) Martin Bell, Nicholas Booth, Brian Clegg, Joe Donnelly, Amanda Lees, Michelle Paver, Carole Stone, Justin Wintle

Tips Redhammer Management accepts submissions from previously published writers only. A limited number of unpublished writers may be approached by the agency through Litopia Writers' Colony and internet writing community at www.litopia.com.

Robin Jones Literary Agency

6b Marmora Road, East Dulwich, London, SE22 0RX
T 020 8693 6062
E robinjones@gmail.com

Contact Robin Jones

Established 2008

Insider Info Actively seeking clients, both new and established authors. Commission rates of 15 per cent for domestic sales, 20 per cent for foreign sales, 15 per cent for film. Does not charge a reading fee. Specializes in personal contact, fast response and detailed feedback.

Considers Commercial and Literary Fiction titles.

Submission Guidelines Will accept unsolicited material. Send query letter with SAE, synopsis and three sample chapters.

Client(s) John Parkin, Fred Nath, Sara Mendes da Costa, Ashley Stokes, Geoffrey Newsome, Paul Lyons

Tips Does offer a criticism service. Robin has worked at four literary agencies, been an international literary scout for seven years, and an editorial consultant for five. Very keen on ideas and philosophy, thrillers, journalism and zeitgeist books, history, biography and autobiography.

Robinson Literary Agency

Block A511, The Jam Factory, 27 Green Walk, London, SE1 4TT
T 020 7096 1460
F 020 7243 6326
E info@rlabooks.co.uk

Contact Managing Director, Peter Robinson

Established 2005

Insider Info Seeking both new and established writers. Commission rates vary for domestic sales and are 20 per cent for foreign sales. Does not charge a reading fee.

Considers General Mainstream/Contemporary Fiction titles.

Submission Guidelines Send query letter with SAE.

Tips Robinson Literary Agency will suggest revisions for any submitted work.

Rogers, Coleridge & White Ltd

20 Powis Mews, London, W11 1JN
T 020 7221 3717
F 020 7229 9084
E info@rcwlitagency.co.uk
W www.rcwlitagency.co.uk

Contact Deborah Rogers (Illustrated, Children's); Gill Coleridge (Illustrated, Children's); Pat White Illustrated, Children's); Peter Straus (Fiction, Biography, Current Affairs, Narrative, History); David Miller (Fiction, Biography, Current Affairs, Narrative, History); Zoe Waldie (Fiction, Biography, Current Affairs, Narrative, History); Catherine Pellegrino (Children's, Young Adult); Hannah Westland (Debut Fiction, Non-Fiction); Laurence Laluyaux (Foreign Rights)

Established 1987

Insider Info Seeking both new and established writers. Aims to respond to queries and proposals within eight weeks. Proposals will be returned if accompanied by SAE. Obtains new clients by recommendation, conference and queries or submissions. Commission rates of 15 per cent for domestic sales and 20 per cent for foreign sales. *Prior to opening the agency Deborah Rogers was an agent and also working in publishing. Gill Coleridge worked at Anthony Sheil Associates and is also President of the Association of Author's Agents. Pat White was an editor and rights director for Simon & Schuster. Peter Straus worked at Hodder & Stroughton, Hamish Hamilton and Macmillan.

Considers Titles in most categories of Fiction.

Submission Guidelines Send proposal package with SAE, synopsis, three sample chapters and author biography.

Recent Sale(s) *The Suspicions of Mr Whicher*, Kate Summerscale (Bloomsbury); *Netherland*, Joseph O'Neill (Fourth Estate); *The Bolter*, Frances Osbourne (Little, Brown)

Tips Rogers, Coleridge & White does not accept submissions by fax or email.

Rupert Heath Literary Agency

E emailagency@rupertheath.com
W www.rupertheath.com

Contact Rupert Heath

Established 2000

Insider Info Actively seeking clients. Accepts simultaneous submissions. Proposals will be returned if accompanied by SAE. Obtains new clients by queries or submissions. Commission rates of 15 per cent for domestic sales and 20 per cent for foreign sales. Does not charge a reading fee.

Considers General Mainstream/Contemporary Fiction titles.

Submission Guidelines Send query letter with SAE and one sample chapter by email.

Tips Rupert Heath prefers to receive submissions by email.

Scott Ferris Associates

Brynfield, Reynoldston, Swansea, SA3 1AE
T 01792 390009
E scottferris@macunlimited.net

Contact Gloria Ferris, Rivers Scott

Established 1981

Insider Info Commission rates of 15 per cent for domestic sales and 20 per cent for foreign sales. Charges an arranged reading fee.

Considers General Fiction titles.

Submission Guidelines Send query letter with SAE.

Tips Scott Ferris does not accept unsolicited manuscripts.

Seven Towers

4 St Mura's Terrace, Strangford Road, East Wall, Dublin 3, Republic of Ireland
E info@seventowers.ie
W www.seventowers.ie

Contact Directors, Sarah Lundberg and Colm Lundberg

Insider Info No unsolicited manuscripts. Catalogue available online.

Considers Children's and Adult Fiction titles, as well as Graphic works.

Submission Guidelines Accepts proposal package (including outline, synopsis and three sample chapters).

Client(s) Oran Ryan, Ross Hattaway, Conor Farrell, Noel Ó Briain

Tips Seven Towers is also a small press and publishes limited editions of works of merit, where Seven Towers does not act as agent to the author, for instance works which may have specified areas of interest but which deserve publication, as well as some collections of poetry and short stories to help showcase new writers.

Sheil Land Associates Ltd

(incorporating Richard Scott Simon Ltd 1971 and Christy & Moore Ltd 1912)

52 Doughty Street, London, WC1N 2LS
T 020 7405 9351
F 020 7831 2127
E info@sheilland.co.uk
W www.sheilland.co.uk

Contact Agents UK & US, Sonia Land, Vivien Green, Piers Blofeld, Ian Drury; Film/Theatre/TV, Sophie Janson, Lucy Fawcett; Foreign, Gaia Banks, Emily Dyson

Established 1962

Insider Info Proposals will be returned if accompanied by SAE. Obtains new clients by queries or submissions. Commission rates of 15 per cent for domestic sales and 20 per cent for foreign sales. Does not charge a reading fee.

Considers Literary and Commercial Fiction, Crime/Thrillers, Drama, Humour, Romance, Science-Fiction and Fantasy titles.

Submission Guidelines Send proposal package with SAE, synopsis, two to three sample chapters and author biography. No children's titles considered.

Client(s) Peter Ackroyd, Benedict Allen, Charles Allen, Pam Ayres, Melvyn Bragg, Steven Carroll, David Cohen, Anna del Conte, Judy Corbalis, Elizabeth Corley, Seamus Deane, Greg Dyke, Rosie Goodwin, Chris Ewan, Jean Goodhind, Robert Green, Susan Hill, Richard Holmes, HRH The Prince of Wales, Ian Johnstone, Irene Karafilly, Richard Mabey, Graham Rice, Robert Rigby, Steve Rider, Martin Riley, Diane Setterfield, Tom Sharpe, Martin Stephen, Jeffrey Tayler, Andrew Taylor, Rose Tremain, Barry Unsworth, Kevin Wells, Prof. Stanley Wells, Neil White, John Wilsher, Paul Wilson and the Estates of Catherine Cookson, Patrick O'Brian, Penelope Mortimer, Jean Rhys, FA Wesley

Tips Sheil Land Associates welcomes new writers and aims to help in the development of their careers.

Shelley Power Literary Agency

✉ 13 rue du Pré Saint-Gervais, 75019 Paris, France
☎ T 0033 1 42 38 36 49
F 0033 1 40 40 70 08
✎ E shelley.power@wanadoo.fr

Contact Shelley Power

Established 1977

Insider Info Seeking both new and established writers. Currently represents 25 clients. Does not accept simultaneous submissions. Aims to respond to queries and proposals within one week and manuscripts within three weeks. Proposals will be returned if accompanied by SAE. Obtains new clients by recommendation and by queries or submissions. Commission

rates of 12.5 per cent for domestic sales, 20 per cent for foreign sales and 20 per cent for film sales. Offers an open-ended written contract with 60 days notice for termination. Does not charge a reading fee.

Considers Crime, Family Saga, Feminist, Glitz, Historical, Literary, Mainstream, Thriller and Women's/Chick Lit Fiction titles.

Submission Guidelines Send query letter with SAE, outline, three sample chapters and author biography by email. No children's books, science-fiction or fantasy considered.

Tips Shelley Power is a British agent who lives in, and therefore works from, Paris. She represents English-language authors only.

Shirley Stewart Literary Agency

✉ 3rd Floor, 21 Denmark Street, London, WC2H 8NA
☎ T 020 7836 4440
F 020 7836 3482

Contact Director, Shirley Stewart (Literary)

Established 1993

Insider Info Actively seeking clients. Proposals will be returned if accompanied by SAE. Obtains new clients by queries or submissions. Commission rates of 10–15 per cent for domestic sales and 20 per cent for foreign sales. Does not charge a reading fee.

Considers Literary Fiction titles.

Submission Guidelines Send query letter with SAE, synopsis and three sample chapters. No science-fiction, fantasy or children's titles.

Tips Shirley Stewart Literary Agency does not accept submissions by fax or on disk.

Sinclair-Stevenson

✉ 3 South Terrace, London, SW7 2TB
☎ T 020 7581 2550
F 020 7581 2550

Contact Directors, Christopher Sinclair-Stevenson and Deborah Sinclair-Stevenson

Established 1995

Insider Info Seeking both new and established writers. Accepts simultaneous submissions. Proposals will be returned if accompanied by SAE. Obtains new clients by queries or submissions. Commission rates of 10 per cent for domestic sales and 15 per cent for foreign sales. Does not charge a reading fee.

Considers General Fiction titles.

Submission Guidelines Send query letter with SAE and synopsis. No science-fiction, fantasy or children's titles.

Tips Sinclair-Stevenson also handles estates, and will suggest revisions on authorized submissions.

Sunflower Literary Agency

BP 14, Lauzerte, 82110, France
E submission@sunflowerliteraryagency.com
W www.aaraulit.com

Contact David Sherriff (Submissions and Correspondence); Senior Editor and Agent, Phillip Adams (Action, Psychological and Techno Thrillers), Miss Stone (Literary Novels and Social Satire)

Established 2003

Insider Info Seeking new writers. Does not accept simultaneous submissions. Proposals will be returned if accompanied by SAE. Obtains new clients by queries or submissions. Commission rates are variable.

Considers Crime, Erotic, Literary, Thriller, Psychological/Techno Thrillers, Satirical and Social Satire Fiction titles.

Submission Guidelines Send a brief query by email, conforming to the guidelines on the website. No romance, 'whodunit', or spirit-world titles considered.

Tips See website for submissions process, as the agency has very strict submission rules. Sunflower is only interested in new authors, or established authors who are changing genre. The agency does not accept unsolicited manuscripts and is usually closed to all submissions in January and February.

The Susijn Agency Ltd

3rd Floor, 64 Great Titchfield Street, London, W1W 7QH
T 020 7580 6341
F 020 7580 8626
E info@thesusijnagency.com
W www.thesusijnagency.com

Contact Founder and Agent, Laura Susijn; Agent, Nicola Barr

Established 1998

Insider Info Actively seeking clients. Aims to respond to queries and proposals within eight weeks. Proposals will be returned if accompanied by SAE. Obtains new clients by queries or submissions. Commission rates of 15 per cent for domestic sales, 20 per cent for foreign sales and 15 per cent for film sales. Does not charge a reading fee.

Considers Literary Fiction titles.

Submission Guidelines Send proposal package with SAE, synopsis and two sample chapters. No romance, sagas, science-fiction, fantasy, children's or illustrated titles.

Client(s) Peter Ackroyd, Robin Baker, Jon Butler & Bruno Vincent, Gwynne Dyer, Travis Elborough, Bi Feiyu, Radhika Jha, Kluun, Kolton Lee, Christine Leunens, Yan Lianke, Tessa De Loo, Karel van Loon, Jeffrey Moore, Tor Norretranders, Mineke Schipper, Rowan Simons, Paul Sussman, Shimon Tzabar, Dubravka Ugresic, Alex Wheatle, Simone van der Vlugt, Henk Van Woerden, Adam Zameenzad

Tips The Susijn Agency are specialists in English- and foreign-language world rights and are interested in authors from various cultures with cross-cultural themes. Does not accept submissions by email, but include an email address with manuscripts for a quick reply.

Tamar Karet Literary Agency

56 Priory Road, London, N8 7EX
T 020 8340 6460
E tamar.karet.agent@btinternet.com

Contact Tamar Karet

Insider Info Actively seeking clients. Accepts simultaneous submissions. Proposal will be returned if accompanied by SAE. Obtains new clients by queries or submissions. Commission rates of 15 per cent for domestic sales and 20 per cent for foreign sales.

Considers Literary Fiction titles.

Submission Guidelines Send proposals package with SAE, synopsis, and two to three sample chapters. No science-fiction, academia, horror, military or children's titles considered.

Tips Tamar Karat does not accept submissions by email, but include an email address with manuscripts for a quick reply.

Tanja Howarth Literary Agency

✉ 19 New Row, London, WC2N 4LA
☎ T 020 7240 5553
F 020 7379 0969
✎ E tanja.howarth@btinternet.com

Established 1970

Insider Info Actively seeking clients. Accepts simultaneous submissions. Proposals will be returned if accompanied by SAE. Commission rates of 15 per cent for domestic sales, and 20 per cent for foreign sales. Does not charge a reading fee.

Considers General Fiction titles.

Submission Guidelines Send query letter with SAE. No children's titles considered.

Tips Tanja Howarth Literary Agency specializes in German translation rights. Does not accept unsolicited manuscripts.

Teresa Chris Literary Agency

✉ 43 Musard Road, London, W6 8NR
☎ T 020 7386 0633

Contact Director, Teresa Chris

Established 1988

Insider Info Actively seeking clients. Accepts simultaneous submissions. Proposals will be returned if accompanied by SAE. Obtains new clients by queries or submissions. Commission rates of 10 per cent for domestic sales and 20

per cent for foreign sales. Does not charge a reading fee.

Considers Crime, Literary and Women's/Chick Lit Fiction titles.

Submission Guidelines Send query letter with SAE, synopsis, and two to three sample chapters. No genre fiction considered.

Tips Teresa Chris Literary Agency welcomes unsolicited proposals.

Toby Eady Associated

✉ 3rd Floor, 9 Orme Court, London, W2 4RL
☎ T 020 7792 0092
F 020 7792 0879
✎ E zaria@tobyeady.demon.co.uk
W www.tobyeadyassociates.co.uk

Contact Managing Director, Toby Eady; Directors, Sama Hammam and Jamie Coleman; Assistant, Pamela Hunt

Established 1968

Insider Info Seeking both new and established writers. Proposals will be returned if accompanied by SAE. Obtains new clients from recommendation, conferences and queries or submissions. Commission rates of 15 per cent for domestic sales and 20 per cent for film/scripts and foreign sales. Written contract is offered, with three months notice required for termination. *Representatives attend the City Literature Writer's Festival in Winchester.

Considers Action/Adventure, Confessional, Historical, Literary, Mainstream and Contemporary Fiction titles.

Submission Guidelines Send proposal package with SAE, outline, synopsis, short author biography and 50 sample pages. No children's books considered.

Recent Sale(s) *Sword Song,* Bernard Cornwell (HarperCollins)

Client(s) Bernard Cornwell, Chris Cleave, Rana Dasgupta, Julia Lovell, Rachel Sieffert

Tips Top-quality research is essential in any submitted material.

UKUnpublished

11a Spa Road, Hockley, Essex, SS5 4AZ
T 01702 204636
E info@ukunpublished.co.uk
W www.ukunpublished.co.uk

Contact Proprietor, David Buttle

Insider Info UKUnpublished is a publisher/agent looking to offer the benefits of both traditional and self-publishing – full publishing, printing, and distribution throughout the UK and the US, but paying up to 44 per cent higher royalties. Editing/proofreading services are not available. Will publish all categories of books, from Children's Fiction to Adult/Erotica, and Technical Non-Fiction to Cookery. Aims to respond to queries and manuscripts within six weeks, however this is considered to be an outside timescale. Visit the website to find out more about the service, or email/write/fax to request a brochure. Prefers to deal directly with the author, instead of through an agent.

Considers Titles in all Fiction genres, including Children's, Adult and Short Story Collections.

Submission Guidelines Visit the website to find out full details about the service and the company, and email David Buttle directly to ask any questions you may have.

Tips UKUnpublished is dedicated to giving as many authors as possible an outlet, to 'let the world share your imagination', while providing a quality and personal service. UKUnpublished also offers accounting and tax services provided by qualified accountants, ensuring that you can concentrate on writing. All royalties are paid regularly.

Uli Rushby-Smith Literary Agency

72 Plimsoll Road, London, WN4 2EE
T 020 7354 2718
F 020 7354 2718

Contact Uli Rushby-Smith

Established 1993

Insider Info Seeking both new and established writers. Will consider simultaneous submissions. Proposals will be returned if accompanied by SAE. Commission rates of 15 per cent for domestic sales and 20 per cent for foreign sales. Does not charge a reading fee.

Considers Literary, General and Commercial Fiction titles.

Submission Guidelines Send query letter with SAE, outline and two to three sample chapters.

Tips Uli Rushby-Smith does not accept submissions on disk.

United Agents

12–26 Lexington Street, London, W1F 0LE
T 020 3214 0800
F 020 3214 0801
E info@unitedagents.co.uk
W www.unitedagents.co.uk

Contact Chair, Lindy Kin; Managing Director, St John Donald; Head of Books, Caroline Dawnay and Simon Trewin; Agents (Books), Robert Kirby, Charles Walker, Rosemary Canter, Rosemary Scoular, James Gill, Anna Webber, Sarah Ballard, Jessica Craig (Adult Foreign Rights) and Jane Willis (Children's Foreign Rights); Agents (Theatre, Film & Television), Hannah Begbie, Duncan Millership, Olivia Homan, Dallas Smith, Lindy King, Maureen Vincent, Ruth Young, Lisa Toogood, Duncan Hayes, Kirk Whelan-Foran

Insider Info Currently handles non-fiction books, novels, television scripts and film scripts. Aims to respond to proposals within four to six weeks. Submission guidelines available online.

Considers Titles in all genres.

Submission Guidelines For books send proposal package (including synopsis, two to three sample chapters and author biography) by email. Submission details to: looking@unitedagents.co.uk

Client(s) Nick Hornby, Anthon Horowitz, John Boyne, Julian Barnes, Justin Cartwright, Scarlett Thomas, Joanna Trollope, Ruth Rendell, Nicki French, Ewan MacGregor, Keira Knightly

Tips UA receives over 200 submissions per week from all areas and responds only to those of interest. Note that they have very detailed submission guidelines on their website, covering each of their departments.

United Authors Ltd

11–15 Betterton Street, London, WC2H 9BP

T 020 7470 8886
F 020 7470 8887
E editorial@unitedauthors.co.uk

Established 1998

Insider Info Seeking both new and established writers. Will consider simultaneous submissions. Proposals will be returned if accompanied by SAE. Obtains new clients by queries or submissions. Commission rates of 12 per cent for domestic sales, 20 per cent for foreign sales and 15–20 per cent for film (and radio) sales. Does not charge a reading fee.

Considers General Fiction Novels and Children's Fiction titles.

Submission Guidelines Send query letter with SAE.

Client(s) Terence Brady, Peter Willet, Charlotte Bingham, the estate of John Bingham

Tips Will suggest revision on any solicited manuscripts.

Vanessa Holt Ltd

59 Crescent Road, Leigh on Sea, Essex, SS9 2PF

T 01702 473787
F 01702 471890
E vanessa@holtlimited.freeserve.co.uk

Contact Director, Vanessa Holt

Established 1989

Insider Info Actively seeking clients. Will consider simultaneous submissions. Proposals will be returned if accompanied by SAE. Obtains new clients by queries or submissions. Commission rates of 15 per cent for domestic sales, 20 per cent for foreign sales and 15 per cent for film sales. Does not charge a reading fee.

Considers Crime, Children's, Literary, Young Adult and General Fiction titles.

Submission Guidelines Send query letter with SAE. No children's illustrated books considered.

Tips Vanessa Holt is interested in books with potential film, television or radio tie-ins. Does not accept unsolicited manuscripts.

Wade & Doherty Literary Agency Ltd

33 Cormorant Lodge, Thomas More Street, London, E1W 1AU

T 020 7488 4171
F 020 7488 4172
E rw@rwla.com
W www.rwla.com

Contact Robin Wade (General Fiction, Non-Fiction and Children's Books); Broo Doherty (General Fiction, Non-fiction, Commercial Women's Fiction and Crime Novels)

Established 2001

Insider Info Actively seeking clients. Currently represents around 30 clients, half of whom are new or previously unpublished writers. Will consider simultaneous submissions. Aims to respond to queries and proposals within seven days and manuscripts within 30 days. Proposals returned if accompanied by SAE. Obtains new clients by recommendation, conferences and queries or submissions. Commission rates of 10 per cent for domestic sales, 20 per cent for foreign sales and 20 per cent for film sales. Written contract offered for extent of publishing, with 30 days notice required for termination. Does not charge a reading fee and does not offer a criticism service. *Attends the annual Crime Writers Association conference in Harrogate, and the Romantic Novelists Association conference in London.

Considers Action/Adventure, Confessional, Crime, Erotica, Ethnic, Experimental, Family Saga, Fantasy, Feminist, Gay/Lesbian, Glitz, Historical, Horror, Humour, Children's, Literary, Mainstream, Mystery, Regional, Religion, Romance, Science-Fiction, Sports, Supernatural, Thriller, Women's/Chick Lit, and Young Adult Fiction titles.

Submission Guidelines Send proposal package with synopsis, author biography and first 10,000 words of sample material, by email or post.

Recent Sale(s) *Dragon Horse*, Peter Ward (Doubleday); *The Secret of Excalibur*, Andy McDermott (Headline)

Client(s) Philippa Ashley, Marion Husband, Caroline Kington, Ray Connolly, Georgina Harding, Helen Oyeyemi, Lance Price, Rachel Trezise, Caroline Carver, Angela Dracup, Steve

Hague, Eve Isherwood, Andy McDermott, Paul Johnston, Louise Cooper, Kimberly Green, Adam Guillain, Steve Alton, Andrea Shavick, Peter Ward, Sameen Ali, Alison Bruce, Steuart Campbell, Sheila Hardy, Neil Hegarty, Brenda James, Prof. WD Rubinstein, Mike Newlands, Lance Price, Ewen Southby-Tailyour, Ayowa Taylor

Watson, Little Ltd

48–56 Bayham Place, London, NW1 0EU
T 020 7388 7529
F 020 7388 8501
E office@watsonlittle.com
W www.watsonlittle.com

Contact Managing Director, Mandy Little; Senior Agent, James Wills

Insider Info Actively seeking clients. Will consider simultaneous submissions. Proposals returned if accompanied by SAE. Obtains new clients by queries or submissions. Commission rates of 15 per cent for domestic sales, 20 per cent for foreign sales and 15 per cent for film sales. Overseas Associates are The Marsh Agency Ltd; Film & TV Associates are The Sharland Organisation Ltd and MBA Literary Agents Ltd; USA Associates are Howard Morhaim Literary Agency (Adult) and The Chudney Organisation (Children's). Does not charge a reading fee.

Considers Women's Fiction, Crime, Children's and Literary Fiction titles.

Submission Guidelines Send query letter with SAE and synopsis.

Recent Sale(s) *Football Dynamo*, Marc Bennetts (Virgin); *Shooting the Moon*, VM Jones (Anderson Press)

Client(s) Helen Armstrong, Adrian Bloom, Robin Cohen, Mark Hanson, Deborah Jaffe, Michael Jordan, Alice Muir, Ian Palmer, Mark Ronan, Rosie Swale, Edward Craig, Robert Giddings, Mukul Patel, Stewart Ross, Wayne Talbot, Henning Wehn, Duncan Cameron, Nicola Hill, Ann Kramer, Karen Saunders, Jane Wright

Tips Watson, Little does not accept email queries or full-length unsolicited manuscripts. The agency also represents illustrators.

The Whispering Buffalo Literary Agency Ltd

97 Chesson Road, London, W14 9QS
T 020 7565 4737
E info@whisperingbuffalo.com
W www.whisperingbuffalo.com

Contact Mariam Keen

Established 2008

Insider Info Actively seeking clients. Commission rates of 12.5 per cent for domestic sales, 20 per cent for foreign sales and film rights. Does not charge a reading fee.

Considers Commercial/Literary, Children's and Young Adult Fiction titles.

Submission Guidelines Accepts query letter with synopsis, three sample chapters and SAE to ensure return of hardcopy material. Pages should be double-spaced, single-sided and A4.

Tips The agency provides a high level of personal representation and also handles merchandising.

William Morris Agency (UK) Ltd

Centre Point, 103 New Oxford Street, London, WC1A 1DD
T 020 7534 6800
F 020 7534 6900
W www.wma.com

Contact CEO, Jim Wiatt; Chairman, Norman Brokaw

Established 1965

Insider Info Seeking both new and established writers. Will consider simultaneous submissions. Proposals returned if accompanied by SAE. Obtains new clients by queries or submissions. Commission rates of 15 per cent for domestic sales, 20 per cent for foreign sales, and 10 per cent for film sales. Does not charge a reading fee.

Considers Novels and General Fiction titles.

Submission Guidelines Send query letter with SAE, synopsis and up to 50 sample pages.

Tips William Morris has worldwide offices and represents both entertainment talent and literary clients.

The Wylie Agency (UK) Ltd

✉ 17 Bedford Square, London, WC1B 3JA
☎ T 020 7908 5900
F 020 7908 5901
✎ E mail@wylieagency.co.uk
W www.wylieagency.com

Contact President, Andrew Wylie

Established 1996

Insider Info Currently handles novels. Considers simultaneous submissions. Proposals returned if accompanied by SAE. Obtains new clients by queries or submissions. Commission rates of ten per cent for domestic sales, and between 15 and 20 per cent for foreign sales. Does not charge a reading fee.

Considers Novels and General Fiction titles.

Submission Guidelines Send query letter with SAE, or query by email. No children's fiction considered.

Client(s) Chinua Achebe, Ken Adam, Chimamanda N Adichie, Arthur Allen, Martin Amis, Laurie Anderson, Matt Bai, Philip Bobbitt, Patricia Bosworth, Paul Collier, Ian Frazier, Al Gore, Tipper Gore, Dennis Hopper, Michael Kantor, Annie Leibovitz, Norman Mailer, Jon McGregor, Louis Menand, Miyuki Miyabe, Thom Mount, Michael O'Brien, Paul Preston, Lou Reed, Salman Rushdie, Jeffrey D Sachs, Robert Schlesinger

Tips The Wylie Agency does not accept unsolicited manuscripts.

LITERARY CONSULTANTS & EDITORIAL SERVICES

Adventures in Fiction

14 Grosvenor Avenue, London, N5 2NR
T 020 7354 2598
E enquiries@adventuresinfiction.co.uk
W www.adventuresinfiction.co.uk

A consultancy that works with writers at all stages in their careers, offering appraisal services for individual manuscripts, as well as a range of ongoing 'mentoring' programmes.

Anne Barclay Enterprises

The Old Farmhouse, Hexworthy, Yelverton, Devon, PL20 6SD
T 01626 208011

Provides editorial services to both published and unpublished authors. Packages include ghost writing, editing, copyediting and assessment of manuscripts.

Chapter One Promotions

Canterbury Court, 1–3 Brixton Road, London, SW9 6DE
T 0845 456 5364
E info@chapteronepromotions.com
W www.chapteronepromotions.com

Chapter One Promotions runs annual short story, poetry and novel competitions, plus children's story and young illustrator's competitions. They provide creative workshops and literary events as well as a critique and proofreading service.

College-on-the-Net

81 Warwick Road, Sutton, Surrey, SM1 4BL
T 020 8642 1063
E Online form
W www.jml.college-on-the-net.co.uk

Mainly offers tutorial courses on a wide range of subjects but also offers an author's appraisal service, where specialists will provide various levels of critique on a manuscript. Clients may use the service as an ongoing course, or as a one off.

Cornerstones

Milk Studios, 34 Southern Row, London, W10 5AN
T 020 8968 0777
E kathryn@cornerstones.co.uk
W www.cornerstones.co.uk

Contact Director, Helen Corner; Managing Editor, Kathryn Robinson

Cornerstones offers a manuscript assessment and advisory service for both children's and adult fiction. They also scout for literary agencies such as Annette Green, Conville & Walsh, LAW, United Agents and others. Authors are asked to ring or email with a query before submitting their complete manuscript.

The Cutting Edge

Archery House, 33 Archery Square, Walmer, Deal, Kent, CT14 7JA
T 01304 371721
F 01304 371416
E jmthurley@aol.com
W www.thecuttingedge.biz

The Cutting Edge offers many services, including manuscript assessment, editorial input, constructive criticism and creative advice, re-writing, presentation for the market, and contractual and business advice. Authors are asked to submit a hardcopy of their completed manuscript along with a cheque for the fees.

Daniel Goldsmith Associates

Unit 17, Percival Lane, Runcorn, Cheshire,
WA7 4UX
T 01928 796576
E lorena@danielgoldsmith.co.uk
W www.danielgoldsmith.co.uk

Book editors and literary consultants.
Assessment reports from £125. Market
assessment for foreign published authors.
Free submission and recommendation to agents
and publishers.

Fish Publishing

Durras, Bantry, Co. Cork, Republic of Ireland
E info@fishpublishing.com
W www.fishpublishing.com

Fish Publishing runs the annual Fish Short
Story Prize with prizes from €300 to €3000.
They also provide a full editorial consultancy
service designed to provide writers with one-
on-one, ongoing, constructive feedback on
their work, whether it is a complete novel or
a proposal package.

The Hilary Johnson Author's Advisory Service

1 Beechwood Court, Syderstone, Norfolk,
PE31 8TR
T 01485 578954
E enquiries@hilaryjohnson.com
W www.hilaryjohnson.com

Offers professional appraisals of authors' novels.
General writing-related advice also given. Also
acts as a scout for a well-known literary agency.

Jan Henley Manuscript Appraisal Service

E jan.henley1@gmail.com
W www.janhenley.co.uk

Published writer Jan Henley (also writing as
Anna Cheska and Juliet Hall) offers a personal
manuscript appraisal service, with links to a
leading literary agent.

Leda Sammarco

E info@ledasammarco.com
W www.ledasammarco.com

Leda Sammarco provides coaching services for
writers at every stage, from the creative process
all the way through to publication.

Linda Acaster

E lindaacaster@yahoo.co.uk
W www.lindaacaster.blogspot.com

In-depth critique of fiction offered by a
published novelist and short story writer,
and former tutor at the Arvon Foundation
and the Open College of Arts.

The Literary Consultancy

Free Word Centre, 60 Farringdon Road,
London, EC1R 3GA
T 020 7324 2563
E info@literaryconsultancy.co.uk
W www.literaryconsultancy.co.uk

Fiction is critiqued. They also scout for leading
agencies.

New Writers Consultancy

35a Lower Park Road, Brightlingsea, Colchester,
Essex, CO7 0JX
T 01206 303607
E submissions@new-writers-consultancy.com

Offers a variety of packages including appraisals,
critiques and editing. Services are provided by
Diana Hayden, an ex BBC worker, editor and
proofreader, and Karen Scott, a published author.
Submissions are accepted by post or email.

Oxford Literary Consultancy

191 The Slade, Headington, Oxford, OX3 7HR
T 01865 751004
E oxfordwriters@mac.com
W www.oxfordwriters.com

Offers manuscript assessment and editing,
proofreading, copy-editing and mentoring

services, as well as acting as a scout for leading literary agencies. They have had a number of previous successes in placing first-time writers with literary agents or publishers.

Reading and Righting

618b Finchley Road, London, NW11 7RR
T 020 8455 4564
E lambhorn@gmail.com
W www.readingandrighting.netfirms.com

A script/manuscript reading and assessment service, that also offers advice on agents and publishers. One-to-one follow-up tuition and mentoring can also be provided, as well as editing of complete manuscripts, websites and blogs. Other services include workshops and lectures.

Real Writers

PO Box 170, Chesterfield, Derbyshire, S40 1FE
E info@real-writers.com
W www.real-writers.com

Offers a manuscript appraisal service by correspondence or email, on either a one-off or an ongoing basis.

S Ribeiro, Literary Consultant

42 West Heath Court, North End Road, London, NW11 7RR
T 020 8458 9082
E sribeiroeditor@aol.com

Freelance services include copywriting and jacket information, editing to publication standards, and detailed manuscript appraisal. Works with writers, small presses and self-published writers.

StorytrackS

16 St Briac Way, Exmouth, Devon, EX8 5RN
T 01395 279659
E mail@margaretjames.com
W www.storytracks.net

Provides manuscript appraisal services. Also offers a ghost-writing service, can run workshops, and may act as a scout for a literary agency.

Susan Wallace

PO Box 95, Liverpool, L17 8WY
T 0844 330 8023
E susanwallace@blueyonder.co.uk
W www.noveleditingservices.com

Journalist and writer. Provides authors with sensitive but stern editing, copy-editing and proofreading to help lift and crystallize manuscripts with a significant, professional polish. Understanding, confidential, thorough and loyal; aims to help bring your work to fruition. Fee for entire manuscript agreed after a test example. Fast turnaround available.

The Writers' Workshop

7 Market Street, Charlbury, Oxfordshire, OX7 3PH
T 0845 459 9560
E info@writersworkshop.co.uk
W www.writersworkshop.co.uk

The team will appraise manuscripts and produce reports, as well as entering into dialogue over the findings of the appraisal. The editors are a team of published writers, most of whom have taught creative writing at university level and/or have won or been shortlisted for major literary awards. They can also provide help in finding agents. Check the website to view their credentials.

The Writing Coach

E Online form
W www.thewritingcoach.co.uk

Run by published novelist Jacqui Lofthouse. Can provide either a reader's report or a full critique.

Writing Literary Consultants

E Online form
W www.writing.co.uk

Provides a range of services from assisting with submissions to publishers, to manuscript appraisals. They also act as scouts for leading literary agents.

USEFUL ORGANIZATIONS

Booktrust

✉ Book House, 45 East Hill, London, SW18 2QZ
☎ T 020 8516 2977
   F 020 8516 2978
   E query@booktrust.org.uk
✎ W www.booktrust.org.uk

Contact Chief Executive, Viv Bird

Booktrust is an independent national charity that encourages people of all ages and cultures to engage with books and the written word. It administers seven book prizes, including the Orange Prize for Fiction. It has many ongoing projects that promote reading, including the Children's Laureate.

The British Fantasy Society

✎ W www.britishfantasysociety.org.uk

Contact President, Ramsey Campbell; Chair, Guy Adams

The British Fantasy Society exists to promote the genres of fantasy, science-fiction and horror in all their forms. It has an active and enthusiastic membership, and runs a number of well-respected awards.

Centerprise Literature Development Project

✉ 136–138 Kingsland High Street, London, E8 2NS
☎ T 020 7254 9632
   E literature@centerprisetrust.org.uk
✎ W www.centerprisetrust.org.uk

Contact Administrator, Susan Yearwood

Centerprise Literature is an arts development agency for the promotion of access to, and enjoyment of, literature in all its forms, through local and community-based initiatives. Centerprise Literature services North and North East London with two parallel programmes of work. Its core programme focuses on providing a through-line of support of writers by offering courses, specialist groups, and one-on-one support. Their magazine, *Calabash*, has a high reputation, focusing on Black and Asian literature. They also run the Hackney Word Festival.

The Crime Writers' Association

☎ T 07780 693144 (press only)
   E info@thecwa.co.uk
✎ W www.thecwa.co.uk

Contact Chair, Lesley Horton; Membership Secretary, Rebecca Tope

The Crime Writers' Association has over 450 members. The minimum qualification for membership is to have at least one published book with a crime theme. The CWA is best known for its various 'Dagger' awards for crime fiction.

Historical Novel Society

   E Online form
✎ W www.historicalnovelsociety.org

Contact Founder/Publisher, Richard Lee

The Historical Novel Society promotes all aspects of historical fiction. It provides support and opportunities for new writers, information for students, booksellers and librarians, as well as a community for authors, readers, agents and publishers. The society publishes the quarterly *Historical Novels Review* magazine.

The Horror Writers Association UK

   E hwa@horror.org
✎ W www.horror.org/uk

The Horror Writers Association UK is the UK chapter of the Horror Writers Association, a worldwide organization of writers and publishing professionals. The HWA is dedicated to the pursuit of professional conduct within the industry, and to creating quality horror literature. Please note that the email contact given is to the HWA central US site.

The Irish Writers' Union

19 Parnell Square, Dublin 1, Republic of Ireland
T 00353 1 872 1302
E iwu@ireland-writers.com
W www.ireland-writers.com

Contact Chair, Helen Dwyer; Secretary, Brid Quinn

The Irish Writers' Union represents the interests of all Irish writers, whether they were born in Ireland or elsewhere. Writers who are Irish by attachment, inclination or persuasion are also welcome to join. The Union offers a model contract for guidance to members and assists in disputes if, or when, things go wrong. It also acts as a watchdog on both contract and royalty payments, for members or for their estate.

New Writing North

Holy Jesus Hospital, City Road,
Newcastle upon Tyne, NE1 2AS
T 0191 233 3850
F 0191 447 7686
E Online form
W www.newwritingnorth.com

New Writing North (NWN) is the writing development agency for the North East of England (the area covered by Arts Council England North East). It aims to create an environment in which new writing in all genres can flourish and develop. It merges individual development work from writers across all media, with educational work and the production of creative projects. It works with writers from different genres and forms to develop career opportunities, new commissions, projects, residencies, publications and live events. NWN manages the Northern Writers' Awards, and also aims to support writers at all stages of their careers through mentoring programmes and the creation of professional development training initiatives and projects.

New Writing South

9 Jew Street, Brighton, East Sussex, BN1 1UT
T 01273 735353
E Online form
W www.newwritingsouth.com

A writing organization open to all creative writers in the South East of England, and also for those seeking creative writers, and to other creative writing agencies, including all producers of dramatic writing. Sister organization of New Writing North.

Public Lending Right

Richard House, Sorbonne Close,
Stockton-on-Tees, TS17 6DA
T 01642 604699
F 01642 615641
W www.plr.uk.com

Under the United Kingdom's PLR Scheme authors receive payments from government funds for the free borrowing of their books from public libraries. To qualify for payment, authors must apply to register their books with the PLR organization. Payments are made annually on the basis of loans data collected from a sample of public libraries in the UK. All authors can benefit from this; indeed books that may not necessarily have been successes in the high street might earn pleasant fees from library borrowing over time. Most writers would be advised to register their titles for PLR.

The Royal Society of Literature

Somerset House, Strand, London, WC2R 1LA
T 020 7845 4676
E info@rslit.org
W www.rslit.org

Contact President, Michael Holroyd; Chair, Anne Chisholm

The Royal Society of Literature is entirely devoted to the promotion and enjoyment of excellence in British writing. Founded in 1820, past and present Fellows (who are elected) include some of the most eminent names in British literature. Membership is open to all. Regular meetings with speakers from the world of literature are held at Somerset House; and members of the public are welcome. The society also has major annual awards for both fiction and non-fiction. It supports the work of writers in many ways, including campaigning for libraries to remain providers of good books above all else, and to keep English literature at the heart of the learning curriculum.

Science Fiction Foundation

✉ 75 Rosslyn Avenue, Harold Wood, Essex, RM3 0RG
🔗 W www.sf-foundation.org

Contact Roger Robinson

The aim of the SFF is to promote science-fiction and bring together those who read, write, study, teach, research or archive science-fiction in Britain and the rest of the world. It also supports science-fiction at conventions, at conferences and at other events that bring those interested in science-fiction together. The four main objectives of the SFF are: to provide research facilities for anyone wishing to study science-fiction; to investigate and promote the usefulness of science-fiction in education; to disseminate information about science-fiction; and to promote a discriminating understanding of the nature of science-fiction. Its main activities include publication of the journal *Foundation: The International Review of Science Fiction*, and supporting the research library The Science Fiction Foundation Collection, at the University of Liverpool.

Scottish Book Trust

✉ Sandeman House, Trunk's Close, 55 High Street, Edinburgh, EH1 1SR
📞 T 0131 524 0160
F 0131 524 0161
🔗 E info@scottishbooktrust.com
W www.scottishbooktrust.com

Contact CEO Marc Lambert; General Manager, Jeanette Harris

Scottish Book Trust is Scotland's national agency for reading and writing. It promotes reading and books. Under its umbrella is Live Literature Scotland, a national initiative that enables Scottish citizens to engage with the nation's authors, playwrights, poets, storytellers and illustrators. It is the only writer bursary scheme of its kind in the UK, subsidizing the cost of 1,200 community visits by writers in all areas

of Scotland, and is extremely popular. More than 500 writers who are available to conduct readings and literary events in Scotland are listed and searchable on the SBT database.

Society for Storytelling

✉ PO Box 2344, Reading, RG6 7FG
📞 T 0118 935 1381
🔗 E Online form
W www.sfs.org.uk

Contact Chair, Martin Manasse; Treasurer, Administrator and Newsletter Editor, Tina Bilbé

The SfS is an open organization that welcomes anyone with an interest in oral storytelling. It aims to provide an information network for oral storytelling, stories, storytellers and storytelling clubs, and organizes storytelling events, such as storytelling festivals. The SfS publishes *Storylines* magazine and the quarterly *Directory of Storytellers*.

The Society of Authors

✉ 84 Drayton Gardens, London, SW10 9SB
📞 T 020 7373 6642
F 020 7373 5768
🔗 E info@societyofauthors.org
W www.societyofauthors.org

Contact Chair, Tracy Chevalier; General Secretary, Mark Le Fanu

The Society of Authors is a non-profit organization, founded to protect the rights and further the interests of authors. The society offers grants to previously published writers who are British by birth and under the age of 40, to benefit them in research and travel. The twice-yearly grants, awarded in April and September, are normally between £1,000 and £2,000 and rarely exceed £4,000. Authors must submit: a copy of their latest published book; a brief history of their writing career; details of their current work; size of advance (if any); names of publishers already approached or working with; overall financial position and why the grant is needed; details of past grants; confirmation of their eligibility to enter; and copies of past reviews (if any). Full application details are available on the website. See entries under Bursaries, Fellowships and Grants and Competitions and Prizes for more information. See the website for details of regional groups, including The Society of Authors, Scotland.

The Society of Authors, Scotland

(See The Society of Authors)

Society of Women Writers & Journalists

✉ c/o Secretary, Wendy Hughes, 14 Laburnum Walk, Rustington, West Sussex, BN16 3QW
🖉 W www.swwj.co.uk

Contact Chair, Jean Morris; Membership Secretary, Wendy Hughes

The UK's longest established organization for professional women writers. The aims of the SWWJ include the encouragement of literary achievement, the upholding of professional standards, and social contact with fellow writers and others in the field, including editors, publishers, broadcasters and agents. It is an international association and is affiliated to women's associations across the world. The society has been accepting male writers as associate members since 2004. See the website for regional contacts and activities. Many of the London meetings are held at The New Cavendish Club, 44 Great Cumberland Place, London W1.

Women Writers Network

✉ Venue: Conway Hall, 5 Red Lion Square, Holborn, London, WC1R 4RL
🖉 E info@womenwriters.org.uk

WWN is a networking group for professional women writers. Most are freelance, some are salaried, and together they represent a wide range of writing interests. WWN is not a writers' circle, but a group formed to help women further their professional development. The usual venue is Conway Hall, on the second Monday of every month – see the website for further details.

The Writer's Compass

✉ NAWE, PO Box 1, Sherrif Hutton, York, YO60 7YU
☎ T 0131 553 2210
E p.johnston@nawe.co.uk
🖉 W www.nawe.co.uk/the-writers-compass.html

Contact Director, Philippa Johnston

The Writer's Compass (formerly Literaturetraining) is the UK's only dedicated provider of free information and advice on professional development for the literature sector. It aims to help writers and literature professionals – at every stage of their career – to invest in themselves and their professional development, so that they can realize their full potential. Writers, and those involved in some way with creating or supporting new writing and literature, will find information on training and professional development opportunities on the website. If advice is needed on how to move forwards professionally, The Writer's Compass can offer various forms of help.

The Writers' Guild of Great Britain

✉ 40 Rosebery Avenue, London, EC1R 4RX
☎ T 020 7833 0777
F 020 7833 4777
🖉 E erik@writersguild.org.uk
W www.writersguild.org.uk

Contact President, David Edgar; Chair, Katharine Way; General Secretary, Bernie Corbett; Admin Assistant, Erik Pohl

The Writers' Guild of Great Britain is the trade union representing writers in television, radio, theatre, books, poetry, film and video games. In television, film, radio and theatre, the Guild is the recognized body for negotiating minimum terms and practice agreements for writers. It campaigns and lobbies on behalf of all writers, and is influential up to government level. Its voice is listened to and its views are respected. Any writer who has received payment under a contract in terms at or above the Writers' Guild minimum terms for at least one piece of work is entitled to become a full member.

ONLINE RESOURCES

Writer's Sites

ABC Writers Network

W www.abcwritersnetwork.co.uk

A free, international writer's forum, originating from Ireland.

All Books Review

W www.allbookreviews.com

A review site, largely for self-published books.

Ascriber/Writers Eyes

W www.writerseyes.org

A showcase site for unpublished or self-published writers. For a small fee you may display your work on the site, which the team claim to promote actively. The site also has sections for news, competitions and events, all of which are free to post in.

Ask About Writing

W www.askaboutwriting.net

A site containing information on writers' awards and competitions. There is also advice on aspects of writing, and advertisements for other services of use to writers.

Ask Oxford

W www.askoxford.com

A spin-off from the Oxford English Dictionary. Includes tips on spelling, grammar and producing better writing, as well as stories of interest from around the globe.

Authonomy.com

W www.authonomy.com

A peer review site, run by HarperCollins, where the top-rated authors for each month receive a free critique from a HarperCollins editor. Several authors have secured publishing deals through Authonomy.com.

Authorbank

W www.authorbank.com

Members can upload a synopsis to be viewed by publishers who are also registered. Publishers can then approach the writer through Authorbank, who can act as literary agents. Authorbank is currently offering this service free of charge to writers.

Author Network

W www.author-network.com

A site with articles, tips and resources for writers.

Author's Den

W www.authorsden.com

A free community site. Content includes book reviews, articles, e-books and more. Members get a free biography page.

Chapter One Promotions

W www.chapteronepromotions.com

A writer's site, which is also a literary agency and consultancy. Authors and illustrators may display their work on the site for a fee. There are details of events and competitions, as well as a section on resources for children.

Characterization Tool for Novelists

W www.synergise.com/p4

A process and tool, available for a fee, that helps novelists to create realistic characters quickly and intuitively based on accepted psychological types. Works both online and offline.

Classic Short Stories

W www.classicreader.com/short-stories.php

An online resource containing complete short stories from a wide range of authors spanning several centuries, including authors such as Honore de Balzac, Anton Chekhov, Edgar Allan Poe and many others.

East of the Web

W www.eastoftheweb.com/short-stories

East of the Web is a British site dedicated to new, previously unpublished fiction, as well as to classic short stories from well-known authors. Genres include children's, crime, general fiction, horror, humour, non-fiction, romance, science-fiction and hyperfiction. See the website for full submission details.

Freelance Writing Organization International

W www.fwointl.com

A Canadian-based members site, which is free to join. Contains many resources for writers, including forums, markets, research resources and more.

The Frontlist

W www.frontlist.com

A site where users can upload samples of their work, and in turn provide several critiques of others' work. Once the critiques have been done, their own work will be put up for critique. Pieces scoring above a certain threshold will be put forward to specialist editors and agents. The Friday Project has published recent high-scoring additions to this site in print. A £10 charge is made to view the critiques of your own work. You do not have to view them if you do not

wish to, but they will still be sent forward if they score highly enough.

Great Writing

W www.greatwriting.co.uk

Great Writing is a volunteer-run online community that was formed after the closure of the BBC's 'Get Writing' service. It is free to join and offers members a chance to submit their own writing to the site for peer review, as well as providing writing forums and chat areas, articles, news and the occasional competition.

Hackwriters

W www.hackwriters.com

A free internet magazine which accepts submissions of travel writing, fiction, lifestyle and social comment, but does not pay any fees.

Horror Writers UK

W www.horrorwriters.net

HorrorWriters.net was specially set up for all writers of horror fiction and screenplays. As well as giving writers the opportunity to post their work and receive valuable and constructive feedback, the site also features many other topics of interest relating to the whole craft of horror writing, such as book reviews, articles and much more. Membership is free.

JBWB Writing Competition

W www.jbwb.co.uk/writingcomps.htm

A detailed list of writing competitions, compiled by the Jacqui Bennett Writers Bureau.

National Novel Writing Month

W www.nanowrimo.com

US site that challenges people to write a 50,000 word novel between 1 and 30 November each year. If you make the deadline, you are a 'winner'. The idea is to encourage fast writing and not necessarily to focus on quality.

Novelists Inc

W www.ninc.com

US-based membership site with advice and practical help for fiction writers. Members' only sections include an agent guide and an email list.

NthPosition

W www.nthposition.com

A free online magazine/e-zine with politics and opinion, travel writing, fiction and poetry, reviews and interviews.

One of Us

W www.oneofus.co.uk

A resource site with articles, writing tips and a discussion forum. Free to access.

Preditors & Editors

W http://pred-ed.com

Preditors & Editors' sole purpose is to provide writers, artists, composers and game designers with information and contacts for the purpose of seeking publication of their work. P&E also maintains a 'Warnings' page, listing known scam artists, vanity publishers and literary fraudsters. They are always seeking information from writers who have been badly treated by agents, publishers or the like.

Prize Magic

W www.prizemagic.co.uk

A site that contains a useful directory of writing competitions and links to them.

Proof Positive Writing Contests

W www.proofpositive.com/contests/ writecontests.php

A US site advertising many writing contests, including those that are open to UK residents.

Pulp.net

W www.pulp.net

Pulp.net is a not-for-profit organization that aims to advance the art and practice of literature, promote the art of literature for the public benefit, and encourage greater participation in literature creation. Pulp.net functions in a similar way to a monthly e-zine, but also hosts a variety of talks, literary events and workshops at venues such as courses, writing conferences and festivals. Pulp.net accepts open submissions of short fiction and will publish as many as three new short stories per issue, from both established and first-time authors.

Reactive Writing

W www.reactivewriting.co.uk

A site dedicated to exploring creative writing on the internet.

Six Sentences

W www.sixsentences.blogspot.com

Six Sentences is a flash-fiction site where each story is told in six sentences. The editor publishes everything that is submitted, and usually publishes six new stories per day.

Slush Pile Reader

W www.slushpilereader.com

A site that showcases authors manuscripts to an audience of online readers. The readers vote upon whether or not the manuscript should be published, and give reviews and criticism. Slush Pile Reader will also publish the most popular submissions.

Trace

W http://tracearchive.ntu.ac.uk

A free online resource linked to Nottingham Trent University. Trace provides a space for writers to meet, communicate, discuss work and be creative. Also offered through the site are courses, a consultancy service and a children's area.

WordCounter

W www.wordcounter.com

A site that allows you to copy and paste text into a field and check for repetitions. In a separate field you may also check your writing for political leanings.

The Workhouse

W www.fictionworkhouse.com

An online literary writer's forum. Registration (free) is required to use the forum.

Write Away

W www.writeaway.co.uk

A membership site, which offers a writers' community forum, access to editors and library information staff, plus the option of paying for appraisal services. The team can also advise on self-publishing and sell your books through the site. Lifetime membership costs from £27.45.

Write Link

W www.writelink.co.uk

A membership site where work in progress is rated by other members. Once the work is at a certain level it gets linked to the resources area, which contains information on paying markets. Each piece published in the resources area earns £20. There is a discussion forum and subscription is free, although if you want the chance to submit work for review you must pay a fee.

Writer Beware

W www.sfwa.org/beware

Writer Beware is the public face of the Science-Fiction & Fantasy Writers of America's Committee on Writing Scams. The site contains discussions of a variety of literary schemes and deceptions, information on how to identify them, advice on how to avoid them, and links to useful online resources. It has been designed so that it can be used by any writer, regardless of subject, style, genre or nationality.

The Writer Gazette

W www.writergazette.com

Provides free writer-related articles, job listings, contests, resources, tips and more – all of which are designed to help improve and promote your writing career. Updated on a weekly basis.

Writers' Circles

W www.writers-circles.com

A directory of writers' circles across the country that is also available to buy in print. The site links to other resources, such as writing competitions, and contains small market directory sections, including agents and magazines.

Writers Free Reference

W www.writers-free-reference.com

A free portal site containing links to many other sites, resources and articles of interest to writers.

Writer's Market (US)

W www.writersmarket.com

A subscription-based site with access to thousands of frequently updated US writing markets, plus advice, tips and resources.

Writers Net

W www.writers.net

A US site containing information for writers, editors, agents and publishers. The site contains lists of US contacts and has a discussion forum.

WritersServices

W www.writersservices.com

A very full site with information, services and advice for writers.

Writing World

W www.writing-world.com

A US site full of articles on writing and publishing. There are also links to freelance job opportunities and a bookshop.

YouWriteOn.com

W www.youwriteon.com

A peer review site where the top five authors for each month receive a free Arts Council-funded critique from top editors and leading literary agents and publishers, including Curtis Brown, Orion and Bloomsbury. The site aims to help new writers develop, and to help talented writers get noticed and published.

BURSARIES, FELLOWSHIPS & GRANTS

The Authors' Foundation

✉ The Society of Authors, 84 Drayton Gardens, London, SW10 9SB
☎ T 020 7373 6642
F 020 7373 5768
✎ E info@societyofauthors.org
W www.societyofauthors.org

Grants are available for writers who are already commissioned by a British publisher to write a full-length work of fiction, poetry or non-fiction. There are also grants for those that have been previously published and can demonstrate a strong likelihood they will be published in Britain again. Money is designed to assist with the research, travel and living costs that a publisher's advance may not cover. The twice-yearly grants, awarded in April and September, are normally between £1,000 and £2,000, and rarely exceed £4,000. Applicants should include: a brief history of their writing career; details of their current work; size of advance (if any); names of publishers already approached, or working with; overall financial position and why the grant is needed; details of past grants; and copies of past reviews (if any). Full application details are available on the website.

Charles Pick Fellowship

✉ School of Literature and Creative Writing, University of East Anglia, University Plain, Norwich, NR4 7TJ
☎ T 01603 592810
F 01603 507728
✎ E charlespickfellowship@uea.ac.uk
W www.uea.ac.uk/lit/awards/pick

A six-month bursary of £10,000 in memory of Charles Pick, a publisher and literary agent. Applicants must be unpublished writers of fictional or non-fictional prose (excluding reports from academic research). Winners will be picked on the strength of their writing proposal and references from editors, agents or accredited creative writing teachers. Fellows must reside at the University of East Anglia. Shared office space and computer facilities will be made available for the Fellow in the School of Literature and Creative Writing. The Fellow will be required to submit written work to a nominated mentor and take part in creative writing research seminars, however there are no teaching duties.

David TK Wong Fellowship

✉ School of Literature and Creative Writing, University of East Anglia, University Plain, Norwich, NR4 7TJ
☎ T 01603 592810
F 01603 507728
✎ E davidtkwongfellowship@uea.ac.uk
W www.uea.ac.uk/lit/awards/wong

An annual grant of around £26,000 to enable a writer to spend a year based at the University of East Anglia writing a work of fiction incorporating an aspect of life in the Far East as a subject matter. Applicants may be of any nationality, and can be a published or an unpublished writer.

European Jewish Publication Society

✉ PO Box 19948, London, N3 3ZL
☎ T 020 8346 1668
F 020 8346 1776
✎ E cs@ejps.org.uk
W www.ejps.org.uk

Contact Dr Colin Shindler

The society supplies grants of up to £3,000 to publishers seeking assistance in the publication of Jewish interest books, both fiction and non-fiction (£1,000 for poetry). Assistance is also given with the marketing and promotion of the title once published. Potential applicants must first approach a publisher, and then the publisher must contact the society. Recent examples of books include: *Photographing the Holocaust* by Janina Struck and *The Arab-Israeli Cookbook* by Robin Soans.

Hawthornden Literary Institute

✉ Hawthornden Castle, International Retreat for Writers, Lasswade, EH18 1EG
☎ T 0131 440 2180
F 0131 440 1989

Hawthornden provides a quiet retreat for up to six writers to concentrate on their work. Writers who win access to this facility are known as Hawthornden Fellows. They become guests of the retreat once they have arrived, but no travel expenses are paid. Application forms can be requested by telephone or fax and must be returned by the end of November for retreats the following year.

North East Literary Fellowship

✉ Arts Council England North East, Central Square, Forth Street, Newcastle upon Tyne, NE1 3PJ
☎ T 0845 300 6200
F 0191 230 1020
✎ E Online form
W www.artscouncil.org.uk/regions/north-east/

A fellowship in association with the University of Durham and the University of Newcastle. Contact the North East branch of Arts Council England for more details and how to apply.

Robert Louis Stevenson Memorial Fellowship

✉ The National Library of Scotland, George IV Bridge, Edinburgh, EH1 1EW
☎ T 0131 623 3700
✎ E media.office@scottisharts.org.uk
W www.nls.uk/about-us/awards

Contact Fiona Morrison Graham

Winners receive a two-month residency at Grez-sur-Loing, Fontainbleu, France, where Stevenson first met his wife Fanny Osborne, funded by the Scottish Arts Council and the National Library of Scotland. Applicants must be writers living in Scotland, or be Scottish by birth. Submit no more than 3,000 words of original work (in progress or recently published), along with a brief statement of how the fellowship would be useful, and a short career history.

The Royal Literary Fund

✉ 3 Johnson's Court, London, EC4A 3EA
☎ T 020 7353 7160
✎ E rlitfund@btconnect.com
W www.rlf.org.uk

Contact General Secretary, Eileen Gunn

The Royal Literary Fund has been continuously helping authors since it was set up in 1790. It is funded by bequests and donations from writers who wish to help other writers. Its committee members come from all walks of literary life and include novelists, biographers, poets, publishers, lawyers and agents. Help is given to writers in many different situations, where personal or professional setbacks have resulted in loss of income. Grants cannot be made for works in progress. Pensions are considered for older writers who have seen their earnings decrease. To apply, contact Eileen Gunn providing a list of your work, including names of publishers, dates, and whether sole author. Of special interest to all involved in writing in higher education is Writing Matters, the RLF report on student writing in higher education. It examines the difficulties many students face in writing effectively, and proposes a range of measures to address these. The report argues that much greater attention should be paid to helping students adjust to the demands of writing at university, and that writing development is a key factor for progress in the higher education sector.

Scottish Arts Council Bursaries

✉ Grants Administration Department, 12 Manor Place, Edinburgh, EH3 7DD
☎ T 0131 226 6051
✎ E help.desk@scottisharts.org.uk
W www.creativescotland.com

A range of grants, which are available for professionals working in the arts, including some in the literature and drama fields. Check the website for details of current offers and application procedures. Applicants should normally live or work in Scotland.

The Society of Authors Charitable Trusts

The Society of Authors, 84 Drayton Gardens, London, SW10 9SB
T 020 7373 6642
F 020 7373 5768
E info@societyofauthors.org
W www.societyofauthors.org

Contact Dorothy Sim

There are currently three funds available for professional freelance writers who experience sudden or temporary financial difficulty. The Francis Head Bequest is open to all writers, particularly those with unexpected health problems. The Authors' Contingency Fund is open to writers (or their dependants) who are in extreme financial difficulty. The John Masefield Memorial Trust is open to poets (or their dependants) who face sudden financial problems. Applications for all three may be made using the form available on the website..

WRITING & PUBLISHING COURSES

Full-Time Courses

Anglia Ruskin University

East Road, Cambridge, CB1 1PT
T 0845 271 3333
E Online form
W www.anglia.ac.uk

BA Writing, BA Writing and Drama, English Literature or Film Studies

Bath Spa University

School of Humanities and Cultural Industires, Bath Spa University, Newton Park Campus, Newton St Loe, Bath, BA2 9BN
T 01225 876268
F 01225 875605
E enquiries@bathspa.ac.uk
W www.bathspa.ac.uk

BA Creative Writing (Single or Joint). Contact Richard Kerridge, r.kerridge@bathspa.ac.uk; MA Creative Writing. Contact Richard Kerridge, r.kerridge@bathspa.ac.uk; MA Writing for Young People. Contact Julia Green, j.a.green@bathspa.ac.uk; PhD Creative Writing. Contact Dr Tracey Brain, t.brain@bathspa.ac.uk

Birkbeck College

Malet Street, Bloomsbury, London, WC1E 7HX
T 020 7631 6000
F 020 7631 6270
E info@bbk.ac.uk
W www.bbk.ac.uk

MA Creative Writing. Contact englishandhumanities@bbk.ac.uk

Blackpool & The Fylde College

Ashfield Road, Bispham, Blackpool, FY2 0HB
T 01253 504343
F 01253 356127
E visitors@blackpool.ac.uk
W www.blackpool.ac.uk

BA English Language, Literature and Writing

Brunel University

Kingston Lane, Uxbridge, Middlesex, UB8 3PH
T 01895 274000
F 01895 232806
E admissions@brunel.ac.uk
W www.brunel.ac.uk

BA Creative Writing. Contact Rose Atfield, English.admissions@brunel.ac.uk; BA English with Creative Writing. Contact Rose Atfield, English.admissions@brunel.ac.uk; MA Creative and Professional Writing. Contact Donna White, donna.white@brunel.ac.uk; MA Creative Writing (The Novel). Contact Donna White, donna.white@brunel.ac.uk; MA Journalism. Contact Donna White, donna.white@brunel.ac.uk

Bucks New University

Queen Alexandra Road, High Wycombe, Buckinghamshire, HP11 2JZ
T 01494 522141
F 01494 524392
E advice@bucks.ac.uk
W www.bcuc.ac.uk

BA Creative Writing with Film Studies, Drama, English Literature, Media Studies, or Digital Video Production (or combinations)

Canterbury Christ Church University

North Holmes Road, Canterbury, Kent, CT1 1QU
T 01227 767700
F 01227 470442
E admissions@canterbury.ac.uk
W www.canterbury.ac.uk

BA Creative and Professional Writing; MA Creative Writing and Prose Fiction

De Montfort University

✉ The Gateway, Leicester, LE1 9BH
☎ T 0116 255 1551
F 0116 257 7533
✏ E enquiry@dmu.ac.uk
W www.dmu.ac.uk

BA Creative Writing (Joint)

Edge Hill University

✉ St Helen's Road, Ormskirk, Lancashire, L39 4QP
☎ T 01695 575171
F 01695 579997
✏ E enquiries@edgehill.ac.uk
W www.edgehill.ac.uk

BA Creative Writing; BA Creative Writing and English; MA Creative Writing

Goldsmiths College

✉ University of London, New Cross, London, SE14 6NW
☎ T 020 7919 7171
✏ E admissions@gold.ac.uk
W www.gold.ac.uk

BA English with Creative Writing; MA Creative and Life Writing; MPhil and PhD in Creative Writing

Grimsby Institute of Further & Higher Education

✉ Nuns Corner, Grimsby, North East Lincolnshire, DN34 5BQ
☎ T 01472 311222
F 01472 879924
✏ E infocent@grimsby.ac.uk
W www.grimsby.ac.uk

BA Professional Writing; MA Professional Writing

Lancaster University

✉ Bailrigg, Lancaster, LA1 4YW
☎ T 01524 65201

 W www.lancaster.ac.uk

BA English Language with Creative Writing; BA English Literature with Creative Writing; BA English Literature, Creative Writing and Practice; MA Creative Writing

Liverpool John Moores University

✉ Faculty of Media, Arts & Social Science, Dean Walters Building, 1 St James Road, Liverpool, L1 7BR
☎ T 0151 231 5175
E massadmissions@ljmu.ac.uk
✏ W www.ljmu.ac.uk

BA Creative Writing

London Metropolitan University

✉ 166–220 Holloway Road, London, N7 8DB
☎ T 020 7423 0000
E admissions@londonmet.ac.uk
✏ W www.londonmet.ac.uk

BA Creative Writing (Single or Joint); BA Creative Writing and English Literature; BA Journalism Studies; MA Professional Writing. Contact humanities@londonmet.ac.uk

London South Bank University

✉ 90 London Road, London, SE1 6EN
☎ T 020 7815 7815
 E enquiry@lsbu.ac.uk
✏ W www.lsbu.ac.uk

BA Writing for Media Arts; BA Creative Writing; MA Media Writing

Loughborough University

✉ Loughborough, Leicestershire, LE11 3TU
☎ T 01509 263171
E postmaster@lboro.ac.uk
✏ W www.lboro.ac.uk

BA Publishing with English; MA Creative Writing; MA Modern & Contemporary Writing

Manchester Metropolitan University

✉ All Saints Building, All Saints, Manchester, M15 6BH
☎ T 0161 247 2000
  F 0161 247 6390
✎ E enquiries@mmu.ac.uk
  W www.mmu.ac.uk

BA Creative Writing (Single and Joint); BA English and Creative Writing. Contact English-hums@mmu.ac.uk; PgDip/MA Creative Writing

Marjon

✉ University College Plymouth, St Mark & St John, Derriford Road, Plymouth, Devon, PL6 8BH
☎ T 01752 636700
✎ E admissions@marjon.ac.uk
  W www.marjon.ac.uk

BA Creative Writing (Joint)

National University of Ireland, Galway

✉ University Road, Galway, Republic of Ireland
☎ T 00353 91 524411
✎ E info@nuigalway.ie
  W www.nuigalway.ie

MA Literature and Publishing; MA Writing

Newcastle University

✉ Newcastle upon Tyne, NE1 7RU
☎ T 0191 222 6000
✎ E enquiries@ncl.ac.uk
  W www.ncl.ac.uk

MA Creative Writing

Newman University College

✉ Genners Lane, Bartley Green, Birmingham, B32 3NT
☎ T 0121 476 1181
  F 0121 476 1196
✎ E admissions@newman.ac.uk
  W www.newman.ac.uk

Creative Writing (Combined Honours Programmes). Contact info.creativewriting@newman.ac.uk

Northumbria University

✉ Ellison Place, Newcastle upon Tyne, NE1 8ST
☎ T 0191 232 6002
  F 0191 227 3903
✎ E er.admissions@northumbria.ac.uk
  W www.northumbria.ac.uk

BA English Literature and Creative Writing; MA Creative Writing

Nottingham Trent University

✉ Burton Street, Nottingham, NG1 4BU
☎ T 0115 941 8418
✎ E hum.undergrad@ntu.ac.uk
  W www.ntu.ac.uk

BA English with Creative Writing

Queen's University Belfast

✉ University Road, Belfast, BT7 1NN
☎ T 028 9024 5133
  F 028 9097 2828
✎ E admissions@qub.ac.uk
  W www.qub.ac.uk

MA English (Creative Writing). Contact pgenglish@qub.ac.uk

Roehampton University

✉ Erasmus House, Roehampton Lane, London, SW15 5PU
☎ T 020 8392 3232
  F 020 8392 3470
✎ E enquiries@roehampton.ac.uk
  W www.roehampton.ac.uk

BA Creative Writing (Single or Joint); MA Creative and Professional Writing; MA Children's Literature

Royal Holloway, University of London

✉ Egham Hill, Egham, Surrey, TW20 0EX
☎ T 01784 434455
F 01784 437520
✎ E admissions@rhul.ac.uk
W www.rhul.ac.uk

BA English and Creative Writing; BA Drama and Creative Writing; MA Creative Writing

Ruskin College, Oxford

✉ Walton Street, Oxford, OX1 2HE
☎ T 01865 554331
F 01865 554372
✎ E enquiries@ruskin.ac.uk
W www.ruskin.ac.uk

BA English Studies (Creative Writing and Critical Practice)

Sheffield Hallam University

✉ City Campus, Howard Street, Sheffield, S1 1WB
☎ T 0114 225 5555
F 0114 225 4449
✎ E enquiries@shu.ac.uk
W www.shu.ac.uk

MA Writing. Contact dsenquiry@shu.ac.uk

Southampton Solent University

✉ East Park Terrace, Southampton, Hampshire, SO14 0YN
☎ T 023 8031 9000
F 023 8022 2259
✎ E ask@solent.ac.uk
W www.ssu.ac.uk

BA Writing Fashion and Culture; BA Writing Popular Fiction; Creative Writing: Industry and Practice

Staffordshire University

✉ College Road, Stoke on Trent, Staffordshire, ST4 2DE

 T 01782 294000
E admissions@staffs.ac.uk
✎ W www.staffs.ac.uk

BA Creative Writing

St Mary's College

✉ Waldegrave Road, Strawberry Hill, Twickenham, TW1 4SX
☎ T 020 8240 4000
F 020 8240 4255
✎ E admit@smuc.ac.uk
W www.smuc.ac.uk

BA Creative and Professional Writing. Contact Peter Dewar, dewarp@smuc.ac.uk

Trinity & All Saints

✉ Brownberrie Lane, Horsforth, Leeds, LS18 5HD
☎ T 0113 283 7100
F 0113 283 7200
✎ E enquiries@leedstrinity.ac.uk
W www.leedstrinity.ac.uk

BA English and Writing

Trinity College Dublin

✉ College Green, Dublin 2, Republic of Ireland
☎ T 00353 1 896 1000
✎ E admissions@tcd.ie
W www.tcd.ie

M.Phil Creative Writing

University College, Falmouth

✉ Woodlane, Falmouth, Cornwall, TR11 4RH
 T 01326 211077
F 01326 213880
✎ E admissions@falmouth.ac.uk
W www.falmouth.ac.uk

BA English with Creative Writing; MA/PgDip Professional Writing

University of Birmingham

✉ Edgbaston, Birmingham, B15 2TT
☎ T 0121 414 3344
  F 0121 414 3971
✐ E English@bham.ac.uk
  W www.birmingham.ac.uk

BA English with Creative Writing;
MA Creative Writing

University of Bolton

✉ Deane Road, Bolton, BL3 5AB
☎ T 01204 900 600
✐ E enquiries@bolton.ac.uk
  W www.bolton.ac.uk

BA Creative Writing (Single or Joint); Creative
Writing and English; BA Media, Writing and
Production; MA Creative Writing (Part-Time)

University of Central Lancashire

✉ Preston, PR1 2HE
☎ T 01772 201201
✐ E cenquiries@uclan.ac.uk
  W www.uclan.ac.uk

Combined Honours Creative Writing

University of Chester

✉ Parkgate Road, Chester, CH1 4BJ
☎ T 01244 511000
  F 01244 511300
✐ E enquiries@chester.ac.uk
  W www.chester.ac.uk

BA Creative Writing (Joint Honours). Contact
Jen Mawson, j.mawson@chester.ac.uk; MA
Creative Writing. Contact Dr Ashley Chantler,
a.chantler@chester.ac.uk

University of Chichester

✉ Bishop Otter Campus, College Lane, Chichester,
West Sussex, PO19 6PE
☎ T 01243 816000
✐ E admissions@chi.ac.uk
  W www.chiuni.ac.uk

BA English and Creative Writing. Contact
english.chiuni.ac.uk; MA Creative Writing.
Contact english.chiuni.ac.uk

University of Cumbria

✉ Lancaster Campus, Bowerham Road,
Lancaster, LA1 3JD
☎ T 01524 384384
✐ E admissionslancaster@cumbria.ac.uk
  W www.cumbria.ac.uk

BA English and Creative Writing

University of Derby

✉ Kedleston Road, Derby, DE22 1GB
☎ T 01332 590500
  F 01332 294861
✐ E askadmissions@derby.ac.uk
  W www.derby.ac.uk

BA Creative Writing (Single and Joint). Contact
adtenquiry@derby.ac.uk; BA Media Writing
(Joint). Contact adtenquiry@derby.ac.uk

University of Dundee

✉ Nethergate, Derby, DD1 4HN
☎ T 01382 383000
  F 01382 388150
✐ E university@dundee.ac.uk
  W www.dundee.ac.uk

MA Writing Culture

University of East Anglia

✉ Norwich, NR4 7TJ
☎ T 01603 456161
  F 01603 458553
✐ E admissions@uea.ac.uk
  W www.uea.ac.uk

BA English Literature with Creative Writing;
MA Creative Writing (Prose); MA Life Writing

University of East London

Docklands Campus, 4–6 University Way, London, E16 2RD
T 020 8223 3000
E study@uel.ac.uk
W www.uel.ac.uk

BA Creative and Professional Writing; MA Writing (Imaginative Practice)

University of Edinburgh

Old College, South Bridge, Edinburgh, EH8 9YL
T 0131 650 1000
F 0131 650 2147
E communications.office@ed.ac.uk
W www.ed.ac.uk

MSc Creative Writing. Contact drose@staffmail.ed.ac.uk

University of Essex

Wivenhoe Park, Colchester, CO4 3SQ
T 01206 873333
F 01206 873598
E admit@essex.ac.uk
W www.essex.ac.uk

BA Creative Writing; MA Literature, Creative Writing

University of Exeter

Streatham Campus, Northcote House, Devon, EX4 4QJ
T 01392 661000
E admissions@exeter.ac.uk
W www.exeter.ac.uk

MA Creative Writing. Contact humanities-pgadmissions@exeter.ac.uk

University of Glamorgan

Pontypridd, Wales, CF37 1DL
T 08456 434 030
F 01443 654050
W www.glam.ac.uk

BA Creative and Professional Writing; M.Phil Writing

University of Glasgow

University Avenue, Glasgow, G12 8QQ
T 0141 330 2000
E pgadmissions@admin.gla.ac.uk
W www.glasgow.ac.uk

MA Creative Writing. Contact seslladmin@arts.gla.ac.uk

University of Gloucestershire

The Park, Cheltenham, GL50 2RH
T 0844 801 0001
F 01242 714827
E admissions@glos.ac.uk
W www.glos.ac.uk

BA Creative Writing; MA Creative and Critical Writing

University of Greenwich

Old Royal Navy College, Park Row, Greenwich, London, SE10 9LS
T 020 8331 8000
F 020 8331 8145
E courseinfo@greenwich.ac.uk
W www.gre.ac.uk

BA Creative Writing; BA Media Writing

University of Hertfordshire

College Lane, Hatfield, Hertfordshire, AL10 9AB
T 01707 284000
F 01707 284115
E admissions@herts.ac.uk
W www.herts.ac.uk

BA Creative Writing (Humanities)

University of Huddersfield

Queensgate, Huddersfield, HD1 3DH
T 01484 422288
E admissionsandrecords@hud.ac.uk
W www2.hud.ac.uk

English Literature with Creative Writing BA(Hons); English Language with Creative Writing BA(Hons); English with Creative Writing

BA(Hons). Contact englishadmissions@hud.ac.uk

University of Hull

Hull, HU6 7RX
T 01482 346311
F 01482 466511
E admissions@hull.ac.uk
W www.hull.ac.uk

BA Creative Writing (Joint Honours);
MA Creative Writing

University of Kent

School of English, Rutherford College,
University of Kent, Canterbury, CT2 7NX
T 01227 823054
F 01227 827001
E english@kent.ac.uk
W www.kent.ac.uk

MA Creative Writing

University of Leeds

Leeds, LS2 9JT
T 0113 243 1751
F 0113 244 3923
W www.leeds.ac.uk

MA Writing for Performance and Publication.
Contact admissions-pci@leeds.ac.uk

University of Manchester

Oxford Road, Manchester, M13 9PL
T 0161 306 6000
E pg-admissions@manchester.ac.uk
W www.manchester.ac.uk

MA Creative Writing. Contact pg-english@manchester.ac.uk

University of Middlesex

Bramley Road, London, N14 4YZ
T 020 8411 5555
E enquiries@mdx.ac.uk
W www.mdx.ac.uk

BA Creative Writing and English Literature;
BA Publishing, Media and Cultural Studies;
BA Creative and Media Writing

University of Northampton

Park Campus, Boughton Green Road,
Northampton, NN2 7AL
T 01604 735500
F 01604 720636
E study@northampton.ac.uk
W www.northampton.ac.uk

BA Creative Writing (Joint)

University of Oxford

Wellington Square, Oxford, OX1 2JD
T 01865 270000
F 01865 270708
W www.ox.ac.uk

MSt Creative Writing. Contact
mstcreativewriting@conted.ox.ac.uk

University of Plymouth

Drake Circus, Plymouth, PL4 8AA
T 01752 600600
E prospectus@plymouth.ac.uk
W www.plymouth.ac.uk

BA English and Creative Writing. Contact
arts.admissions@plymouth.ac.uk: MA/PgDip
Creative Writing. Contact artspostgrad@plymouth.ac.uk

University of Portsmouth

University House, Winston Churchill Avenue,
Portsmouth, Hampshire, PO1 2UP
T 023 9284 8484
F 023 9284 3082
E info.centre@port.ac.uk
W www.port.ac.uk

BA Creative and Media Writing. Contact create.
admissions@port.ac.uk: BA Creative Writing
(Joint). MA Creative Writing. Contact create.
admissions@port.ac.uk

University of Salford

Salford, Greater Manchester, M5 4WT
T 0161 295 5000
F 0161 295 5999
E course-enquiries@salford.ac.uk
W www.salford.ac.uk

BA English and Creative Writing; BA Journalism
and English (Joint); MA Creative Writing:
Innovation and Experiment. Contact Ruth Potts,
r.potts@salford.ac.uk

University of St Andrews

St Andrews, Fife, KY16 9AJ
T 01334 476161
E admissions@st-andrews.ac.uk
W www.st-andrews.ac.uk

M.Litt Creative Writing (Fiction)

University of Strathclyde

16 Richmond Street, Glasgow, G1 1XQ
T 0141 552 4400
F 0141 552 0775
E contact-facultyofarts@strath.ac.uk
W www.strath.ac.uk

BA Journalism and Creative Writing (Joint)

University of Sussex

Sussex House, Brighton, BN1 9RH
T 01273 606755
F 01273 678335
E pg.enquiries@sussex.ac.uk
W www.sussex.ac.uk

MA Creative Writing; MA Creative and
Critical Writing

University of Wales, Aberystwyth University

Department of English, Hugh Owen Building,
Aberystwyth, SY23 3DY
T 01970 622534
F 01970 622530
E english@aber.ac.uk
W www.aber.ac.uk/english

BA English Literature and Creative Writing;
MA Creative Writing

University of Wales, Bangor University

Bangor, Gwynedd, LL57 2DG
T 01248 351151
E admissions@bangor.ac.uk
W www.bangor.ac.uk

BA English Language with Creative Writing;
BA English with Creative Writing; BA Creative
Writing and Media Studies. Contact lingadmin@
bangor.ac.uk; PhD/Mphil Creative Writing.
Contact Dr Raluca Radulescu r.radulescu@
bangor.ac.uk

University of Wales Trinity Saint David

Carmarthen, Wales, SA31 3EP
T 01267 676767
F 01267 676766
E Online form
W www.trinitysaintdavid.ac.uk

BA English with Creative Writing; MA Creative
Writing. Contact Paul Wright, p.wright@
trinitysaintdavid.ac.uk

University of Wales, Newport

Information Centre, Caerleon Campus,
Lodge Road, Newport, NP18 3QT
T 01633 432432
F 01633 432046
E uic@newport.ac.uk
W www.newport.ac.uk

BA Creative Writing (Joint)

University of Wales, Swansea

Singleton Park, Swansea, SA2 8PP
T 01792 205678
F 01792 295157
W www.swansea.ac.uk

MA Creative and Media Writing

University of Wales Institute, Cardiff

✉ Howard Gardens, Cardiff, CF24 0SP
☎ T 029 2041 6070
F 029 2041 6286
✐ E uwicinfo@uwic.ac.uk
W www3.uwic.ac.uk

BA English and Creative Writing. Contact Dr Spencer Jordan, sjordan@uwic.ac.uk

University of Warwick

✉ Coventry, CV4 7AL
☎ T 024 7652 3523
F 024 7646 1606
✐ E ugadmissions@warwick.ac.uk
E pgadmissions@warwick.ac.uk
W www.warwick.ac.uk

BA English Literature and Creative Writing; MA Writing: MA Translation, Writing and Cultural Difference

University of Westminster

✉ 309 Regent Street, London, W1B 2UW
☎ T 020 7911 5000
F 020 7911 5858
✐ E course-enquiries@westminster.ac.uk
W www.westminster.ac.uk

BA English Literature and Creative Writing; BA Linguistics and Creative Writing

University of Winchester

✉ West Hill, Winchester, SO22 4NR
☎ T 01962 841515
F 01962 842280
✐ E course.enquiries@winchester.ac.uk
W www.winchester.ac.uk

BA Creative Writing; MA Creative and Critical Writing

University of Wolverhampton

✉ Millennium City Building, City Campus South, Wulfruna Street, Wolverhampton, WV1 1LY

☎ T 01902 321000
✐ E enquiries@wlv.ac.uk
W www.wlv.ac.uk

BA Creative and Professional Writing (Joint); BA Media and Cultural Studies

Part-Time Courses

ACS Distance Education

✉ PO Box 4171, Stourbridge, DY8 2WZ
☎ T 0800 328 4723
F 020 7681 2702
✐ E info@acsedu.co.uk
W www.acsedu.co.uk

Writing, publishing and journalism courses by correspondence.

AD Services (Scotland) Ltd

✉ Suite 15, The Beckford Business Centre, 28 Beckford Street, Hamilton, ML3 0BT
☎ T 01698 307171
F 01698 307140
✐ E info@ad-services-scotland.co.uk
W www.ad-services-scotland.co.uk

Distance learning courses in fiction writing and journalism.

Adult College, Lancaster

✉ White Cross Education Centre, Quarry Road, Lancaster, LA1 3SE
☎ T 01524 60141
F 01524 581137
✐ E adcollege.info@ed.lancscc.gov.uk
W www.theadultcollege.org

Part-time creative writing courses.

Alston Hall

✉ Alston Lane, Longridge, Preston, PR3 3BP
☎ T 01772 784661
F 01772 785835
✐ E alstonhall.general2@lancashire.gov.uk
W www.alstonhall.com

A range of day, evening and weekly courses on writing and literature.

Arvon National

Free Word, 60 Farringdon Road, London, EC1R 3GA
T 020 7324 2554
E london@arvonfoundation.org
W www.arvonfoundation.org

Residential writing courses across four properties in Devon, Scotland, Shropshire and West Yorkshire.

Aspiring Writers

47 Old Exeter Road, Tavistock, Devon, PL19 0JE
T 01822 615610
E info@aspiringwriters.co.uk
W www.aspiringwriters.co.uk

Courses and workshops on every aspect of writing with a creative and practical approach. Residential weekends can also be arranged.

Ballyfermot College of Further Education

Ballyfermot Road, Ballyfermot, Dublin 10, Republic of Ireland
T 00353 1 626 9421
F 00353 1 626 6754
E info@bcfe.cdvec.ie
W www.bcfe.ie

Evening classes in creative writing, journalism and screenwriting.

Beginning to Write

United Reform Church, 30 Fisherton Street, Salisbury, SP2 7RG
E susandown5@aol.com
W www.salisburywriters.co.uk

Beginner's writing course. Contact Susan Down.

Belfast Institute

Belfast Metropolitan College, Brunswick Street, Belfast, BT2 7GX
T 028 9026 5265
E central_admissions@belfastmet.ac.uk
W www.belfastmet.ac.uk

Adult learning and vocational courses in writing, media and journalism. Formed by the merger of the Belfast and Castlereagh College on 1 August 2007.

Belstead House Education & Conference Centre

Belstead House, Sprites Lane, Ipswich, Suffolk, IP8 3NA
E belstead.house@educ.suffolkcc.gov.uk

Offers a range of residential courses.

Birkbeck College

Birkbeck College, University of London, Malet Street, Bloomsbury, London, WC1E 7HX
T 0845 601 0174
F 020 7079 0641
E info@bbk.ac.uk
W www.bbk.ac.uk

Short courses and adult learning classes for various types of writing.

Blackpool & The Fylde College

Ashfield Road, Bispham, Blackpool, Lancashire, FY2 0HB
T 01253 504343
F 01253 356127
E visitors@blackpool.ac.uk
W www.blackpool.ac.uk

Adult community learning, and access courses in creative writing.

Bournemouth Adult Learning

Ensbury Avenue, Bournemouth, Dorset, BH10 4HG
T 01202 451950
F 01202 451989
E bal.enquiries@bournemouth.gov.uk
W www.bournemouth.gov.uk/Education/Adults

Various adult learning courses.

Brighton Writers' Workshop

Varndean College, Surrenden Road, Brighton, East Sussex, BN1 6WQ
T 01273 546604
F 01273 542950
E Online form
W www.varndean.ac.uk

Writing courses for adults.

Brockenhurst College

Lyndhurst Road, Brockenhurst, Hampshire, SO42 7ZE
T 01590 625555
E adulteducation@brock.ac.uk
W www.brock.ac.uk

Wide range of adult courses.

BSY Group

Oakwood, Dunsland Cross, Devon, EX22 7YT
T 0800 731 9271
E info@bsygroup.co.uk
W www.bsygroup.co.uk

Distance learning courses, including creative writing.

Buckingham Adult Learning

Data Centre, Evreham, Swallow Street, Iver, SL0 0HS
T 0845 045 4040
F 01753 783756
E studentenquiries@buckscc.gov.uk
W www.adultlearningbcc.ac.uk

Adult creative writing courses.

Burnley College

Princess Way, Burnley, Lancashire, BB12 0AN
T 01282 733373
E student.services@burnley.ac.uk
W www.burnley.ac.uk

Adult creative media courses.

Burton Manor

The Village, Burton, Neston, Cheshire, CH64 5SJ
T 0151 336 5172
F 0151 336 6586
E enquiry@burtonmanor.com
W www.burtonmanor.com

Variety of short residential and non-residential writing courses.

Bury Adult & Community Learning Service

Bury Adult Education Centre, 18 Haymarket Street, Bury, BL9 0AQ
T 0161 253 7501
E student.services@bury.gov.uk
W www.bury.gov.uk/EducationAndLearning/

Community courses in creative writing.

Caboodle Retreats

Caboodle Cottage, 69 Southwold Road, Wrentham, Beccles, Suffolk, NR34 8JE
T 01502 676107
F 01502 676107
E info@caboodleretreats.co.uk

Runs various courses and writing holidays.

Cambridge Institute of Continuing Education

Institute of Continuing Education, University of Cambridge, Madingley Hall, Madingley, Cambridge, CB3 8AQ
T 01223 746262
F 01223 746200
E registration@ice.cam.ac.uk
W www.ice.cam.ac.uk

Offers a wide variety of creative writing courses.

Carlow College

College Street, Carlow, Republic of Ireland
T 00353 59 915 3200
F 00353 59 914 0258
E infocc@carlowcollege.ie
W www.carlowcollege.ie

Offers creative writing courses.

Castle College Nottingham

Maid Marian Way, Nottingham, NG1 6AB
T 0845 845 0500
E learn@castlecollege.ac.uk
W www.castlecollege.ac.uk

Wide range of media courses.

Central Bedfordshire College

Kingsway, Dunstable, Bedfordshire, LU5 4HG
T 0845 355 2525
E enquiries@centralbeds.ac.uk
W www.centralbeds.ac.uk

Various media examination courses.

Central Saint Martins College of Art & Design

Southampton Row, London, WC1B 4AP
T 020 7514 7015
F 020 7514 7016
E shortcourse@csm.arts.ac.uk
W www.csm.arts.ac.uk

Evening and weekend courses on all types of writing.

Chapter Centre

Market Road, Cardiff, CF5 1QE
T 029 2031 1050
E enquiry@chapter.org
W www.chapter.org

Offers writing workshops and competitions.

Charles Street Community Education Centre

16 Charles Street, Newport, NP20 1JU
T 01633 656656

Short courses in writing.

Cheadle & Marple Sixth Form College

Cheadle Road, Cheadle Hulme, Stockport, Cheshire, SK8 5HA
T 0161 486 4602
F 0161 482 8129
E info@camsfc.ac.uk
W www.camsfc.ac.uk

Adult learning courses in creative writing.

Chesterfield College

Infirmary Road, Chesterfield, S41 7NG
T 01246 500500
F 01246 500587
E advice@chesterfield.ac.uk
W www.chesterfield.ac.uk

Part-time, adult and community courses.

City College Brighton & Hove

Pelham Street, Brighton, East Sussex, BN1 4FA
T 01273 667788
F 01273 667703
E info@ccb.ac.uk
W www.ccb.ac.uk

Full- and part-time certificates and diplomas in writing and journalism.

City Lit

Keeley Street, Convent Garden, London, WC2B 4BA
T 020 7492 2600
E infoline@citylit.ac.uk
W www.citylit.ac.uk

A wide range of writing and journalism short courses. New courses added on a regular basis.

City of Bath College

Avon Street, Bath, BA1 1UP
T 01225 312191
F 01225 444213
E courses@citybathcoll.ac.uk
W www.citybathcoll.ac.uk

Part-time creative writing courses.

City of Bristol College

College Green Centre, St George's Road, Bristol, BS1 5UA
T 0117 312 5000
F 0117 312 5053
E enquiries@cityofbristol.ac.uk
W www.cityofbristol.ac.uk

Part-time adult courses in various types of writing.

City University Courses for Adults

Northampton Square, London, EC1V 0HB
T 020 7040 5060
F 020 7040 5070
E Online form
W www.city.ac.uk/conted/cfa.htm

Courses for adults in writing and journalism. Contact robert.lastman.1@city.ac.uk, T 020 7040 8237

Coleg Powys

Llanidloes Road, Newtown, Powys, Wales, SY16 4HU
T 0845 408 6200
F 01686 622246
E Online form
W www.coleg-powys.ac.uk

Access courses in writing and literature.

Comberton Village College

West Street, Comberton, Cambridgeshire, CB23 7DU
T 01223 264721
F 01223 264548

E commed@comberton.cambs.sch.uk
W www.combertonvc.org

Offers various community courses.

The Complete Creative Writing Course

The Groucho Club, 45 Dean Street, Soho, London, W1D 4QB
E maggie@writingcourses.org.uk
W www.writingcourses.org.uk

Original, advanced residential writing courses.

Conway Education Centre

Conway Mill, 5–7 Conway Street, Belfast, BT13 2DE
T 028 9024 8543
F 028 0923 0427
E Online form
W www.conwayeducation.com

Various writing courses.

The Creative Writers Workshop

PO Box 1, Kinvara, Co. Galway, Republic of Ireland
T 00353 86 252 3428
E creativewriting@ireland.com
W www.thecreativewritersworkshop.com

Creative writing workshops and retreats using right-brain/left-brain techniques in locations across Ireland. Contact Irene Graham.

CTJT

Forum House, Stirling Road, Chichester, West Sussex, PO19 7DN
T 01243 381998
E Online form
W www.ctjt.biz

Online courses in most spheres of writing, journalism, proofreading and editing.

Dillington House

Dillington House, Illminster, Somerset, TA19 9DT
T 01460 258648
F 01460 258615
E dillington@somerset.gov.uk
W www.dillington.co.uk

Residential and day courses in literature and creative writing.

Dingle Writing Courses

Ballintlea, Ventry, Co. Kerry, Republic of Ireland
T 00353 66 915 9815
F 00353 66 915 9815
E info@dinglewritingcourses.ie
W www.dinglewritingcourses.ie

Various weekend writing courses for all levels of experience.

Doncaster College

The Hub, Chappell Drive, Doncaster, DN1 2RF
T 01302 553553
F 01302 553559
E infocentre@don.ac.uk
W www.don.ac.uk

Various media courses.

Dublin College of Management & IT

College House, 10 Southern Cross Business Park, Bray, Co. Wicklow, Republic of Ireland
T 00353 1 286 5783
F 00353 1 633 5544
E info@cmit.ie
W www.cmit.ie

Distance learning courses in journalism and fiction writing.

The Earnley Concourse

Earnley Concourse, Earnley, Chichester, West Sussex, PO20 7JN
T 01243 670392
F 01243 670832
E info@earnley.co.uk
W www.earnley.co.uk

Various literature courses.

Eastleigh College

Chestnut Avenue, Eastleigh, SO50 5SF
T 023 8091 1299
F 023 8032 2133
E goplaces@eastleigh.ac.uk
W www.eastleigh.ac.uk

Part-time creative writing courses.

East Moors Community Education Centre

Sanquahar Street, Splott, Cardiff, CF24 2AD
T 029 2046 2858
F 029 2046 2858
E eastmoorsac@cardiff.gov.uk
W www.cardiff.gov.uk

Various community courses.

Edinburgh University

Office of Lifelong Learning, University of Edinburgh, 11 Buccleuch Place, Edinburgh, EH8 9LW
T 0131 650 4400
F 0131 662 0783
E oll@ed.ac.uk
W www.lifelong.ed.ac.uk

Wide variety of adult learning courses, including aspects of creative writing.

Emerson College

Emerson College, Forest Row, East Sussex, RH18 5JX
T 01342 822238
F 01342 826055
E info@emerson.org.uk
W www.emerson.org.uk

Various weekend and short courses in literature and creative writing.

Essex Live Literature Courses

 Essex Libraries, Goldlay Gardens, Chelmsford, Essex, CM2 6WN
T 01245 284981
E malcolm.burgess@essexcc.gov.uk

Various literature events, including writing courses. Contact Malcolm Burgess.

Exeter College

Centre for Creative Studies, Victoria Yard, Off Queen Street, Exeter, EX4 3SR
T 0845 111 6000
F 01392 205913
E info@exe-coll.ac.uk
W www.exe-coll.ac.uk

Courses in 'writing for fun and publication' and creative writing. Print journalism certification course.

Exeter Phoenix

Bradninch Place, Gandy Street, Exeter, EX4 3LS
T 01392 667081
E education@exeterphoenix.org.uk
W www.exeterphoenix.org.uk

Various community classes and workshops.

Farncombe Estate

Farncombe Estate Centre, Broadway, Cotswolds, Worcestershire, WR12 7LJ
T 0333 456 8580
F 01386 854350
E enquiries@farncombeestate.co.uk
W www.farncombeestate.co.uk

Weekend courses on various types of writing and literature.

Fire in the Head

T 01548 821004
E roselle@fire-in-the-head.co.uk
W www.fire-in-the-head.co.uk

Various residential and day courses for writers at locations across the south of England.

Galway Arts Centre

47 Dominick Street, Galway City, Republic of Ireland
T 00353 91 565886
F 00353 91 568642
E info@galwayartscentre.ie
W www.galwayartscentre.ie

Various writing courses and events, as part of the literature and arts programme.

Guildford Institute

 Ward Street, Guildford, Surrey, GU1 4LH
T 01483 562142
E info@guildford-institute.org.uk
W www.guildford-institute.org.uk

A range of part-time writing courses.

Harrow College

Harrow on the Hill Campus, Lowlands Road, Harrow, HA1 3AQ
T 020 8909 6000
E enquiries@harrow.ac.uk
W www.harrow.ac.uk

Part-time media courses.

Havering Adult College

Bower Park, 472 Havering Road, Romford, Essex, RM1 3NH
T 01708 764238
F 01708 3433089
E enquiries-adultcollege@havering.gov.uk
W www.havering.gov.uk/hac

Adult learning courses in creative writing.

Hereward College

 Bramston Crescent, Tile Hill, Coventry, CV4 9SW
T 024 7646 1231
F 024 7669 4305
E enquiries@hereward.ac.uk
W www.hereward.ac.uk

Full- and part-time courses in media and creative studies. The college has a particularly well-developed programmed for disabled students.

Higham Hall

Higham Hall College, Bassenthwaite Lake,
Cockermouth, Cumbria, CA13 9SH

T 01768 776276
F 01768 776013
E admin@highamhall.com
W www.highamhall.com

Day and residential courses in literature
and writing.

The Institute of Creative Writing

Overbrook Business Centre, Poolbridge Road,
Blackford, Wedmore, BS28 4PA

T 0800 781 1715
F 01934 713492
E Online form
W www.inst.org/authors

Distance course on creative writing and
getting published.

Irish Writers Centre

19 Parnell Square, Dublin 1, Republic of Ireland

T 00353 1 872 1302
F 00353 1 872 6282
E info@writerscentre.ie
W www.writerscentre.ie

Wide range of part-time courses on writing.

Killaloe Hedge-School of Writing

4 Riverview, Ballina, Killaloe, Co. Clare,
Republic of Ireland

T 00353 61 375217
F 00353 61 375487
E Online form
W www.killaloe.ie/khs

Various weekend writing courses and
workshops. Contact David Rice.

Kilroy's College

26 York Street, London, W1U 6PZ

T 0845 300 4259

E homestudy@kilroyscollege.ac.uk
W www.kilroyscollege.co.uk

Distance learning courses in creative writing
and journalism.

Knuston Hall Residential College

Irchester, Wellingborough, Northamptonshire,
NN29 7EU

T 01933 312104
F 01933 357596
E enquiries@knustonhall.org.uk
W www.knustonhall.org.uk

Residential college running various short
writing courses.

Lambeth College

Brixton Centre, 56 Brixton Hill, Lambeth,
London, SW2 1QS

T 020 7501 5010
E courses@lambethcollege.ac.uk
W www.lambethcollege.ac.uk

Pre-entry, foundation degrees and certification
courses in journalism. A short, part-time,
creative writing course is also available.

Learning Curve

Leader Cottage, Blainslie, Galashiels, TD1 2PR
T 01896 860661
E edesk@learning-curve.org
W www.learningcurve-uk.com

Various correspondence courses in writing
and copywriting.

Leicester City Council

New Walk Centre, Welford Place, LE1 6ZG
T 0116 252 7000
E lifelonglearning@leicester.gov.uk
W www.leicester.gov.uk

Community classes in creative writing.

Leicestershire County Council

County Hall, Glenfield, Leicester, LE3 8RA
T 0116 232 3232
E communityed@leics.gov.uk
W www.leics.gov.uk

Creative writing classes at various locations around Leicestershire. Contact Louise Robinson.

Liberato

E Online form
W www.liberato.co.uk

Writing retreats and courses in Suffolk and Greece. Also provides editorial services.

London College of Communication

Elephant and Castle, London, SE1 6SB
T 020 7514 6500
E info@lcc.arts.ac.uk
W www.lcc.arts.ac.uk/training

Wide range of short courses in writing and journalism. Currently under review, check website for details.

The Lotus Foundation

16 Lancaster Grove, Swiss Cottage, London, NW3 4PB
T 020 7794 8880
E Online form
W www.lotusfoundation.org.uk

Courses, workshops, therapy and poetry groups.

Manchester Adult Education Service

Victoria Mill Adult Learning Centre, Lower Vickers Street, Manchester, M40 7LJ
T 0800 083 2121
E adult-education@manchester.gov.uk
W www.manchester.gov.uk/adulteducation

Community creative writing courses across Manchester.

Marlborough College Summer School

Marlborough College, Marlborough, Wiltshire, SN8 1PA
T 01672 892200
F 01672 892207
E Online form
W www.mcsummerschool.org.uk

July summer school with adult courses and workshops in creative writing disciplines.

Mary Immaculate College, University of Limerick

Department of English and Literature, Mary Immaculate College, University of Limerick, Republic of Ireland
T 00353 61 313632
E eugene.obrien@mic.ul.ie
W www.mic.ul.ie/creativewriting/creativewriting3.htm

A creative writing course based around a series of workshops.

Middlesex University Summer School

Summer School Office, Middlesex University, Trent Park, Bramley Road, London, N14 4YZ
T 020 8411 5782
F 020 8411 2297
E sschool@mdx.ac.uk
W www.mdx.ac.uk/summer

Summer school runs from June to August and includes several courses on writing for different types of media.

Morley College

61 Westminster Bridge, London, SE1 7HT
T 020 7928 8501
F 020 7928 4074
E enquiries@morleycollege.ac.uk
W www.morleycollege.ac.uk

Part-time creative writing courses for beginners.

National Academy of Writing

E rena@thenationalacademyofwriting.org.uk
W www.thenationalacademyofwriting.org.uk

Diploma in writing, covering various genres. There is a strict application process to be followed before being accepted onto the full diploma course.

National Extension College

The Michael Young Centre, Purbeck Road, Cambridge, CB2 8HN
T 0800 389 2839
F 01223 400321
E info@nec.ac.uk
W www.nec.ac.uk

Distance learning courses on creative writing, writing for money, writing short stories and writing humour.

North Warwickshire & Hinckley College

Hinckley Road, Nuneaton, Warwickshire, CV11 6BH
T 024 7624 3000
F 024 7632 9056
E the.college@nwhc.ac.uk
W www.nwhc.ac.uk

A range of certificated writing courses.

North West Kent College

Oakfield Lane, Dartford, DA1 JT
T 0800 074 1447
F 01322 629468
E course.enquiries@nwkcollege.ac.uk
W www.nwkcollege.ac.uk

Part-time and full-time foundation degree in professional writing. Contact Neil Nixon.

Oaklands College

St Albans Smallford Campus, Hatfield Road, St Albans, Hertfordshire, AL4 0JA

T 01727 737000
E advice.centre@oaklands.ac.uk
W www.oaklands.ac.uk

Journalism and media studies A-level, and part-time course in creative writing.

Open College of the Arts

Michael Young Arts Centre, Redbrook Business Park, Wilthorpe Road, Barnsley, S75 1JN
T 0800 731 2116
F 01226 730838
E enquiries@oca-uk.com
W www.oca-uk.com

A range of workshops.

Open University

Literature Department (Faculty of Arts), The Open University, Walton Hall, Milton Keynes, MK7 6AA
T 0845 300 6090
F 01908 654806
E Online form
W www.open.ac.uk/arts/literature/creative-writing.htm

Short beginners courses in creative writing.

Oxford University Department for Continuing Education

Rewley House, 1 Wellington Square, Oxford, OX1 2JA
T 01865 270360
E enquiries@conted.ox.ac.uk
W www.conted.ox.ac.uk

Courses: MSt Creative Writing – two years part-time; Undergraduate Diploma Creative Writing – two years part-time; Summer Programme in Creative Writing – three-week residential course; Creative Writing Summer School – several one-week residential courses; Online course in Creative Writing –ten online sessions; Part-time classes in New Ways to Write, The Craft of Writing.

Oxford University Summer School

Oxford University Department for Continuing Education, Rewley House, 1 Wellington Square, Oxford, OX1 2JA
T 01865 270396
F 01865 270429
E oussa@conted.ox.ac.uk
W www.conted.ox.ac.uk/oussa

July summer school, running a variety of writing courses and workshops.

Perth College

Perth College UHI, FREEPOST TY333, Perth, PH1 2BR
T 01738 877000
F 01738 877001
E pc.enquiries@perth.uhi.ac.uk
W www.perth.ac.uk

Creative writing leisure courses.

Peterborough Regional College

Park Crescent, Peterborough, PE1 4DZ
T 0845 872 8722
F 01733 767986
E info@peterborough.ac.uk
W www.peterborough.ac.uk

Part-time journalism and creative writing courses.

Plunket College

Swords Road, Whitehall, Dublin 9, Republic of Ireland
T 00353 1 837 1689
F 00353 1 836 8066
E info@plunketcdvec.ie
W www.plunketcollege.ie

Short evening course in creative writing.

Queens University, Belfast School of Education

Lifelong Learning, School of Education, 69/71 University Street, Belfast, BT7 1HL

T 028 9097 3323/5941
F 028 9097 5066
E education@qub.ac.uk
W www.qub.ac.uk/edu

Open learning courses in creative writing.

Regent Academy

Lyne Akres, Brandis Corner, Devon, EX22 7YH
T 0800 378281/01409 220415
F 01409 220416
E info@regentacademy.com
W www.regentacademy.com

Distance learning courses in many aspects of writing, publishing and the media.

Reid Kerr College

Renfew Road, Paisley, Renfrewshire, PA3 4DR
T 0800 052 7343
F 0141 581 2204
E sservices@reidkerr.ac.uk
W www.reidkerr.ac.uk

Runs a creative writing course.

Richmond Adult Community College

Parkshot, Richmond, TW9 2RE
T 020 8843 5907
F 020 8332 6560
E info@racc.ac.uk
W www.racc.ac.uk

Range of part-time writing courses including screenwriting, creative writing and comedy writing.

Rotherham College of Arts & Technology

Town Centre Campus, Eastwood Lane, Rotherham, S65 1EG
T 08080 722777
E info@rotherham.ac.uk
W www.rotherham.ac.uk

Offers a part-time advanced creative writing course.

Scottish Universities International Summer School

✉ 21 Buccleuch Place, Edinburgh, EH8 9LN
☎ T 0131 650 4369
  F 0131 662 0275
✎ E suiss@ed.ac.uk
  W www.summer-school.hss.ed.ac.uk/suiss/

An annual summer school, which includes a creative writing course in cooperation with the Edinburgh International Book Festival (in August).

SG Media Training

☎ T 020 7794 0288
✎ E susangrossman@tiscali.co.uk
  W www.susangrossman.co.uk

Individual mentoring, 'Life's a Pitch' workshops, and distance learning, on all aspects of getting published, from writing book or feature proposals to how to be a successful journalist or travel writer. Inside information offered by an experienced magazine editor, journalist and BBC broadcaster, currently a visiting lecturer in journalism at two London universities.

South Essex College

✉ Luker Road, Southend-on-Sea, Essex, SS1 1ND
☎ T 0845 52 12345
  F 01702 432320
✎ E learning@southessex.ac.uk
  W www.southessex.ac.uk

Diploma in advanced publishing and weekend courses in creative writing.

South Nottingham College

✉ West Bridgford Centre, Greythorn Drive, West Bridgford, Nottingham, NG2 7GA
☎ T 0115 914 6400
  F 0115 914 6444
✎ E enquiries@snc.ac.uk
  W www.snc.ac.uk

Part-time creative writing courses.

Spread the Word

✉ 77 Lambeth Walk, London, SE11 6DX
☎ T 020 7735 3111
  F 020 7735 2666
✎ E info@spreadtheword.org.uk
  W www.spreadtheword.org.uk

Courses, workshops and advice for London-based writers.

Stevenson College Edinburgh

✉ Bankhead Avenue, Edinburgh, EH11 4DE
☎ T 0131 535 4600
  F 0131 535 4708
✎ E info@stevenson.ac.uk
  W www.stevenson.ac.uk

Open access creative writing courses.

St Helens College

✉ Town Centre Campus, Water Street, St Helens, Merseyside, WA10 1PP
☎ T 01744 733766
  F 01744 623400
✎ E Online form
  W www.sthelens.ac.uk

Adult workshops in creative writing.

Stonebridge Associated Colleges

✉ Stonebridge House, Ocean View Road, Bude, Cornwall, EX23 8ST
☎ T 0845 230 6880
  F 01288 355799
✎ E info@stonebridge.uk.com
  W www.stonebridge.uk.com

Wide range of short-term distance learning courses in writing and journalism.

Strode College

✉ Strode College, Church Road, Street, Somerset, BA16 0AB
☎ T 01458 844400
  F 01458 844411

E Online form
W www.strode-college.ac.uk

Part-time creative writing courses.

Study House

Writers College, 8 Hillswood Avenue, Kendal, Cumbria, LA9 5BT
T 01539 724622
E Online form
W www.study-house.co.uk

Certificates in fiction writing and journalism.

Swanwick Writers' Summer School

Hayes Conference Centre, Alfreton, Swanwick, Derbyshire, DE55 1AU
E Online form
W http://swanwickwritersschool.co.uk

One week summer school in August, dedicated to writing courses. For all levels of experience.

Swarthmore Education Centre

2–7 Woodhouse Square, Leeds, West Yorkshire, LS3 1AD
T 0113 243 2210
F 0113 243 2210
E info@swarthmore.org.uk
W www.swarthmore.org.uk

Creative writing courses.

Ty Newydd

Llanystumdwy, Cricieth, Gwynedd, LL52 0LW
T 01766 522811
E post@tynewyyd.org
W www.tynewydd.org

Residential writing courses.

UCD Adult Education Centre

Library Building, University College Dublin, Belfield, Dublin 4, Republic of Ireland

T 00353 1 716 7123
F 00353 1 716 7500
E adult.education@ucd.ie
W www.ucd.ie/adulted/courses

Adult courses in creative writing.

UK Open Learning

69 Lowther Street, Whitehaven, Cumbria, CA28 7AD
T 0800 043 4288
E sales@uk-open-learning.com
W www.uk-open-learning.com

Distance learning courses in writing, journalism and editing.

University of Bristol

Senate House, Tyndall Avenue, Bristol, BS8 1TH
T 0117 928 9000
E admissions@bristol.ac.uk
W www.bris.ac.uk

Short courses and day courses in creative writing, contact English-lifelong@bristol.ac.uk. Part-time diploma in creative writing.

University Centre Hastings

Havelock Road, Hastings, East Sussex, TN34 1DQ
T 0845 602 0607
E information@uch.ac.uk
W www.uch.ac.uk

Short courses in writing, poetry and screenwriting.

University College Falmouth

Woodlane, Falmouth, Cornwall, TR11 4RH
T 01326 211077
F 01326 213880
E admissions@falmouth.ac.uk
W www.falmouth.ac.uk

Summer schools on novel writing and writing for children.

University of Dundee

Continuing Education, University of Dundee,
Level 2, Tower Building, Dundee, DD1 4HN
T 01382 383000
F 01382 201604
E conted@dundee.ac.uk
W www.dundee.ac.uk/learning/conted

Adult creative writing courses.

University of East Anglia

Continuing Education, Faculty of Social
Sciences, University of East Anglia, Norwich,
NR4 7TJ
T 01603 591451
F 01603 451999
E cont.ed@uea.ac.uk
W www.uea.ac.uk/contedu

Certificates and diplomas in creative writing,
screenwriting, fiction and poetry. Also runs
creative writing and literature day schools.

University of Glasgow

Department of Adult and Continuing
Education, St Andrew's Building, 11 Eldon
Street, Glasgow, G3 6NH
T 0141 330 1835
F 0141 330 1821
E c.robertson@educ.gla.ac.uk
W www.gla.ac.uk/departments/adulteducation/

Part-time creative writing courses.

University of Hull

Centre for Lifelong Learning, University of Hull,
49 Salmon Grove, Hull, HU6 7SZ
T 01482 465666
E cll@hull.ac.uk
W www2.hull.ac.uk

Creative writing evening course.

University of Kent

School of English, Rutherford College, University
of Kent, Canterbury, Kent, CT2 7NZ
T 01227 827133
F 01227 827001

E english@kent.ac.uk
W www.kent.ac.uk

Part-time certificates and diplomas in creative
writing subjects. Run at a range of locations
across Kent.

University of Liverpool

Continuing Education, University of Liverpool,
126 Mount Pleasant, Liverpool, L69 3GR
T 0151 794 6900
E conted@liverpool.ac.uk
W www.liv.ac.uk/conted

Part-time courses in creative writing and
getting published.

University of Newcastle

School of English Literature, Language
& Linguistics, Percy Building, Newcastle
upon Tyne, NE1 7RU
T 0191 222 7625
F 0191 222 8708
E english@ncl.ac.uk
W www.ncl.ac.uk/elll/about/creative/

Short courses in various types of creative
writing. Also runs spring and summer schools
on creative writing, and hosts many other
writing events – such as readings.

University of Sheffield

Institute for Lifelong Learning, University
of Sheffield, 196–198 West Street, Sheffield,
S1 4ET
T 0114 222 7000
F 0114 222 7001
E till@sheffield.ac.uk
W www.shef.ac.uk/till/

Certificate in creative writing. Also runs a range
of creative writing and general interest courses.

University of St Andrews

University of St Andrews Creative Writing
Summer Programme, St Katharine's West,
16 The Scores, St Andrews, Fife, KY16 9AX

T 01334 462275
F 01334 463330
E rmd10@st-andrews.ac.uk
W www.st-andrews.ac.uk/admissions/ug/int/summerschools/

Summer school for creative writing.

University of Strathclyde

Centre for Lifelong Learning, 7th Floor, Graham Hills Building, 40 George Street, Glasgow, G1 1QE
T 0141 548 4287
F 0141 553 1270
E learn@cll.strath.ac.uk
W www.strath.ac.uk/cll/

Evening and weekend classes in many types of writing.

University of Sunderland

North East Centre for Lifelong Learning, 2nd Floor Bedson Building, Kings Road, Newcastle upon Tyne, NE1 7RU
T 0191 515 2800
F 0191 515 2890
E lifelong.learning@sunderland.ac.uk
W www.cll.sunderland.ac.uk

Wide range of adult education courses in literature, writing and getting published.

University of Sussex

Centre for Community Engagement, Mantell Building, University of Sussex, Falmer, Brighton, BN1 9RF
T 01273 678300
F 01273 873715
E cce@sussex.ac.uk
W www.sussex.ac.uk/cce

Open courses.

University of the Arts, London

272 High Holborn, London, WC1V 7EY
T 020 7514 6000
E admissions@arts.ac.uk
W www.arts.ac.uk

Many short courses on writing, editing, journalism and publishing, at various centres in London.

University of Warwick

Centre for Lifelong Learning, Westwood Campus, University of Warwick, Coventry, CV4 7AL
T 024 7615 1155
E cll@warwick.ac.uk
W www2.warwick.ac.uk/study/cll/open_courses

Adult short courses in creative writing, journalism and publishing.

Urchfont Manor College

Urchfont, Devizes, Wiltshire, SN10 4RG
T 01380 840495
F 01380 840005
E Online form
W www.urchfontmanor.co.uk

Residential courses, day courses and study tours on creative writing topics.

Wakefield Adult & Community Education Service

Manygates Education Centre, Manygates Lane, Sandal, Wakefield, WF2 7DQ
T 01924 303302
E aces@wakefield.gov.uk
W www.wakefieldaces.net

Creative writing community course.

Waterford Institute of Technology

Adult & Continuing Education Office, WIT, Cork Road Campus, Waterford, Republic of Ireland
T 00353 51 302040
E ace@wit.ie
W www.wit.ie

Creative writing evening class.

The Watermill at Posara

The Mill, Posara, Fivizzano, 54013 Italy
T 020 7193 6246
E Online form
W www.watermill.net

Offers a wide range of residential creative writing courses.

Workers Educational Association

4 Luke Street, London, EC2A 4XW
T 020 7426 3450
F 020 7426 3451
E national@wea.org.uk
W www.wea.org.uk

Voluntary provider of adult learning, including courses in creative writing, publishing and journalism. Search the website by location to find the nearest course.

Writers Bureau

Sevendale House, 7 Dale Street, Manchester, M1 1JB
T 0845 345 5995
T 0161 236 9440
E studentservices@writersbureau.com
W www.writersbureau.com

The Writers Bureau offers home study creative writing courses, with individual guidance from expert tutors and flexible tuition. Courses cover style, presentation, copyright, and how to sell your writing in different markets. They cater for a wide range of skill levels, including beginners, and cover articles, short stories, journalism, novels, romances, historicals, writing for children, writing for television and writing for radio and theatre, among other subjects. Details are free on request and a 15-day trial period is available, as well as the option for a full refund if not successful.

Writers' News Home Study

5th Floor, 31–32 Park Row, Leeds, LS1 5JD
T 0113 200 2917
F 0113 200 2928

E homestudy@writersnews.co.uk
W www.writersnews.co.uk

Nine home-based writing courses. Contact the Home Study Coordinator for a free prospectus.

Writers Reign

Fortress Publishing, 1 Delta Road, Hutton, Brentwood, Essex, CM13 1NG
T 01277 226840
E editor@writersreign.co.uk
W www.writersreign.co.uk

The WritersReign website is for all aspiring writers. It has a comprehensive pool of articles covering many interesting and exciting topics, as well as frequently updated writing and poetry competition listings. It also has an impressive array of links to other writers' websites and a software page with details about some useful products you may not know about. WritersReign also offers a free article writing e-course.

WriteWords

PO Box 850, St Albans, AL1 9BE
E admin@writewords.org.uk
W www.writewords.org.uk

Range of email correspondence courses on different types of writing and publishing.

The Writing College

16 Magdalen Road, Exeter, EX2 4SY
T 01392 499488
F 01392 498008
E enquiries@writingcollege.com
W www.writingcollege.com

Offers a creative writing correspondence course.

Writing Holidays, Writers' Seminars & Workshops

Felicity Fair Thompson, 39 Ranelagh Road, Sandown, PO36 8NT
T 01983 407772
F 01983 407772

E info@learnwriting.co.uk
W www.learnwriting.co.uk

Organizes writers' retreats and conferences.

Written Words

5 Queen Elisabeth Close, London, N16 0HL
T 020 8809 4725
E henrietta@writtenwords.net
W www.writtenwords.net

Intensive workshops for fiction writers. Also
offers private tutorials for novels/short stories.
Full manuscripts welcomed.

COMPETITIONS & PRIZES

Arthur C Clarke Award for Science Fiction

✉ 60 Bournemouth Road, Folkestone, Kent, CT19 5AZ
☎ T 01303 252939
✐ E chairofjudges.clarkeaward@gmail.com
W www.clarkeaward.com

Competition/Award Director Paul Billinger

Established 1986

Insider Info The Arthur C Clark Award for Science Fiction is presented for the best science-fiction novel of the year, as selected from a shortlist. The award is presented annually and the prize consists of a trophy and £2,010 (for the 2010 award and increasing by £1 annually). The winning book is picked by a jury panel. This competition is open to writers from any nationality, provided their book is in English and published in the UK.

Genres Science-Fiction

Submission Guidelines Titles must be previously published in the UK between 1 January and 31 December in the current year.

Tips Novellas (less than 30,000 words) and short story collections are not eligible for this award. Entries should be made by the book's publishers.

Authors' Club First Novel Award

✉ 40 Dover Street, London, W1S 4NP
☎ T 020 7499 8581
F 020 7409 0913
✐ E authors@theartsclub.co.uk

Competition/Award Director Stella Kane

Established 1954

Insider Info The Authors' Club award is presented to a promising work of fiction written by a British author and published in the UK. The award is presented annually, with prize money of £1,000.

Genres Novels

Submission Guidelines Submissions must be previously published full-length novels by first-time authors.

Tips Entries are usually nominated by publishers.

Betty Trask Awards

✉ 84 Drayton Gardens, London, SW10 9SB
 T 020 7373 6642
F 020 7373 5768
✐ E Online form
W www.societyofauthors.org/betty-trask

Insider Info These awards are sponsored by the Society of Authors and presented for the best debut, due to be published, or unpublished novel by a writer under the age of 35. Novels should be romantic or traditional and the prize will not be awarded to experimental fiction. Several prizes may be presented in one year and prize money totals £25,000 and should be used for periods of foreign travel.

Genres Fiction, Novels

Submission Guidelines Submissions must be received by the end of January each year. Guidelines/entry forms are available on the website. Writers should be Commonwealth citizens and must not have had work published other than the novel submitted. Unpublished writers should submit a copy of the manuscript. Published writers should send a book, proof of manuscript via their publisher. Mark for the attention of Dorothy Sym.

Chapter One Promotions International Novel Competition

✉ Canterbury Court, 1–3 Brixton Road, London, SW9 6DE
☎ T 0845 456 5364
F 0845 456 5347
✐ E info@chapteronepromotions.com
W www.chapteronepromotions.com

Insider Info This is an open competition for unpublished novels. Only the first two chapters and the closing chapter are required, and the novel need not have been finished. The competition is held every two years. The winner will receive support in completing their work, which will be published and available through the Book Cellar and Amazon.

Genres Novels

Submission Guidelines Submissions must be received by 28 February each year. There is a fee of £20 per novel. Titles should be previously unpublished.

Tips There is no word count and entries may be submitted by post or online. Entrants must declare if their work has been submitted to any other competitions, agents or publishers.

Cinnamon Press Novel Writing Award

Meirion House, Glan yr afon, Tanygrisiau, Blaenau Ffestiniogg, Gwynedd, LL41 3SU
E jan@cinnamonpress.com
W www.cinnamonpress.com

Insider Info An award aimed at allowing new writers their first full-length novel publication. Writers are invited to submit the first 10,000 words of their work. The award is offered twice yearly. The top five based on the samples will be invited to submit their full novel. The winner receives £400 and a contact for their novel of between 60,000 and 80,000 words to be published by Cinnamon Press. Open to any writer who has never had a full-length novel published.

Genres Novels

Submission Guidelines Submissions must be received between 30 June and 30 November each year. Guidelines are available on the website. The entry fee is £20 per novel. Novels must be previously unpublished.

Tips Novels do not necessarily need to be finished at the closing date but writers need to be able to provide the full work within two months of the closing date if they are shortlisted. Work should be double spaced on single-sided sheets. Handwritten entries will not be accepted.

Debut Dagger

Crime Writer's Association Debut Dagger, PO Box 273, Boreham Wood, Herts, WD6 2XA
E Online entry form.
W www.thecwa.co.uk/daggers/debut

Insider Info The Debut Dagger award is sponsored by the Crime Writers' Association. It is an award designed to help launch the careers of unpublished crime writers and is presented annually. The prize consists of £700 and two tickets to the CWA Duncan Lawrie Dagger Awards, including a night's stay for two in a hotel. All shortlisted entrants receive a selection of crime novels and professional critiques of their entries, and will also be invited to the awards dinner. The award is open to any writer who has not previously had a novel published. Previously published writers in non-crime fiction areas (including self-published writers) should email for advice on their individual eligibility.

Genres Crime Fiction

Submission Guidelines Submissions must be received between 1 November and 7 February each year. Guidelines for submissions are available on the website. Submit the first 3,000 words and a 500–1,000 word synopsis of the rest of the novel. Include a signed entry form, information for which is on the website. There is also the facility for online entry. There is a fee of £25 per story. The novel must be previously unpublished.

Tips Crime novels only, although 'crime' can be interpreted broadly. For a style guide and advice on writing crime novels, visit the website. Winning the Debut Dagger doesn't guarantee you'll get published, but it does mean your work will be seen by leading agents and top editors.

The Dundee International Book Prize

E literarydundee@gmail.com
W www.dundeebookprize.com

Established 1996

Insider Info Sponsored by Birlinn Ltd and the University of Dundee. Normally awarded every two years. The winning writer receives £10,000 and the publication of their novel.

Genres Fiction, Novels

Submission Guidelines See website for deadline. Entrants must not have had a novel previously published. Children's novels are not eligible.

Tips There are no restrictions on theme or style. Entries must be made by email as a Word document; see website for details.

The Elizabeth Goudge Trophy

E jan@jan-jones.co.uk
W www.rna-uk.org

Insider Info An annual competition sponsored by the Romantic Novelists' Association. Writers are invited to submit entries based on a romance theme set by the Chairman. The winner is presented with a silver bowl at the conference.

Genres Fiction

Submission Guidelines Work should be previously unpublished.

Tips Open to RNA members only.

Harry Bowling Prize for New Writing

StorytrackS, 16 St Briac Way, Bystock, Exmouth, Devon, EX8 5RN
W www.harrybowlingprize.net

Established 2000

Insider Info An award for the best opening chapter and synopsis of a novel set in London. In memory of Harry Bowling, a successful writer who set much of his work in London. Held every two (even) years, the overall winner receives £1,000 and runners up receive £100 each. Judges include Jane Morpeth (Harry Bowling's Editor at Hodder Headline) and Laura Longrigg (his Agent at MBA). Entrants must not have published any adult works of fiction before, however they may have published short stories, scripts for television and radio, non-fiction and children's fiction and non-fiction.

Genres Fiction

Submission Guidelines Submissions should be received by 31 March each year. Guidelines are available online. Entry fee of £10.

Tips Submit up to 5,000 words and a 500-word synopsis by post, along with an entry form (available from the website), entry fee and SAE if receipt is required. A list of criteria that the judges are looking for is published on the website – read this thoroughly before entering.

Impress Prize for New Writers

Impress Books Ltd, The Innovation Centre, University of Exeter Campus, Rennes Drive, Exeter, Devon, EX4 4RN
T 01392 262301
F 01392 262303
E enquiries@impress-books.co.uk
W www.impress-books.co.uk

Contact Dr Richard Willis

Established 2007

Insider Info Offers a prize of a publishing contract with Impress Books. Winners aim to be published the year following the award.

Genres No specific genre

Submission Guidelines Open to new writers who have not previously published a book-length publication. Submissions should be in the form of a proposal, biography and sample chapter up to 6,000 words. Entry date for year of entry and full details can be found on the website.

Tips The prize is designed to publish new, innovative writing talent.

The Joan Hessayon New Writers' Scheme Award

E melaniehilton@tiscali.co.uk
W www.rna-uk.org

Competition/Award Director Roger Sanderson

Insider Info Sponsored by the Romantic Novelists' Association. Awarded annually for a debut published romance novel from a member of their New Writers' Scheme. The writer must still be a member of the New Writers' Scheme at the time of the award and the winning novel in particular must have been developed through the scheme.

Genres Fiction, Novels

Submission Guidelines The book must either be published or under contract with a publisher.

Tips Any unpublished romantic novelist may apply to join the New Writers' Scheme. Entry forms are available from the website and fees are £90. Members will have access to all the events and services of the RNA and will be entitled to a manuscript appraisal service.

Leaf Books Writing Competitions

Gti Suite, Ty Menter, Navigation Park, Aberycynon, CF45 4SN
T 029 2081 0726
E contact@leafbooks.co.uk
W www.leafbooks.co.uk

Competition/Award Director Sam Burns

Established 2005

Insider Info Ongoing competitions for fiction, short stories, micro-fiction and poetry. Each competition is run in order to get the winning entries into print. Prize consists of publication in a Leaf book and £150. Judged by named judges, or a panel of readers. Rights to submitted material remains with the author upon entry. Competition open to any writer.

Genres Fiction

Submission Guidelines Guidelines and entry form available via SAE. Entry fee varies. Work should be previously unpublished.

Tips Read the guidelines on the website.

McKitterick Prize

84 Drayton Gardens, London, SW10 9SB
T 020 7373 6642
F 020 7373 5768

E info@societyofauthors.org
W www.societyofauthors.org

Insider Info Sponsored by the Society of Authors. Awarded for a first full length novel by a writer over the age of 40. Awarded annually, the winner receives £4,000. The writer must be over the age of 40 on 31 December in the year of submission.

Genres Novels

Submission Guidelines Guidelines available on the website. Previously published entries must have appeared in print between 1 January and 31 December the previous year. Accepts unpublished entries.

Tips Send four copies of the book (if published), or the first 30 pages of the manuscript (if unpublished), to Paula Johnson, Awards Secretary at the Society of Authors. Entries are normally invited from late summer.

Melissa Nathan Award for Comedy Romance

4 Connaught Gardens, PO Box 56923, London, N10 3YU
E Online form
W www.melissanathan.com

Insider Info The Melissa Nathan Award is presented to a writer of a comedy romance title published during the previous year. The prize was set up by Nathan, a writer, before she died in 2006 and was first awarded in 2007. The winner receives a prize of £5,000 and a trophy.

Genres Romance/Comedy Novels

Submission Guidelines Use the online form on the website where there is an option to click on 'enter competition', for more information. Publishers should send six copies of nominated titles.

Tips Entries should link the two main elements – comedy and romance – together in a way that is 'compelling and natural'. The inaugural winner was bestseller Marian Keyes.

National Association of Writers Groups Creative Writing Competitions

✉ PO Box 9891, Market Harborough, LE16 0FU
E secretary@nawg.co.uk
W www.nawg.co.uk

Insider Info The NAWG runs a variety of annual competitions including the NAWG/ Writers' News Short Story Competition. Other categories have included: Mini-Tale; Denise Robertson Trophy for the Best Group Anthology; Best Limerick; Free Verse Poem; Children's Poem; Collection of Five Poems; Open Short Story; Short Story (with given last line); Children's Short Story; Novel (previously unpublished); Non-Fictional Article in 'how-to' mode; and Fantasy/Science-Fiction. Awarded annually, each category has different prizes but there are often small cash prizes, books and trophies on offer.

Genres Fiction, Non-Fiction, Poetry, Novels, Articles, Short Stories, Story Collections

Submission Guidelines There are various entry fees. Works should be unpublished.

Tips Details of further competitions, categories and closing dates will be published on the website along with shortlisted and winning entries from previous years.

Noma Award for Publishing in Africa

✉ PO Box 128, Witney, Oxfordshire, OX8 5XU
T 01993 775235
F 01993 709265
E maryljay@aol.com
W www.nomaaward.org

Competition/Award Director Mary Jay

Established 1979

Insider Info Sponsored by Kodansha Ltd, Japan. An annual $10,000 award for a book by an African writer and published by an independent/autonomous African publishing house domiciled on the continent. Scholarly works, literature and children's books are eligible. Submission and entry must be made by publisher; maximum of three entries. The purpose is to encourage African scholars and writers to publish with African publishers, rather than abroad, with a view to strengthening African publishing. Judged by a panel of African and international scholars and book experts, chaired by Walter Bgoya, Tanzanian publisher. No entry fee. The writer must be an African national, wherever resident.

Genres Fiction, Non-Fiction, Poetry, Essays, Children's, Novels, Short Stories, Drama

Submission Guidelines Deadline for entry is the end of April each year. Guidelines and entry forms do not need SAE; they can be posted, emailed, or downloaded from the website. Previously published entries must appear in print between 1 January and 31 December the previous year.

Tips If interpretation of guidelines gives rise to questions of eligibility, the Secretariat can advise.

Opening Pages Competition

E andrea@ukauthors.com
W www.ukauthors.com

Insider Info Sponsored by volunteer readers, professional editors and the UKA Press to support UK Authors writing site activities, this annual competition offers detailed feedback on the opening 3,000 words of a book. Run annually, 'feedback entrants' receive a five page detailed assessment on their writing, 65 pages of writing advice, and six to ten independent reader reports.

Submission Guidelines Entry fee is £15 per entry, and £18 per feedback entry. Work should be unpublished.

Tips The winning entry is offered publication by UKA Press, and shortlisted entries are invited to submit their work to be considered for publication. Check the UK Authors website for more details.

FESTIVALS & CONFERENCES

Aspects Festival

North Down Heritage Centre, Bangor,
Co. Down, BT20 4BT
T 028 9127 8032
W www.northdown.gov.uk

Dates Late September

A series of events to celebrate Irish writing.
Many guest speakers across various genres
of writing.

Athlone Literary Festival

Custume Place, Athlone, Co. Westmeath,
Republic of Ireland
T 00353 87 7914899
E literaryathlone@gmail.com
W www.athlone.ie/literaryfestival

Dates September

Formerly know as the John Broderick Weekend,
which celebrated the work of Broderick. It is
now a broader literary festival. Guest speakers
include writers, poets, agents and academics.

Arthur Miller Centre International Literary Festival

Literary Festival Administrator, HUM Faculty
Office, University of East Anglia, Norwich,
NR4 7TJ
T 01603 592286
E literaryevents@uea.ac.uk
W www.uea.ac.uk/hum/litevents

Dates Spring and Autumn

An annual festival of events and talks by well-
known writers.

Ballymena Arts Festival

Briad Arts Centre, Ballymena, Co. Antrim,
BT43 7DR
T 028 2563 5900
E braid.enquiries@ballymena.gov.uk
W www.thebraid.com

Contact Rosalind Lowry

Dates March/April

A general arts festival that offers a varied
programme of activities including music, dance,
theatre, comedy and storytelling.

Bath Literature Festival

Bath Festivals Ltd, Abbey Chambers,
Kingston Buildings, Bath, BA1 1NT
T 01225 462231
F 01225 445551
E info@bathfestivals.org.uk
W www.bathlitfest.org.uk

Contact Artistic Director, Sarah LeFanu

Dates February/March

Ten days of literary events, encompassing
writing in all its forms. The festival is fast gaining
a reputation for presenting the very best in
local, national and international writers to an
ever-increasing audience.

Beverley Literature Festival

Wordquake, Council Offices, Skirlaugh,
East Riding of Yorkshire, HU11 5HN
T 07920 451010
E john.clarke@eastriding.gov.uk
W www.beverley-literature-festival.org

Contact Festival Director, John Clarke

Dates October

A series of literature events and readings,
including some to live music. A children's
programme runs alongside the main festival.

Birmingham Book Festival

T 0121 303 2323
W www.birminghambookfestival.org

Contact Artistic Director, Jonathan Davidson;
Programme Manager, Sara Beadle; Project
Manager, Lucy Wood

Dates October

An annual festival of books and writing. The
festival is a not-for-profit charity and also runs an
extensive 'writers in schools' programme (Write
On! – Adventures in Writing) and undertakes
year-round events and activities.

Bournemouth Literary Festival

BLF, 20a Parkwood Road, Bournemouth,
Dorset, BH5 2BH
T 01202 417535
E info@bournemouthliteraryfestival.co.uk
W www.bournemouthliteraryfestival.co.uk

Contact Director and Founder, Lillian Avon

Dates September/October

Bournemouth's international and multicultural
literary festival offers events for both adults and
children, including authors' news, views and
reviews, competitions, parties, performances
and workshops. Each year has a theme, or set
of themes, with events spread across September
and October.

Brighton Festival

12a Pavilion Buildings, Castle Square,
Brighton, BN1 1EE
T 01273 700747
E info@brightonfestival.org
W www.brightonfestival.org

Contact Press Manager, Shelley Bennett

Dates May

Brighton Festival features and exciting
programme of theatre, dance, music, books
and debate, children's and family shows, and
outdoor spectacle.

The Budleigh Salterton Literary Festival

11 East Terrace, Budleigh Salterton,
Devon, EX9 6PG
E smward@mail.com

Contact Artistic Director, Susan Ward

Dates September

The festival combines high-profile authors (2010
included Carol Ann Duffy, Kathy Lette and
Simon Brett) with workshops and opportunities
for local authors.

Buxton Festival

3 The Square, Buxton, Derbyshire, SK17 6AZ
T 01298 70395
F 01298 72289
E info@buxtonfestival.co.uk
W www.buxtonfestival.co.uk

Contact Artistic Director, Andrew Greenwood

Dates July

A music and literature festival, with an emphasis
on opera

Cambridge Wordfest

7 Downing Place, Cambridge, CB3 2EL
T 01223 515335
E admin@cambridgewordfest.co.uk
W www.cambridgewordfest.co.uk

Contact Festival Director and Founder,
Cathy Moore

Dates April/November

A three-day literature festival with events for
adults and children, taking place in the ADC
Theatre. Also runs a Winter Wordfest one-day
festival in November, as well as the Wordfest
Summer School.

Canterbury Festival

Festival Office, 8 Orange Street,
Canterbury, Kent, CT1 2JA
T 01227 452853

E info@canterburyfestival.co.uk
W www.canterburyfestival.co.uk

Contact Festival Director, Rosie Turner; Festival Adminstrator, Sylviane Martell

Dates October

The Canterbury Festival is Kent's International Arts Festival, the largest festival of arts and culture in the region. It attracts an audience of nearly 80,000 people, to over 200 events across two weeks.

The Charleston Festival

The Charleston Trust, Charleston Firle, Lewes, East Sussex, BN8 6LL
T 01323 811626
E info@charleston.org.uk
W www.charleston.org.uk/charlestonfestival

Dates May

The Charleston Festival is held in May and hosts a programme of literary events, workshops and readings by guest speakers.

Chester Literature Festival

Chester Railway Station, 1st Floor West Wing Offices, Station Road, Chester, CH1 3NT
T 01244 405637
E info@chesterfestivals.co.uk
W www.chesterfestivals.co.uk/literature

Contact Katherine Seddon

Dates October

A literature festival with workshops, readings and other events.

Chichester Festivities

Canon Gate House, South Street, Chichester, West Sussex, PO19 1PU
T 01243 528356
E info@chifest.org.uk
W www.chifest.org.uk

Dates June/July

An arts festival across various venues in Chichester, including workshops, talks and readings from literary speakers.

City of London Festival

Fitz Eylwin House, 25 Holborn Viaduct, London, EC1A 2BP
T 020 7583 3585
F 020 7353 0455
E admin@colf.org
W www.colf.org

Contact Festival Director, Ian Ritchie; General Manager, Lindsey Dear

Dates June/July

An arts festival offering a varied programme including opera, literature, installations and exhibitions of visual arts, film screenings and architecture walks and talks. Many of the bigger events are broadcast by the BBC.

County Bookshop Peak Festival (Spring & Autumn)

Countrybookshop, Hassop Station, Nr Bakewell, Derbyshire, DE45 1NW
W www.countrybookshop.co.uk/peakfestival

Dates May/June and October/November

Two large literary festivals, in spring and autumn, held in the Peak District with many well-known authors. The Peak District Book of the Year Award is also presented as part of the festival.

The Cuirt International Festival of Literature

Galway Arts Centre, 47 Dominick Street, Galway, Republic of Ireland
T 00353 91 565886
F 00353 91 568642
E dani@galwayartcentre.ie
W www.galwayartscentre.ie/cuirt

Contact Dani Gill

Dates April

A festival of around 6,000 visitors, offering an eclectic mix of Irish and international writers. Includes readings, signings and workshops.

Derbyshire Literature Festival

Venues across Derbyshire

T 01773 831359
E alison.betteridge@derbyshire.gov.uk
W www.derbyshire.gov.uk/festival

Contact Literature Development Officer, Alison Betteridge

Dates June

A biennial festival that takes place during the first two weeks in June. The next festival is in 2012. The festival takes place in venues all over Derbyshire and aims to encourage people to become involved in all kinds of literature and storytelling events.

Dorchester Festival

Dorchester Arts Centre, School Lane, The Grove, Dorchester, Dorset, DT1 1XR
T 01305 266926
E enquiries@dorchesterarts.org.uk
W www.dorchesterfestival.co.uk

Dates May

A local arts festival with a few literary events.

Dromineer Literary Festival

Ballycommon, Nenagh, Co. Tipperary, Republic of Ireland
T 00353 87 690 8099
E Online form
W www.dromineerliteraryfestival.ie

Contact Chair, Pat Kelly; Secretary, Eleanor Hooker

Dates September

A weekend festival. The programme includes readings, storytelling and competitions.

Dublin Writers Festival

Dublin City Arts Office, The Lab, Foley Street, Dublin 1, Republic of Ireland
T 00353 1 222 5455

E info@dublinwritersfestival.com
W www.dublinwritersfestival.com

Contact Festival Director, Jack Gilligan; Programme Director, Liam Browne

Dates June

A five-day writer's festival typically featuring over 40 Irish and international writers and poets, journalists, political commentators, and even lawyers for a series of readings, discussions, debates and public interviews. Some events are specifically for children.

Durham Book Festival

DCA (Durham City Arts), 2 The Cottages, Fowler's Yard, Back Silver Street, Durham City, DH1 3RA
T 0191 375 0763
E enquiries@durhamcityarts.org.uk
W www.bookfestival.org.uk

Dates October

The longest running and largest literature festival in the North East comprising a range of literary events, readings, workshops and talks across Durham City and County.

Edinburgh International Book Festival

5a Charlotte Square, Edinburgh, EH2 4DR
T 0131 718 5666
F 0131 226 5335
E admin@edbookfest.co.uk
W www.edbookfest.co.uk

Contact Festival Director, Catherine Lockerbie

Dates August

A world-class festival of literature and books, with around 220,000 visitors. Generally features over 600 authors, both new and famous, from over 30 different countries. A large selection of events for toddlers, young readers, teenagers and young adults also runs alongside the main festival programme.

Ennis Book Club Festival

25 Willsgrove, Cahercalla, Ennis, Co. Clare, Republic of Ireland
T 00353 87 972 3647
E info@ennisbookclubfestival.com
W www.ennisbookclubfestival.com

Dates March

A three-day festival celebrating books of all types and genres. The festival is designed with the reader in mind and aims to attract book clubs and book lovers from Ireland and abroad. Events include readings, lectures, music, workshops, exhibitions, cookery demonstrations and more.

Festival at the Edge

Festival at the Edge, The Morgan Library, Aston Street, Wem, Shropshire, SY4 5AU
T 01939 236626
E info@festivalattheedge.org
W www.festivalattheedge.org

Contact Sue Chand

Dates Third weekend in July (Friday to Sunday)

Major UK Storytelling festival in Much Wenlock, Shropshire. Offers an exciting programme of storytelling and music performances including new storytelling commissions, open spot storyrounds, tales around the fire, workshops (both story and music), a full children's programme, craft stalls, on-site catering and camping. A family-friendly event.

Folkestone Literary Festival

T 01303 858500
E info@quarterhouse.co.uk
W www.folkestonebookfest.com

Contact Festivals Manager, Roberta Spicer

Dates November

Offers a range of different activities, literary workshops, screenings and discussions taking place over the course of nine days. The festival also runs a short story competition and a series of children's events.

Frome Festival

25 Market Place, Frome, BA11 1AH
T 01373 453889
E office@fromefestival.co.uk
W www.fromefestival.co.uk

Contact Founder, Martin Bax; Creative Director, Martin Dimery

Dates July

A community arts festival with a literature element. The ten-day festival typically features over 150 events, from pop culture to horticulture.

Guildford Book Festival

Venues around Guildford

T 01483 444334
E director@guildfordbookfestival.co.uk
W www.guildfordbookfestival.co.uk

Contact Festival Director, Glenis Pycraft

Dates October

Talks, workshops and events, in and around Guildford. 2009 was the 20th anniversary of the festival.

Harrogate Crime Writing Festival

Raglan House, Raglan Street, Harrogate, North Yorkshire, HG1 1LE
T 01423 562303
F 01423 521264
E crime@harrogate-festival.org.uk
W www.harrogate-festival.org.uk/crime

Contact Festival Coordinator, Erica Morris

Dates July

Launched in 2003 the Theakstons Old Peculier Crime Writing Festival has grown into the largest literary crime fiction event of its kind, and has achieved international acclaim for its programming, organization and festival atmosphere. Over 7,000 people including writers, editors, publicists, reviewers, press and aficionados attend the Festival each July.

The Humber Mouth Literature Festival

City Arts Unit, Hull City Council, 4th Floor
Kingston House, Bond Street, Hull, HU1 3ER
T 01482 300300
E humbermouth@gmail.com
W www.hullcc.gov.uk

Contact Festival Director, Maggie Hannan;
Festival Assistant, Colin Hurst

Dates June

The Humber Mouth Literature Festival takes
place in Hull during the last two weeks of June,
presenting a wide range of events featuring
authors, speakers and artists from the UK and
around the world.

Ilkley Literature Festival

Manor House, 2 Castle Hill, Ilkley,
West Yorkshire, LS29 9DT
T 01943 601210
F 01943 817079
E admin@ilkleyliteraturefestival.org.uk
W www.ilkleyliteraturefestival.org.uk

Contact Festival Director, Rachel Feldberg;
Adminstrator, Gail Price

Dates October

A two-week literature festival sponsored
by Skipton Building Society. The festival
includes a free fringe programme and a
children's programme.

Jewish Book Week

Jewish Book Council, ORT House,
126 Albert Street, London, NW1 7NE
T 020 7446 8771
F 020 7446 8777
E info@jewishbookweek.com
W www.jewishbookweek.com

Dates February/March

A week celebrating Jewish books and writing
with international speakers and events for
children.

King's Lynn Literature Festival

c/o Anthony Ellis, Hawkins Solicitors,
19 Tuesday Market Place, King's Lynn,
Norfolk, PE30 1JW
T 01553 691661
E enquiries@lynnlitfests.com
W www.lynnlitfests.com

Contact Chairman, Anthony Ellis

Dates March

A fiction festival in March held over a weekend.
Programmes include presentations from
international writers in different genres.

King's Sutton Literary Festival

Festival Tickets, 4 Church Avenue, King's Sutton,
Banbury, Oxon, OX17 3RJ
T 01295 810108
E info@kslitfest.co.uk
W www.kslitfest.co.uk

Contact Jackie Bradley

Dates March

A weekend festival of literary events, sponsored
by the *Banbury Guardian*, including readings
and guest speakers.

Knutsford Literature Festival

76 Glebelands Road, Knutsford, Cheshire,
WA16 9DZ
T 01565 722738
E festival@knutsfordlitfest.org
W www.knutsfordlitfest.org

Dates October

A small, independent festival, offering a range
of literary events.

Lewes Live Literature Festival

✉ PO Box 2766, Lewes, East Sussex, BN7 2WF
☎ T 0797 2037612
E info@leweslivelit.co.uk
✐ W www.leweslivelit.co.uk

Contact Artistic Director, Mark Hewitt

Dates October

The festival programme includes creative writing workshops, spoken word performances, readings, music, film, and visual arts events. LLL runs creative writing workshops throughout the year and stages a young people's festival of words that takes place in Lewes during June.

Lincoln Book Festival

Venues around Lincoln

☎ T 01522 545458
E Online form
✐ W www.visitlincolnshire.com

Contact Karen Parsons

Dates May

The Lincoln Book Festival programme includes talks, workshops, discussions, exhibitions and performances. There are also a wide range of activities and events for children and young readers, including the Lincolnshire Young People's Book Award.

Lit.Com

Venues around Lincolnshire

☎ T 07974 263538
E info@litdotcom.com
✐ W www.litdotcom.com

Dates October

A festival of literature and comedy, including live author events, the very best in UK stand up, film showings, theatre for families, poetry performances and writing workshops, a major exhibition, discussion groups, free-giveaways and design and craft sessions for kids. Held at various venues across North East Lincolnshire.

Lit Fest

✉ The Storey, Meeting House Lane, Lancaster, LA1 91TH
☎ T 01524 62166
✐ W www.litfest.org

Contact Artistic Director, Andy Darby

Dates November

An annual festival focusing on literature, poetry and writing. Includes newly commissioned performances each year. Literature development continues throughout the year in Lancaster.

London Literature Festival

✉ Southbank Centre, Belvedere Road, London, SE1 8XX
☎ T 0844 875 0073
E customer@southbankcentre.co.uk
✐ W www.londonlitfest.com

Dates July

London Literature Festival is a new festival of literature, ideas, creative writing and performance taking place at the South Bank Centre. The festival lasts two weeks and also had many events for children.

Lowdham Book Festival

✉ The Bookcase, 50 Main Street, Lowdham, NG14 7BE
☎ T 0115 966 3219
E janstreeter@thebookcase.co.uk
✐ W www.lowdhambookfestival.co.uk

Contact Jane Streeter/Ross Bradshaw

Dates June

Lowdham Festivals runs a major summer book festival with many different arts events, including talks, readings and live music.

Manchester Literature Festival

✉ Beehive Mill, Jersey Street, Ancoats, Manchester, M4 6JG
☎ T 0161 236 5555

E admin@manchesterliteraturefestival.co.uk
W www.manchesterliteraturefestival.co.uk

Contact Festival Director, Cathy Bolton; Festival Administrator/Events Manager, Jon Atkin

Dates October

Manchester Literature Festival produces a programme of readings and events showcasing the best in regional and national independent publishing, writing and production. It aims to challenge the boundaries of what is traditionally understood to be a literature event and also aims to promote internationalism, diversity and independence.

Mere Literary Festival

Mere, Wiltshire, BA12 6EG
E info@merelitfest.co.uk
W www.merelitfest.co.uk

Contact Festival Administrator, Adrienne Howell

Dates October

An annual festival beginning on the second Monday of October. Events include talks, readings, workshops, shows and activities for children. Also runs the Mere Literary Festival Short Story Competition, with the awards ceremony taking place on the last day of the festival.

National Eisteddfod of Wales

40 Parc Ty Glas, Llanishen, Cardiff, CF14 5DU
T 0845 4 090300
F 029 2076 3737
E gwyb@eisteddfod.org.uk
W www.eisteddfod.org.uk

Contact Festival Organizer, Hywel Wyn Edwards

Dates August

The National Eisteddfod of Wales is a major arts and culture festival, attracting around 160,000 visitors annually. It aims to promote Welsh language and culture and also provides a launch pad for Wales' most talented new performers.

NAWG Open Festival of Writing

PO Box 9891, Market Harborough, LE16 0FU
E secretary@nawg.co.uk
W www.nawg.co.uk

Contact Festival Administrator, Mike Wilson

Dates September

A weekend of workshops, seminars, readings, tutorials and fringe activities led by National Association of Writers' Groups tutors.

Oundle Festival of Literature

Ticket Sales, Oundle Tourist Information Centre, 14 West Street, Oundle, Peterborough PE8 4EF
T 01832 274333
E Online form
W www.oundlelitfest.org.uk

Contact Chair, Nick Turnbull

Dates Spring/Autumn

A festival of fiction, theatre, poetry, history, politics, travel, gardening, cuisine, environmental issues and a community events programme. Some events are free, others are paid for.

Quite Literary

The Plough Arts Centre, 9–11 Fore Street, Great Torrington, Devon, EX38 8HQ
T 01805 624624
E mail@theploughartscentre.org.uk
W www.theploughartscentre.org.uk

Contact Director, Richard Wolfenden Brown

A year-round programme of literature events in and around Torrington. There are readings, workshops and community events.

Redbridge Book & Media Festival

3rd Floor, Central Library, Clements Road, Ilford, Essex, IG1 1EA
T 020 8708 2855
E arts&events@redbridge.gov.uk
W www.redbridge.gov.uk

Dates April/May

A festival of the written word in all its forms, including film screenings and performances, workshops, industry talks and visits from well-known writers and performers. The media element to this festival, alongside the more traditional literature events, makes it unique.

Richmond upon Thames Literature Festival

London Borough of Richmond upon Thames, The Arts Service, Orleans House Gallery, Riverside, Twickenham, TW1 3DJ
T 020 8831 6494
F 020 8940 7568
E artsinfo@richmond.gov.uk
W www.richmond.gov.uk/literature_festival

Contact Festival Programmer, Penny Bowles

Dates November

A series of high-profile writers, from biographers, novelists and poets to leading figures from film, politics and media, give lectures on aspects of writing and literature.

Royal Court Young Writers' Festival

Royal Court Theatre, Sloane Square, London, SW1W 8AS
T 020 7565 5000
F 020 7565 5001
E studio@royalcourttheatre.com
W www.royalcourttheatre.com

Contact Artistic Director, Dominic Cooke

Dates January/March

A biennial festival, the next of which will take place in 2012. Young people under the age of 26 may submit scripts to win the chance to see them developed and performed.

Rye Arts Festival

PO Box 33, Rye, East Sussex, TN31 7YB
T 01797 22442
E Online form
W www.ryefestival.co.uk

Contact Chairman, Catherine Bingham

Dates September

One of the top ten small festivals in the UK, providing a diverse mixture of musical, literary and theatrical events with the emphasis on quality, intellectual weight, style and fun. The visual arts are also very well catered for with the galleries running shows especially for the festival.

The Sunday Times Oxford Literary Festival

Christchurch, St Aldates, Oxford, OX1 1DP
T 01865 286074
E info@oxfordliteraryfestival.com
W www.oxfordliteraryfestival.com

Contact Festival Director, Sally Dunsmore

Dates March/April

Workshops and talks on many literary topics, including writing in different genres, and publishing. Generally has around 350 visiting authors. Children's literature is a special focus and there are plenty of events and workshops for children, as well as workshops on how to write for them.

Swindon Festival of Literature

Lower Shaw Farm, Shaw, Swindon, Wiltshire, SN5 5PJ
T 01793 771080
E swindonlitfest@lowershawfarm.co.uk
W www.swindonfestivalofliterature.co.uk

Contact Festival Director, Matt Holland

Dates May

A two-week festival with workshops, talks and speakers on literature and writing, in and around Swindon. Includes a family and children's weekend.

The Telegraph Hay Festival

The Drill Hall, 25 Lion Street, Hay-on-Wye, HR3 5AD
T 01497 822620
F 01497 821066
E admin@hayfestival.com
W www.hayfestival.com

Contact Festival Director, Peter Florence

Dates May/June

Hay-on-Wye is a paradise for lovers of secondhand books. The *Telegraph* Hay Festival is a major UK festival, which includes talks from a number of famous literary personalities. Webcasts and podcasts of events are made available, and the festival is generally covered on Sky Arts, Radio 4 and the *Telegraph* website. The Hay Festival is now an international event, with festivals in Cartagena, Bogota, Alhambra and Segovia.

The Times Cheltenham Literature Festival

109-111 Bath Road, Cheltenham, Gloucestershire, GL53 7LS
T 01242 774400
E judith.ludenbach@cheltenhamfestivals.com
W www.cheltenhamfestivals.com

Contact Artistic Director, Sarah Smyth

Dates October

Ten days of literary workshops, events and performances, including some big name speakers. More information is available on the festival website and via podcasts on *The Times* website.

Tŷ Newydd Festival

Tŷ Newydd, Llanystumdwy, Criccieth, Gwynedd, LL52 0LW

T 01766 52811
F 01766 523095
E post@tynewydd.org
W www.tynewydd.org

Dates April

A biennial festival, the next of which will be held in 2011. It is a weekend festival with a poetry programme in both Welsh and English.

Ulster Bank Belfast Festival at Queen's

8 Fitzwilliam Street, Belfast, BT9 6AW
T 028 9097 1197
E festivalservice@qub.ac.uk
W www.belfastfestival.com

Contact Festival Director, Graeme Farrow

Dates October

A festival of arts – including music, theatre, film and writing. Previous festivals have featured over 450 visiting artists.

Warwick Words

The Court House, Jury Street, Warwick, CV34 4EW
T 07944 768607
E info@warwickwords.co.uk
W www.warwickwords.co.uk

Contact Patron, Andrew Davies

Dates October

A festival of literature and the spoken word. Workshops, talks, performances and children's events are part of the programme.

Ways With Words Literature Festivals

Droridge Farm, Dartington, Totnes, Devon, TQ9 6JG
T 01803 867373
F 01803 863688
E Online form
W www.wayswithwords.co.uk

Contact Festival Directors, Kay Dunbar and Stephen Bristow

Dates March, July and November

Runs highly regarded literature festivals at several locations across the UK: Keswick (March); Dartington (July); Southwold (November). Also runs retreats and events overseas.

Wellington Literary Festival

Venues around Wellington

T 01952 567697
E welltowncl@aol.com
W www.wellington-shropshire.gov.uk

Dates October

A series of free events and talks in Wellington, with several guest speakers.

Wells Festival of Literature

Venues around Somerset

T 01749 679459
W www.wlitf.co.uk

Dates October

A series of lectures and workshops on various topics within literature and writing. Also runs annual short story and poetry competitions.

Welsh Writing in English Annual Conference

Swansea University, Parc Singleton Park, Swansea, SA2 8PP
E Daniel.g.Williams@swansea.ac.uk
W www.swansea.ac.uk/english/awwe/AnnualConference

Contact Conference Organizer, Dr Daniel Williams

Dates March

An annual weekend conference centred around Welsh writing in English, with a different theme every year.

West Cork Literary Festival

13 Glengarriff Road, Bantry, Co. Cork, Republic of Ireland
T 00353 27 52789
E info@westcorkliteraryfestival.ie
W www.westcorkliteraryfestival.ie

Contact Artistic Director, Denyse Woods

Dates July

A week of literary events for writers, including the annual launch of the Fish Publishing anthology and short story prize.

Wigtown Book Festival

County Buildings, Wigtown, Newton Stuart, Dumfries & Galloway, DG8 9JH
T 01988 402036
E mail@wigtownbookfestival.com
W www.wigtownbookfestival.com

Contact Festival Director, Adrian Turpin

Dates September/October

An annual festival in Wigtown, Scotland's national book town. Programme includes readings and events at various locations in Wigtown.

Winchester Writers' Conference

Faculty of Arts, University of Winchester, West Hill, Winchester, Hampshire, SO22 4NR
T 01962 827238
E barbara.large@winchester.ac.uk
W www.writersconference.co.uk

Contact Founder/Director, Barbara Large

Dates June/July

A weekend of workshops, events and talks. Also runs a book fair.

Word

Office of External Affairs, University of Aberdeen, King's College, Aberdeen, AB24 3FX
T 01224 273874
F 01224 272086

E word@abdn.ac.uk
W www.abdn.ac.uk/word

Contact Artistic Director, Alan Spence

Dates May

A large festival with over 10,000 visitors.
Programme includes readings, workshops,
music sessions, art exhibitions, children's
activities and film screenings.

World Book Day

W www.worldbookday.com

Dates March

World Book Day was designated by UNESCO as
a worldwide celebration of books and reading,
and is marked in over 100 countries around the
globe. The UK World Book Day is celebrated
on a different date to the International World
Book Day to ensure that it falls within school
term time. Special £1 books are created, and
there are lots of events in schools throughout
the country. *The Bookseller* and National Book
Tokens Ltd host and sponsor the day.

Worlds Literature Festival

Writers Centre, 14 Princes Street, Norwich,
NR3 1AE
E Online form
W www.writerscentrenorwich.org.uk

Contact Marketing Director, Katy Carr

Dates June

A festival founded in 2008, with various
events including author readings, creative
workshops, debates and lectures on writing
and environmental issues.

Writers' Holiday at Caerleon

E gerry@writersholiday.net
W www.writersholiday.net

Contact Anne Hobbs

Dates July

A six-day residential conference for everyone,
from beginners to the more experienced.
Around 150 delegates attend.

Writers' Week

24 The Square, Listowel, Co. Kerry,
Republic of Ireland
T 00353 68 21074
F 00353 68 22893
E info@writersweek.ie
W www.writersweek.ie

Contact Máire Logue; Chairman, Michael Lynch

Dates May/June

Writers' Week is a literary festival devoted to
the cause of writers. It aims to guide, direct
and enthuse the emerging writer, to befriend
the established writer and provide a practical
platform for their artistic output. This ideal is
achieved through annual literary competitions,
three-day workshops, readings, seminars,
lectures, book launches and other events.
Writers' Week aims to be inclusive and to make
the arts accessible to everybody. To succeed
with this ambition they have put in place a
broad and comprehensive literary programme
to cater for all tastes.

Writing on the Wall

The Kuumba Imani Millennium Centre,
4 Princes Road, Liverpool, L8 1TH
T 0151 703 0020
E info@writingonthewall.org.uk
W www.writingonthewall.org.uk

Contact Festival Administrator, Janette Stowell

Dates May

A not-for-profit organization that runs a series
of literature related events. These are designed
to encourage young people and the wider
community to take part.

INDEX